WIT
UTSA LIBRARIES

D0842484

RENEWALS 458-4574

WITHDRAWN
UTSA LIBRARIES

CEO

CORPORATE LEADERSHIP
IN ACTION

CEO

CORPORATE LEADERSHIP

IN ACTION

HARRY LEVINSON

AND

STUART ROSENTHAL

Basic Books, Inc., Publishers

NEW YORK

LIBRARY
The University of Texas
At San Antonio

Library of Congress Cataloging in Publication Data

Levinson, Harry.
  CEO: corporate leadership in action.

  Includes index.
  1. Executives--United States—Biography.
  2. Leadership--United States—Case studies. I. Rosenthal,
Stuart   II. Title. III. Title: C.E.O.
HC102.5.A2L48 1984   658.4'2'0926   83–46085
ISBN 0–465–00790–2

Copyright © 1984 by Harry Levinson and Stuart Rosenthal
Printed in the United States of America
Designed by Vincent Torre
10 9 8 7 6 5 4 3 2 1

LIBRARY
The University of Texas
At San Antonio

To those leaders

who shared their experiences,

their privacy, their achievements,

and their frustrations

so that the rest of us

might learn

Contents

Acknowledgments

IN ADDITION to the executives who shared their precious time with us, we are indebted to Lisa Serini, Joanne Park, Maria Milas, Linda McCormick, Marie-Claire Ording, and Marcia Atwood, who transcribed the interviews and typed and retyped the thousands of pages that ultimately were distilled into this book; and to Kristen Walter, Lisa Collins, and Denise Cronan for the hours they spent copyreading and checking. John Elder made important editorial suggestions at critical, frustrating junctures and creatively edited the manuscript. Marilyn Farinato did her usual fine job of coordinating our multiple tasks and enabling us to have the comfort of knowing all the details were in hand. Martin Kessler, president of Basic Books, not only set us on this task but was a continuous source of guidance and support. To all of them our heartfelt thanks.

HARRY LEVINSON
STUART ROSENTHAL

CEO

CORPORATE LEADERSHIP
IN ACTION

1

Why Bother?

"LEADERSHIP," writes the historian James MacGregor Burns, "is one of the most observed and least understood phenomena on earth."[1] Indeed, there are untold volumes on leadership. Why, then, bother to write still another book about it? Because, although ours is a business-dominated society, we have so little detailed discussion of business leadership. There are business chronicles, stories of great corporations and their achievements, some exposés, and other vehicles of self-justification. There are descriptions of ends attained, of outcomes. There are news reports of spectacular executive success. But nowhere is there specific documentation of the characteristic behavior of business leaders. Nor is it easy to define what a business leader is. The business world is an arena for achievers. Some are great financial manipulators. Some are spectacular marketeers. Some are technical innovators. Some build and rebuild communities. Are they leaders? They are executives, perhaps, but not always leaders.

We cannot always learn, and certainly not fully, about leadership from theorists or from contemporary "leaders." Nor can we learn fully from great political leaders. Gandhi was charismatic and revolutionary. His leadership made the British yield India, but until the recent popularity of the movie *Gandhi,* there was little evidence in contemporary India that he even existed. De Gaulle was similarly charismatic. He inspired a defeated France, but he left it with only echoes of stirring words. By way of contrast, the leaders of the American Revolution created an adaptive structure—a mode of organizing people and activities that was capable of changing itself when necessary—to sustain the ideals they verbalized. Similarly, there have been great businessmen— Carnegie, Rockefeller, Sloan, Ford, Harriman—who created mammoth businesses, most of which have adapted poorly to their environment. Their organizations have had difficulty enduring for, among other things, they were without the kind of adaptive structure that could either generate ideals or sustain them.

Sociologists argue that when large organizations falter and fail it is because of bureaucratic rigidity, which Marxist economists contend is the result of capitalistic oligarchic power. Such structural explanations attribute failure to the way the business is organized or the economy is managed. But we know from military experience that while one battalion might have high morale, few casualties, and great combat success, a comparable battalion might have quite the opposite. The same is true of comparable manufacturing plants in the same corporation. Other factors being relatively equal, the most significant difference between one organization and another is neither sociological nor economic. Rather, it lies in a leadership style that gives direction, evolves structure, and allocates power. That leadership style is most relevant to much of contemporary management when it can be viewed in the context of a highly structured organization with established traditions and a long history of how things are done. Since entrepreneurs have their own unique psychology, we are interested in those who assumed leadership of ongoing businesses. What does leadership involve in highly organized settings? That is the animating theme of this book.

Options

If we are to try to understand leadership style, we have several options. One is to classify it, as do most research studies on leadership. We can do that by using labels: autocratic, democratic, laissez-faire.[2] Or characterizations: the craftsman, the jungle fighter, the company man, the gamesman.[3] Or by placing the leadership style on axes: person-oriented versus production-oriented.[4] Or by differentiating the achievement-oriented from the power-oriented or the affiliation-oriented.[5] Or we can characterize their temperaments: intuitive versus analytical. Another way is to try to measure leadership style after defining the traits, qualities, skills, or behaviors that characterize it. We might speak of Theory X and Theory Y,[6] System 4[7] or Model II.[8] Finally, we can assess outcome: what did the leader achieve—in dollars, growth of organization, profitability, return on investment, innovation—the end rather than the means.

Characterizations of this kind are descriptive generalizations about modal behavior. The rubrics are drawn from group averages. We may recognize the broad outlines of specific people, or even their reflections or shadows, but never the people themselves. The generalization, by definition, is never detailed enough to fully describe how an individual actually behaved over time. In effect, it is a gross slice of a group. It cannot tell us much about the *how* or the *why* of leadership, nor about the application of a given style, by a given person, to a given situation. Only now and then, through an occasional paragraph, do we get a glimpse of a person acting, a view of the *how*, of the means rather than the end.

Contemporary management literature argues that a fundamental function of a leader is to create meaning for his followers that will facilitate their commitment and identification. As sociologists Trudy Heller and Jon Van Til put it, "Certain individuals emerge as leaders because of their role in framing experience in a way that provides a viable basis for action, e. g., by mobilizing meaning, articulating and defining what has previously remained implicit or unsaid, by inventing images and meanings that provide a focus for new attention, and by consolidating, confronting or changing prevailing wisdom."[9]

Such works offer us anecdotal data, abstractions from those data, and theory built on abstractions. It is our contention that if we are to learn about leadership from leaders, we must examine a specific person in a specific context. Therefore, our crucial concern is with what the leader actually does, day by day, to build followers and knit them into an organization that can sustain them. The empirical research literature on leadership does not touch significant leaders. While there is much data on the behavior of managers, we have few concrete behavioral specifics about those leaders in top management responsible for building organizations. This is a very serious deficiency. For we have learned that when people are promoted on the basis of having achieved certain objectives, what they bring to their new roles is the continuity of their behavior rather than any particular past attainments. And the behavior that enabled them to achieve results in their earlier roles may or may not enable them to continue to achieve results in their new roles.

For all these reasons we felt it important to document actual business leadership behavior. This book is about the *how* of leadership. It speaks to how the chief executive of an established organization interacts with others, how he projects what kind of an image, how he uses others, and what he does through people to create a different social system with a structure, values, and a behavioral style that give rise to a modified organizational personality. To move toward that end, leaders evolve staffing patterns and modes of developing succession. They breathe new life into their organizations and give them new vision. We are therefore concerned with how they communicate their own personal views of what the organization should be and how they inculcate these personal views into those who follow and who become major components of their organizations. We are interested in how they communicate "who we are" as an organization and "what we are" as a cohesive, functional organizational system. We are interested in the interplay between the person as leader and the interactive organization that follows.

A recent survey of theory and research on leadership lists 5,000 references in nearly 900 pages. For all of that, editor Bernard M. Bass concludes, "It would be instructive to gather behavioral data on an identified current group of charismatic business, military, church, and government leaders nominated by their subordinates because of the strong emotional bonding that has been established between the leaders and their subordinates and because the subordinates credit the leader for their transformed need structure and goal attainments."[10] We report on just such a group.

In 1979 we began to study the behavior of six chief executive officers (CEOs) of major American corporations—General Electric Company, Citicorp, AMAX Inc., Monsanto Company, International Business Machines Corporation, and New York Times Company—to learn *how* such a leader accomplished his mission. How did he get done what he got done? How did he move a large established bureaucratic organization to sustain its adaptive mode?

We are a clinical psychologist and a psychiatrist who have been teachers, consultants, and students of organizations and leadership problems —Levinson for thirty years, Rosenthal for thirteen; we are also involved in executive roles. We undertook this study for a number of reasons. Primary among them was our wish to keep learning about a field that is central to our work as professional consultants, teachers in schools of management and executive seminars, and writers about various executive and managerial problems. Although leaders operate in a multitude of ways, our hope was that we might elaborate certain common elements in practice, orientation, perception, and attitude that would help us understand more about organizational, particularly business, leadership. From extensive clinical and consulting experience we have long recognized the difficulties of changing organizations for even the most capable of executives. Therefore we also hoped to uncover those inhibiting factors that keep a leader from achieving what he has set out to achieve and how those limiting factors operate. Further, we were particularly interested in examining the degree of pressure that is created for people in these roles and how they handle that strain.

It is a curious fact that those who are at the top of their classes, whether in military academies or business schools, do not necessarily become the most successful leaders or the most competent practitioners of leadership. What is it, then, that enables some to rise to the top and, even more important, build structure and inculcate values that make them leaders rather than administrators? Is it enough to be in the right place at the right time, as some of our subjects have been? Obviously not. It is one thing to be in place, it is another to lead successfully. Clearly, personality factors are crucial. Many top-ranked management and military students are good analysts of theoretical problems but cannot translate ideas into action; or they cannot take charge, inspire followers, or gain the respect and trust of superiors that enables them to be promoted. It has been said that Churchill's words coming from Chamberlain would hardly have had the same effect. Some manage to get to high positions by manipulative skill, only to be found wanting in crisis. Our definition of "successful" must take account of how leaders manage the ups and downs to sustain organizational perpetuation. Finally, we thought the contemporary literature too glib and prescriptive. We felt it important to spell out in detail the behavior of leaders who were truly leaders by anyone's criteria.

Method

It is one thing to want to learn about the behavior of leaders and another to go about documenting that behavior. We had several choices. The first and most obvious one was to follow executives around and take notes on their behavior, a method that has been widely used at lower levels. But this approach didn't hold much promise because, unlike studies at lower levels where people remain essentially within a plant or within a limited territory, top leaders go everywhere. Their work takes them literally around the world and into such a range of activity that to document their varied behavior one would have to be with them every moment for a long period of time. Those requirements precluded firsthand observation as a method, although we could have the advantage of observation in our visits to their work settings and our time with them and their colleagues.

We might have approached the problem from a historical point of view, but that would produce history and not the data of observation. Much of what has been written about these executives and their companies is contemporary history. Finally, we could take advantage of the fact that there are some who have observed each of these leaders over an extended period of time during their close work association and so could tell us about how they did what they did. Those observations would complement our interviews with the leaders themselves. We chose that method.

The interview—the method of asking—has a long and noble history. As clinicians, it is our basic tool. It also has advantages for the interviewee. "How do people benefit from being interviewed?" asks psychologist Nevitt Sanford. "They have a chance to say things for which there had not previously been an appropriate audience. They can put into words some ideas and thoughts that had been only vaguely formulated. When these are met with attention and interest, self-esteem rises. People who are interviewed have a chance to reflect on their lives, to take stock, to think out loud about alternatives. . . ."[11]

Having chosen our method, the major issue still remained: which leaders would we choose and why? Someone once asked Margaret Mead why she had chosen the tribe she did. She replied that it was the first one she came to. In a certain sense, we did the same. We sought leaders of established major American business organizations—not the temporary projects of Silicon Valley, which do not yet have traditions, characteristic practices, or well-defined structures. Such established businesses, after all, have come to be models of work organizations that employ large populations and make major capital expenditures. Their practices are emulated by other companies. In that sense, their leaders are indeed significant leaders.

We first approached two chief executives with whom Harry Levinson had had previous contact—Ian K. MacGregor of AMAX and Thomas J.

Watson, Jr., of IBM. There was already an established bond of trust with them, and they readily agreed to participate in the study. Then, in order to have a diversified population, we approached the others—Reginald H. Jones of General Electric, Walter B. Wriston of Citicorp, John W. Hanley of Monsanto, and Arthur O. Sulzberger of the *New York Times*—whom we did not know. We deliberately did not choose any executives with whom we were or had been in consultation. We were indeed fortunate in our selection. We did not know, when we started, that in each instance the leader we chose had rebuilt his organization to new heights, that each had had to change things radically to survive. Nor did we know that all but one had risen through the ranks of his company. We knew only that each was the respected head of a prominent and successful business and each had been in the role long enough to have established his own reputation. Each had a reputation for stability, integrity—and leadership. As coincidence would have it, we discovered that two of the executives were serving on the corporate boards of two others—Hanley on Citicorp and Wriston on General Electric.

Most people would assume that all successful leaders could be characterized as "warriors" since they are all engaged in a highly competitive effort and operate from a strong sense of self-confidence. Their obvious achievements speak for themselves; the respect that others hold for them is reinforcing testimony to their right to that feeling. According to the literature they should have good ego strength and positive self-regard.

The leaders we interviewed were indeed warriors. They warred by building not a pastiche called a conglomerate but solid, integrated, evolutionary organizations. Theirs were multimillion dollar decisions whose outcomes might not be known for years, and they would have to bear the anxiety such uncertainty brings with it. Like most other human beings, from time to time they, too, doubted themselves. For them, that doubt was translated into attack rather than paralysis or retreat. They are extraordinary in the risks they take and the burdens they bear, yet they are ordinary in the psychological costs of that strain.

We asked each of these six leaders if he would be willing to be interviewed and to allow us to interview a half dozen or so colleagues, whom he would name, who had worked with him or were presently working with him and had observed his behavior firsthand. Our intent, we indicated, was to try to understand how a leader exerted an impact on the organization he headed, how he got done what he got done. We were not interested in exposés or justifications or evaluating leadership performance, but rather in understanding and reporting the *how*. We began the work in 1979. Busy executives were difficult to schedule. We did not finish the last interview until May, 1983.

We realized, of course, that in asking each of our CEOs to name those who had observed his behavior and who might be interviewed, we opened ourselves to certain elements of distortion. No matter. We could count on the overlapping perceptions and the repetition of experiences for some confirmation. We also knew that even when there is internal consistency to the information that comes from different people, one may be getting systematic distortion. But at least one learns about that person as seen through a range of lenses, although there may be a similar distortion in each. We cannot altogether discount that distortion, nor at the same time can we take it to be sufficient reason for rejecting the observations. There may be different later observations that will round out the perceptions, but for the moment these are the most accurate perceptions we have.

In some organizations there is a certain inherent constraint in the way people talk about each other and their leadership. That constraint is partly a product of the personalities of the individuals involved and partly a product of organizational values and behavior. There wasn't much we could do about that circumspection and, short of living in the organization itself over an extended period of time, it would be difficult to achieve the freedom of expression that ideally would provide us greater detail. In general, despite our pledge of confidentiality and anonymity, our observers were cautious in their direct or implied criticism of the CEO. This was especially the case in General Electric.

The questions we asked are spelled out in the appendix. They were intended to provide the chief executive interviewee with an opportunity to tell us something about his ego ideal, that never quite attainable goal that each of us constantly pursues and that for some becomes the basis for organizational goals. Subsequent questions helped to illuminate the relationship of the leader and his board, the potential gap between them, and the degree to which the leader, coming into his role, anticipated what he had to do to achieve his goals for the corporation. We also needed to know how the leader saw himself and how he regarded the company from a psychological viewpoint. The leader's self-image would also reveal his degree of insight about himself and his own behavior and about the feedback that he would get from other people about himself. The leader could tell us how he tried to establish operating modes in his organization, with what success and what lessons; he could also tell us what changes he could not effect. We expected our questions to illuminate some of the bases of the leader's strivings and the limits of his attainment.

From these many interviews (all of the interviewees were usually interviewed at least twice in two-hour sittings using the outline in the appendix), from the annual reports and many books written on the respective companies, as well as what has appeared in the managerial literature, we distilled the material to its present size. As much as possible, we tried to avoid repetition and to still maintain our focus on the CEO's behavior and his impact on his organization. Necessarily, much has been left out, much that would have been interesting and sometimes even amusing, but we believe that the essence of the individual leader's behavior is contained in these pages.

We asked each interviewee to check the transcript of his or her (one of the observers was a woman) interview for accuracy. When the penultimate chapter drafts were completed, we sent them to the individual chief executive subjects and asked each to review the chapter draft for accuracy of detail and possible distortion. We had promised each in advance that we would do so in the interest of accuracy because none of the interviewees would see any of the typescripts of the interviews of his colleagues, nor had he seen either preliminary drafts or the data from those interviews. Indeed, some of the biographical information our observer informants gave us was not accurate, and some that was hearsay could not be confirmed in other interviews. However, this procedure did not allow for substantive changes by the chief executive subject. It surprised us that none asked to alter remarks and observations that were critical of him. We expected them to be defensive; that, after all, is human. But, as John Hanley said, "If that's the way they see me, that's the way they see me." Some were concerned about the criticism of their predecessors and one, Walter Wriston, felt that only the record was worthy of consideration. To investigate feelings, thoughts, and behavior was for him an invasion of privacy.

This is not a psychological analysis of these executives. We did not attempt to address the question, "Why?" To do that would require highly detailed intimate life histories, and to discuss the *why* of identifiable living persons would raise serious ethical questions. We felt that if we specified the behavior as reported by the person himself and those who observed him, the reader would be free to make whatever inferences he or she wished. We proposed to let the behavior speak for itself. Although it was not our intent to offer psychological analysis, from time to time we have made an occasional psychological observation. Of course, our own questions and our own editing of the material necessarily makes for a certain point of view, and, no doubt, at times, even some distortion. Part of that distortion arises from the fact that we came to admire our chief executive subjects, foibles and all, for their significant achievements. It shows. There is no way of avoiding that kind of human limitation.

Another part of that distortion is necessarily a product of our biases about leadership. Our point of view is that some leaders want to be leaders and see themselves as leaders. Others rise to the occasion. In either case they see what has to be done and they do it. They provide stability and support while defining goals and providing reassurance. Sometimes they become leaders when they become angry about something, catch fire, and start to lead. The leader's mistakes outshine others' modest successes. Leaders state needs, formulate goals, and institute realistic methods for reaching them. They inspire and help others develop competences they need to serve the organization effectively. Managers become leaders when they learn to take a stand, to take risks, to anticipate, initiate, and innovate.

Leaders have a personal strategy, often vague, but nevertheless a blueprint that guides their careers. Leaders understand that big plans start small. Priorities and timing are of the essence. Step by step they build their integrated structure beneath them, not a single Maginot line but each step a platform for building more. They know what they do best and like best, and how to make those preferences and abilities valuable to others. They have a sense of what they want and a realistic, if not always conscious, understanding of how to get it. The leader is goal-obsessed. The goal may not be altogether clear, but the leader is always thinking about what should be done and how it can be accomplished, both in terms of life goals and organizational attainment. Their mental pictures of themselves as they would like to be in the future have an idealistic and idealized quality; therefore we speak of them as ego ideals. There is an intense striving for personal purpose which is translated into striving for organizational purpose, as differentiated from objectives and definable goals. And they become the leaders of others when they create the conditions for identification with themselves and thereby with the organization. By so doing they become the psychological glue that binds their followers together on behalf of the organization. The personal strategies of leaders, in the service of their ego ideals, breathe new life into their organizations and attract others to their efforts, to sharing their vision and their sense of purpose.

Leaders work at getting support—from above, below, and way off on the peripheries. Early in their careers, they sense who likes them, trusts them, and appreciates them, and they find ways for these people to support their efforts. Leaders understand that without supporters, they simply won't have the power to pursue their ideals. But they also understand that no supporter has to be behind all the leader's goals, or even to fully understand what the leader is after. Generally, leaders are especially alert to people who respond positively to them—and they are astute at assessing how these people can give them leverage to get things done. Leaders get support because they give support. They seek people out, listen to their concerns, and help them understand and resolve the problems they confront. Leaders understand that disappointment and defeat are inevitable in everyone's experience, and they help people anticipate and cope with them. Leaders also help others become more competent by sharing their skills, expertise, and political sophistication. They put their energy behind other people's projects and find ways for others to share in their own success.

Leaders also build support by holding themselves up as models whom others want to emulate. They teach others how to persevere in the face of defeat, how to develop their abilities, and how to pursue goals that are worthy. Though leaders may demand more of their subordinates than other bosses do, their followers willingly give their best because they know they are doing more, learning more, and growing more than they thought possible. Leaders ultimately hold on to their followers because they impart great excitement and enthusiasm about their own work and devotion to the organization, and in that way spark their supporters' creative energies.

Leaders are able to use their power base and implement their strategies because they are thinkers as well as doers. When a program, product, or strategy isn't working, they don't throw up their hands—they figure out what has to be done, confident that their efforts can make the future better than the present. Leaders enjoy conceptualizing, projecting, fantasizing. Where others dread ambiguity, leaders welcome it, seeing opportunities to shape new directions. True leaders are not afraid to take over a failing unit or company, embark on a risky long-term venture, or face a sea of conflicting pressures: they welcome the challenge. And they know full well that safe ventures quickly go stale and never lead to significant success.

Because leaders are always figuring out how they can try new methods, take on more responsibilities, develop their people, and serve their organizations in new ways, they are never bored. They immerse themselves in their work because they love the process, and they seek the gratifications of mastery, usefulness, and creativity. Ultimately leaders are captivated by what their work means. They appreciate the larger social context of their work, and they shape their work to the significant social contribution they hope to make.

It is true that many people demand such perfection of leaders that no one could possibly measure up. Indeed, some demand that of themselves. But leaders cannot be leaders if they are driven by intense internal demand that denies them patience, timing, and flexibility. No leader can lay a major problem to rest in a matter of months, or sometimes, even years. Though necessarily heroic models, leaders cannot expect of themselves the wisdom to right the ills of the world. Wise leaders are those who are willing to propose, attempt, and initiate. They are leaders because they are ready to act when others are still confused, afraid, and indecisive. Leaders test their powers and expand their horizons, generating a life of creative activity that is, in itself, a gratification. Richard Nixon admired de Gaulle's view of a leader as one who aims high, shows that he has vision, acts on the grand scale, and so establishes his authority over the generality of men who splash in shallower waters.[12] We agree.

Despite our experience and our biases, we learned much that surprised us (which we discuss fully in chapter 8). For example, we did not anticipate the degree of self-doubt several of our leaders verbalized, nor the effectiveness with which they mastered it. Although Levinson wrote a book, *Executive*,[13] urging executives to be teachers, we did not anticipate the huge amount of time leaders at this level spent developing other people and ensuring succession. Nor did we appreciate the significance of the huge amount of money these leaders risked in research and capital expenditures as investments in an ambiguous future. Although the popular literature has it that the best place for innovation is in garages—in "the skunkworks"—the reality is that massive sums are required for systematic research. These sums were risked in three cases by leaders who were not themselves technically trained, and who overruled their own engineers and scientists to commit their companies to distant technical horizons. Despite much of the managerial literature advocating that management hang loose, all of the leaders were directive and demanding. Although they made a point of almost never giving orders, they got what they wanted because they didn't tolerate for long not getting it. We were surprised by how willingly five of the six men handed over the reins to their successors, though each could have maneuvered to hold on longer. Finally, we were surprised that these leaders themselves were so willing to talk to us, and so easy to talk to. We were also struck by their modesty.

These, then, are our synopses of the experiences of six leaders, all of whom headed major corporations at the time of the interviews, one of whom still does. We think that what we have written accurately describes these men as they practiced their leadership and provides a reasonable basis for understanding their impact on their organizations. The reader can now test that understanding and share our surprises.

Reginald H. Jones

GENERAL ELECTRIC COMPANY

FRED BORCH had been catching hell. *Fortune, Forbes,* and *Dun's Review* all had taken him to task for General Electric's losses, which reduced its 1970 profits below those of 1969. As CEO, he had been confronted with the need to pour money into three seemingly bottomless economic holes: computers, nuclear power, and aircraft engines. He had not foreseen inflation, the escalation of computer costs, or the near-collapse of the aircraft industry. Perhaps each of these major investments could have been managed one at a time, but three? Hardly. In addition, GE was under antitrust attack, which demanded inordinate attention from Borch. But none of these, he told a *Forbes* reporter, involved decision making as difficult as the ongoing organizational and personnel decisions. He was deeply immersed in structuring a new corporate staff, for "no one man," the next CEO, could handle it all. The business press speculated on his successor.[1]

Outsiders had predicted that vice-chairman Jack Parker would get the job. Some insiders were sure it would be vice-chairman Walter D. Dance. Borch chose Reg Jones. (Everyone at GE called him Reg, which rhymes with Peg. The nickname came from his wife, Grace.) Jones, like other GE top managers, had worked his way up through the managerial ranks, starting as a managerial trainee and spending eight years as a traveling auditor. Borch had put him in charge of strategic business planning as financial vice-president. The planning group came up with the concept of strategic business units as a method for arranging GE's 10 groups, 50 divisions, and 166 departments. These units would focus primarily on medical care, transportation, plastics, and power generation. Jones had also been instrumental in getting GE out of the computer business by selling their computer interests to Honeywell.

Jones was a demonstrably competent general manager. What's more, he had a reputation for doing his homework and great popularity among his GE colleagues. Said one World War II–vintage observer, "He had Eisenhower's political instincts and affability, [General] George Marshall's overall perspective, and an intimidating intellectual capacity." A trim, highly controlled person, described by one reporter as almost pedagogical, Jones knew GE inside out. He also understood that GE would survive only with public permission, that social and economic justice must modify free markets. He therefore had a strong interest in changing the political and social climate in which business operated. He was also a gentle person. His prodigious memory and financial knowledge might well enable him to be on top of GE's business, but his gentleness might well inhibit his face-to-face control of those who needed that kind of control.

When, in June, 1972, Fred Borch told him he was to be Borch's successor, Reg Jones's knees were shaking—a phenomenon not new to him. "I'm not overly imbued with self-confidence," he explained later. Snide remarks had it that most GE top executives were graduates of obscure midwestern engineering schools. Jones was an Easterner, a business school graduate with a major in finance. In GE the financial role usually carried negative, critical, penny-pinching connotations.

Jones demurred at first because "I was uncertain about external aspects of the job, like meeting the President of the United States, or a foreign political personality." He was not then known for his skill in dealing with people outside the corporation, nor was he considered a community leader. Borch reminded him of his successful negotiations with presidents Nixon and Pompidou.

In September, 1972, before he became chairman, Borch had sent Jones to try to arrange with Pompidou a joint effort in aircraft engine development and nuclear power generation. Pompidou was a hard-sell. He asked Reg why France needed General Electric's technology, and, besides, Westinghouse had already been in the nuclear game and was more cooperative. Reg had to persuade Pompidou of General Electric's value to France and of the merits of his company. Once having done that, he had to persuade the U.S. government to allow the arrangement to go through; the government was then very much concerned about the possibility that American companies seeking foreign business might give away American technology, which would have a significant impact on the United States' competitive position. Therefore, Reg had to get President Nixon to convince the executive branch of the government to go along with this project since from the standpoint of international trade and the standpoint of providing employment for American workers, it was critical that the government approve and support that effort. Reg made these points to George Shultz who was then secretary of the treasury. Shultz in turn persuaded Nixon to go along with the General Electric position. It was to this successful negotiating experience that Fred Borch was referring. "Yes, but my knees were shaking then," Jones protested, still unconvinced he was the right person for the job. Borch showed him the ratings of the contenders, which both he and the board of directors had made. That unanimous endorsement ended Jones's resistance. Despite his trepidation, he began to reexamine the company that was to be his to guard and lead—the largest diversified industrial company in the world.

Reg knew he faced serious problems. The outside world saw in GE a corporate monolith, robust with managerial depth. Its record 1972 sales of $10.2 billion were double the figure of ten years before. Its 12 percent net earnings gain resulted in an all-time high in net earnings per share, 17.5 percent on shareholders' equity and 12.7 percent on investment for the year. The price of GE stock ranged from 20 to 25 times earnings. There was a record $10 billion backlog of unfilled orders. And GE had a heritage of technical leadership which dated back to its founding in 1878 as the Edison Electric Light Company. Financial advisers touted GE as a good investment value for the long term because of its size and diversification; its financial resources, including its conservative accounting methods; its technical prominence; and its leadership in the market place.

But inside, it was another story. There were ominous signs and symptoms of internal inefficiency and ineffectiveness. Some spoke of them as the six crises:

1. The company's working capital was anemic. Its heavy investment in facilities left it cash poor. The cash drain was so horrendous that GE

came close to losing its AAA credit rating. It had borrowed $300 million to pay the bills because the company had run out of cash.

2. The Corporate Executive Office, the multiple-role top management structure formed by Borch in 1968, was comprised of Jones and three vice-chairmen. Like all hydra-headed structures, it did not function well. The vice-chairmen had "cognizance" over certain groups, with ambiguous, collective responsibilities for the company as a whole. The group executives who reported to them were not sure whether they had a single boss or multiple bosses.

3. Although international sales had increased 60 percent and international net income had tripled between 1968 and 1972 (to 16 and 17 percent of GE's 1972 sales and earnings, respectively), Jones saw no undergirding business strategy. Nor was there a managerial strategy or one for international succession management. There were a significant number of add-on, international acquisitions that had little realistic upside potential and increasingly ominous downside risk.

4. There were threats and potential threats on all sides. The investment community could threaten GE's high price/earnings ratio. Increasing governmental controls and a congressional threat to impose larger taxes on overseas operations of U.S. companies could force many of those operations out of existence, severly reduce earnings and domestic jobs, and cripple the U.S. competitive position in world markets, including that of GE. There was the never-ending task of building public understanding of the vital need for profit in a competitive market economy.

5. Union contract negotiations loomed for 1973. They had never been easy for GE. The company had experienced a three-month strike in 1969/1970, its first company-wide strike in twenty-six years.

6. Jones had a nagging suspicion that GE's technological lead was eroding and competitors might have achieved parity, even superiority, in some areas. Its technological "firsts" had produced a "not-invented here" mind set; its scientists took a negative view of others' innovations.

But the picture wasn't all negative. Jones had inherited a company of residual health, and he could see the gains Borch had made over what he had inherited. Jones took his leadership conception from the 1972 GE annual report motif. The caption on the cover read, "General Electric today; one company unified by its technological heritage that began with electric lighting." GE, then, would shine from a core. It would be integrated around technologies. It would illuminate and lead the way.

Head of the "Family"

But where to begin? To understand that question in context, one has to know the ethos of GE. Outsiders say that the GE monogram is stamped on the rear ends of its people. And well it might be, given the average of twenty-five years that senior managers have been with the company. They share knowledge, traditions, a history, a value system, and a self-image. From early on it is drummed into GE managers that the company's image must be protected at the expense of short-term gains that compromise quality or integrity. Though the company was shaken by a price-fixing scandal that sent some GE vice-presidents to jail, high standards of "ethical entrepreneurship," moral integrity, hallmark quality, and technical leadership had long been integral to GE's self-image.

Despite its size, its many divisions, and the enormous range of its products, GE is not a conglomerate. GE's monogram is affixed to all products. (Hotpoint added "Made by General Electric" on its appliances.) That monogram constitutes a banner and a franchise under which everyone wins or loses—the "toaster rubs off on the turbine" theory—fostering the "one company" image. When Ralph J. Cordiner, Borch's predecessor, decentralized GE in the early 1950s into 110 businesses, managers were continuously reminded they were still part of GE. Loyalty is highly valued, first to the company as a whole and then to one's businesses. Self-aggrandizement is not tolerated. In fact, some believe that when *Fortune* featured Dr. Thomas A. Vanderslice as a potential successor to Jones, that killed his chances.

Loyalty is exemplified in another way. No one interviewed for this chapter, even those who had left the company, would say much that was negative about Jones or GE. Nor would they speak with financial reporters who sought to interview former GE executives about their GE experiences. That loyalty, together with strong hierarchical control and entrepreneurial-minded managers, makes for extreme responsiveness to corporate signals. When Fred Borch gave the signal that the company had to become international, according to Jones, "You couldn't go into the airport at Frankfurt any day of the week without seeing two or three GE people moving through Frankfurt at the same time." GE managers rushed pell mell to buy up companies—too many of which had to be divested in the next five years.

"GE has a unique culture. It's a family. We enjoy each other. We don't lose many in the family of GE people. We're so supportive of each other," said Jones. "We try desperately to save an individual who has failed, by placing him in a job that better matches his capacities, in order that that individual can make a contribution to the organization. We save many people. There is a renaissance of these people in many instances." This is not merely pious talk. In one case, Jones demoted a failing group head to a regional vice-presidency where the latter's customer contact and business expertise won him respect. In another, a senior executive requested demotion to a position in which he subsequently gained accolades.

The easy give-and-take informality that marks and promotes the network of friendships and collegial fellowship at GE is expressed in the emphasis on teamwork. GE executives come from many origins. There are said to be no old school ties or ethnic or regional cliques among them. Plaudits are shared with the group, and competition is muted and gentlemanly. An observer might even say that it is suppressed. This may explain the insiders' image of the company as having a low incidence of politics. The expression of caring and concern for people is balanced by a reverence for analytical, objective approaches to business. Some attribute this to the large numbers of scientists and engineers in the organization. Conservative comportment in dress and speech (profanity raises eyebrows) is paralleled by marked financial conservatism. "It's a mature company, balanced, sound, solid, one of the most financially conservative companies," Jones remarked, adding, "A foreign visitor once said, 'The company reminds me of a staid old woman who looks both ways before going across the street.'"

Another facet of the company's character had nearly led to a financial rout. "I knew that GE traditionally never gives up on anything," Jones told a reporter as he replayed his role in the venture into computer manufacturing, and in the 1970 retreat. An early booster of entry into computers, Jones, then financial vice-president, sounded the alarm in 1970 to reassess that costly effort. "We never appreciated the size of the opportunity and we never devoted the resources to it that we should have," Jones told the *Wall Street Journal.* He was a key member of the task force assigned the job of reexamining the venture. They proposed and won approval for immediate withdrawal, and Jones was asked to execute it. His and others' analyses showed GE's strength in international markets and Honeywell's in the United States, GE's strength in the largest and smallest computer lines, Honeywell's in the middle. Combining the two product lines and the marketing organizations would create a strong competitor, an outcome that negotiator Jones impressed upon Honeywell as well as the Justice Department. He spent nine months negotiating the deal. Out of the subsequent sale to Honeywell, GE recouped $240 million of its losses.[2] Pundits note that had GE delayed a year or two longer, it would have had to close out that business at a far greater loss. Many believe, as Jack Parker said, it was literally Jones's crowning achievement.[3]

There was no organizational revolution when Jones took over. He knew he had to work "with the grain." It was not a matter of going along to get along; he abhorred the prospect of a GE turned bureaucratic. But Jones grasped that the grain—GE's traditions, its culture—was the transducer through which he would harness, energize, stabilize, and steer this leviathan through whatever economic seas it might encounter.

Liquidity

GE's rapid growth of the 1960s had allowed slack in the reins of financial controls. By late 1973 the liquidity problem was compounded by rising interest rates, cash management problems, double-digit inflation, the financial plight of the electric utilities (major customers), the reality of a serious business downturn, and the energy crisis with its high costs and material shortages. Jones insisted on attention to financial fundamentals—balance sheets, cash flow, return on investment, and costs. Getting receivables down was accomplished mostly by teaching the *whys* and *hows* to the top layer in the company.

Jones had not been known to be a good public speaker. In his earliest speeches as president, he chain-smoked while he read his notes. In one of his first appearances at GE's Crotonville, New York, training center, he made a brief courtesy appearance with a ten-minute presentation that disappointed his managers and left them wondering what he had said.

Reg was very much aware of the fact that he was not an outstanding public speaker, and that he needed to improve his podium skills in order to do well as a chief executive. By reading books on speechmaking he learned to respond to the short attention span of his listeners and to recognize the need for pointed examples, humor, and dramatic quality. He listened to recordings of his own speeches. And, essentially, he became a good speaker by polishing his own skills rather than by formal training. Now he took to the stump. In sessions with individuals or staffs of component organizations, his message was consistent. "We've got to stop the hemorrhaging. We have to learn how to manage cash . . . because we're in desperate straits. You must each find ways to cut inventories, to reverse the course of receivables. We're cutting back on appropriations."

Only when this behemoth began to turn around and it was obvious that the crisis was clearly behind them did Jones cease his jawboning. In 1975 Jones went out of his way to tell his people, "My God, if you can turn this General Electric Company around, there's nothing you guys can't do. Look what you did with this. You turned this cash situation around in six months."

Structure

Reg Jones and the three vice-chairmen, all of whom had been contenders for his office, now had to learn to work with each other despite their respective feelings. As would Ian MacGregor and Jack Hanley in the chapters to come, Jones had to cope with contenders who remained. Describing his experiences managing the disappointment and hostility of former rivals who became his subordinates as he moved through the ranks, he said, "I took the soft approach, coaxed them, let them work out their hostility by my being humble and friendly." By June, 1973, six months into his new role, he had dissolved the vague vice-chairman "cognizance" concept. Instead, he made each vice-chairman directly responsible for certain designated operating groups and corporate staff components. Responsibilities and accountabilities became clearer. Each was also able to be a "vocal advocate" for his groups in the competition for financial and personnel resources. This change from cognizant to direct responsibility wasn't accepted instantly. How did Jones deal with the initial resistance to this role change? "I wouldn't accept the responsibility. When we were in a meeting, when they asked me what I was going to do about a problem, I asked, 'What are you going to do about it? You are responsible for the operation. Do it. Tell me what you intend to do and then do it.' "

Anticipating major thrusts on the fiscal front and others, Jones began to realign the management system at the top. (Realignment to enhance competitive adaptation was tackled by each of our CEOs.) Executives unable or unwilling to meet his standards were replaced over the years, according to insiders, by a phalanx of more competitive hands-on, hard-nosed, broad-gauge operating executives. (This, too, characterizes the direction each CEO took.)

The six corporate staff senior vice-presidents together with the Corporate Executive Office (the chairman and three vice-chairmen) now comprised a new structure, the Corporate Policy Committee, "a forum for reviewing and communicating matters of broad corporate concern." Jones was laying the groundwork for the later dissolution of the corporate executive staff. Jones had R. L. Johnson, vice-president of executive manpower, report directly to him. Like Borch, he would be preoccupied with succession from the beginning. He would not leave the development of managers to chance, nor relegate it to a staff function.

In 1973, Jones initiated a company organization study to formulate a long-range plan into 1981/1982 for an evolving structure that would provide orderly succession and manageability of the greatly enlarged organization he anticipated. He had no specific idea of what that structure should look like. He began by thinking out loud with Johnson and some of his staff. He told them he was unsure where the ensuing discussions would lead, but he wanted help in preparing a detailed outline for a future discussion with top management of the company. He rambled, thinking aloud about some major outline headings and some concepts he wanted to have included. He asked them to keep integrating their continuing discussions into an evolving report. He supplemented the staff's detailed notes of these meetings with his own preliminary notes. He, himself, was known for near-verbatim, highly legible notetaking in outside meetings. This process of consultative thinking which led to a formal document was only the beginning of what was to become a trademark of Jones's style and effectiveness. He would soon gather the best and the brightest staff expertise to assault external threats as well.

Jones had collected 160 items in notes to himself about managment issues. In August, 1973, he began to clarify and document his "Management Style and Related Convictions" (a collection of ideas from the 160 he had noted). Some were maxims, some guidelines, some directives to himself. These included:

1. Minimize ambiguity. (Change the functions of the vice-chairmen and the corporate executive staff, and ensure that people know the purpose of a meeting—decision-making meetings versus review meetings versus communications meetings.)

2. Do your homework. (This becomes more critical as you attain higher responsibility, see the big picture, and know enough details to personally perform "validity tests." Be willing to read in depth and breadth.)

3. The necessity of strategic planning. ("Surprises" are a cardinal sin. See each business situation for what it is and not through one's emotional glasses of what one might like to think it is. Make strategic planning a way of life.)

4. Personal relationships. (Have a firsthand knowledge of your customers and their needs, knowing people as *individuals;* listen with both ears and be willing to "level" with people and to be "leveled" with.)

5. Decision making. (Provide a vehicle that fosters consensus—tempered by the willingness to make decisions where consensus is not achieved. Be ready to stimulate, implement, and live with change. Be prepared to take difficult or unpopular remedial actions where results continue to fall below objectives. Be willing to take risks, make mistakes, and learn from them, and afford one's subordinates the same opportunity.)

6. Put on the "company hat." (Be willing to accept actions that may have a negative impact upon a particular component but are in the best interests of the company as a whole.)

These became part of what Jones called his personal road map.

Strategy

Reg Jones counted on GE's pioneering strategic planning system (implemented in 1970) "to help us accelerate our investments in areas of real potential and to limit our commitments in less promising areas." He elevated the planning function to report directly to himself and stepped up the divestiture program. The outcome was dramatic. GE divested more businesses in 1973 and 1974 than in all of its many previous years. That move increased both cash flow and quality of earnings, although removing low profit businesses from GE's portfolio also reduced its diversity. Crediting top officers with the felicitous turn of events was vintage Jones and GE culture. However, implementing divestitures often required Jones's personal touch. "No one wanted to liquidate his empire," he recalled. His basic control mechanism was resource allocation—but with a twist. Jones instituted inflation-adjusted measures in capital budgeting for individual businesses and projects to ensure that new investments earned rates of return appropriate to their risks. He simply told some managers, "You have no money to continue."[4]

Those were the exceptions. Jones preferred gentle persuasion. He confided to an associate, "I have not issued an edict . . . but I tell you, it's very tempting. But we can't run the company by edicts because it's not fair to the businesses, because you don't know what the right edict should be for each business." That belief was restated again and again in our interviews with the CEOs.

There were times when push came to shove for, despite his manifest patience, underneath, like all people of strong conscience, Jones is an impatient man. When executives dragged their feet on the changes that had been recommended, he was not above precipitating action by demanding to know why. Executives had to present tightly reasoned briefs to justify budget requests. "Where does the business stand relative to competition? What have been the significant trends? What share of the market do you have? What new products do you have coming on-stream? How much have you invested in new engineering?" Shades of the Wharton graduate student whose penchant was to question intellectual economic orthodoxy! In the case of one marginal business, the operating executive made a few lame attempts to explain his request, then painfully acknowledged Jones's juggernaut of facts and concluded that the best strategic alternative was to sell or close his business. Jones assented, only to have the executive plead the impossibility of its liquidation on historical grounds—"GE has always been in this business." Reg assuaged the executive's guilt about altering the GE self-image by pointing to other examples of divestiture, saying, "If we can't see a way to make it go, then let's get out." He helped them find potential buyers or partners.

Reg Jones's style in strategic planning was aggressive probing and penetration in a context of underlying and continuous support for the individual. He used his strength to strengthen individuals and the organization. By so doing, he also modeled a standard and method of leadership. His ability to discern inconsistencies in reported business plans was quickly noted by operating executives. His painstaking preparation for a business meeting prodded subordinates to do likewise. His tone and his focus on the reality that confronted them all soothed the inevitable anxiety about being exposed and punished that accompanies the

actions of a charismatic leader. His hard-nosed business approach fit a
GE culture that venerated professionalism and operating competence.

Jones immersed himself in the business plans of the new forty-three
strategic business units. These basic business entities were of varied
sizes that could grow from department to division to group. Each was
responsible for planning and resource allocation to serve a specific
product/market segment. He inaugurated, and then conscientiously
read and digested, the monthly three-page "Review and Estimate of
Operations" report of the forecasts, sales, and net income from each of
the then two hundred profit centers. He also saw the incoming weekly/
monthly order reports for the entire company. Under later circumstances, intimates thought that these activities were too trivial for him
to continue.

Although his queries did not indict or insult, some senior executives
thought that he got a kick out of catching them off guard. His "gotchas"
kept them on their toes. His questions weeded out inconsistency and
jargon. "How did you derive this? Would you explain that term to me?"
Jones relentlessly but gently forced people to achieve clarity. He as-
serted high standards by pulling new perspectives into discussions,
which elevated the level of discourse. "Reg made suggestions that were
far beyond what you would expect from a financial man," commented
William H. Dannler, a retired GE vice-chairman, in a feature article
about Jones's performance as a financial vice-president. "Although he
might be talking with others about spending money, he'd chime right
in on marketing or on technical matters. In time, he got to be considered a good backup man on anything . . . but he was the best financial
man I ever met."[5]

In the summer of 1972, shortly after becoming president of GE, Reg
Jones moved from the GE domestic stage to the international one. A
cornerstone of his strategy was the reinvigoration of the international
business. Certain strategic business units were expected to develop
specific programs in specific parts of the world. In the first major test
of his mettle in that new role and in that broader strategic arena, Jones
met with President Pompidou of France to discuss GE's hoped-for role
in that nation's aircraft engine program. After an early morning arrival
in Paris, he spent the afternoon closeted with an associate, fine-tuning
his presentation for the thirty-minute, 5 P.M. meeting. He was able to
read, understand, and speak a little French, so he polished a few apt
phrases for the meeting. He was acutely aware that his business arguments would not be conclusively persuasive, so he framed his proposals
within the perspective of the broader, eighty-year relationship between

GE and France and cast that perspective into the future. It worked! Knees shaking, he came through with distinction. During the relaxed cocktail hour and dinner on the plane home when the day's triumph was replayed, he left no doubt he was pleased with himself. From the outset he knew that GE's future would be strongly influenced by outside political forces, themselves a product of economic and social issues. The French connection had given him confidence and, more significantly, tapped a latent reservoir of concern, interest, and skills.

Jones's international travel during his months as president and later as chairman highlighted his penchant—some say fetish—for punctuality. Early one morning, one of Jones's associates who had joined him in mid-itinerary, still suffering from jet lag, was awakened by a Danish bellhop. He dressed, packed, and rushed to the lobby only to find Reg had taken the first car to the airport—for a chartered plane that was not leaving until all company personnel were aboard. When he arrived at the airport, the associate found Jones unperturbed; the plane left on schedule. Two GE executives who had concluded contract negotiations were in Madrid, the last stop for Jones and his party on that trip. Jones assented to their flying home on the company plane. Cautioned by the savvy associate—"Be on time. In fact, be early because Reg will, for sure, be in the car moving at 7 A.M."—they met the associate the next morning on an elevator to the lobby for a 6:15 checkout. There Jones, checked out, paced about the lobby waiting for an airport car scheduled for a 7 A.M. departure.

External Threats

Recognizing in those early months that he would have to engage the outside world, Reg appointed Robert Fegley as the first full-time staff assistant for chief executive officer communications and stationed Fegley almost within earshot of his own office—a managerial gesture that signaled Reg's imminent plunge into the external relations aspects of his role. Reg included his communications expert in meetings in which issues and strategy were discussed. To stay on the same wave length, they exchanged reading material (Reg requested book reviews, including a summary and underline of key passages).

Jones simultaneously focused his efforts on regaining the company's near-term financial equilibrium. He ventured into the investment community to protect the premium price/earnings ratio. "I stuck our collective necks out with the investment community to run 'counter economy' and, solely for internal consumption, set a target of 10 percent annual earnings growth over time—not for each year regardless of the economic cycle." Late in 1974, he confided, "I did this because I felt we all could pull it off—that our management always responded to a challenge. I did it also because I saw no other way to convince the investment community that our premium P/E ratio had continuing merit." (GE did not retain its premium. Subsequent market forces dropped stock prices generally.)

Over the longer range, Jones was concerned with maintaining a profitable growth rate (earnings, not merely fat sales) that would exceed the growth of the U.S. Gross National Product. Accordingly, he declared his goal to internationalize the company—to acquire a greater share of markets that were growing faster than those of the United States—which he supported by publicly urging government initiatives to enhance the U.S. competitive position abroad.

Contract Renewal

Prior to 1973, GE's labor relations policies and attitude toward the coalition of unions that represented nearly half of its employees had been tough. But preliminary informal discussions with the unions gave Jones cause for optimism about the upcoming contract negotiations. Himself inexperienced at labor negotiations, Jones worked in harness with John F. Burlingame, a relatively new, but knowledgeable, vice-president of corporate employee relations. They reversed GE's tough stance to one of genuine give-and-take negotiations and emerged with a new thirty-seven-month contract.

Technical Erosion

GE's Research and Development Center was renowned. It was supplemented by the activities of more than one hundred laboratories associated with product operations. Two GE scientists had won Nobel

Prizes. The company led all others by winning 8 of the awards for "the 100 most significant new technical projects," in a competition conducted by Industrial Research, Inc. It obtained 1,116 patents in 1973. Almost 13,000 employees holding college technical degrees were at work in research, development, and engineering. Jones increased the company-funded part of the 1973 research and development budget by 10 percent to $330 million. (The rest of the research funding was contract research. Total research funding in 1973 was $845 million.) None of this relieved his apprehensions about the company's technological position.

Jones's lack of technical competence may explain his paradoxical success in fathoming the business implications of technical issues. "I don't understand this, let me ask a stupid question," he would say. These "stupid questions" led to further attempts at clarification, with less jargon. If the response was still too technical, he would ask for further explanation in simpler language, pressing for successive clarifications to get an increasingly precise answer. "I know if he's [a technical manager] trying to snow me. I keep plumbing the issue until I get to the business essence of it. I would then repeat this same process with four to five people, and see what shades could be discovered, and how they would reply to the same questions." Reg would make tentative suggestions about what to do, and see what kind of reply this would elicit from the technologists. "There was something of an osmosis of understanding," he said about his immersion in the eddies of expert opinion.

At the 1974 Belleair* management meeting he interjected a downbeat note into that traditionally upbeat event, exhorting managers to analyze the company's failures as well as triumphs, and to learn from them. "I told them we have to get better in technology." As did Thomas Watson of IBM (chapter 6), Jones sensed the importance of technical advances that his own technical people did not yet grasp.

*From 1924 to 1956 the company held annual three-day summer conferences in the camp milieu of GE-owned Association Island in the St. Lawrence River, a rite of passage for young managers when they attained a certain level of responsibility. Initiates met the top officers; all wore first-name badges, were filled in on the business and its objectives, and given an inspirational talk along with fun and games. Association Island was considered "the home of the GE spirit" and constituted initiation into GE management. Expense, flooding, and inadequate size for the expanding company forced a move to the Hotel Bellevue Biltmore in Florida, a site chosen by Ralph Cordiner. The old grande dame 1890s structure, largest of its kind, featured superb individual service, thirty-six holes of golf, and antique-style furnishings. Borch used it, and Jones insisted on keeping it despite pressures to change to a meeting place with more modern decor. Reg identified it as the new Association Island, publicizing its availability to management for company conferences.

To stimulate the researchers and technicians Jones asked a group of internal and external (McKinsey and Co.) technologists to prepare a fifteen-volume report on the frontiers and directions of technology. He explained his position to them: "I want you to know I initiated, personally, the *Technology Study,* to see where our strengths and weaknesses are, a hundred years after Edison. And I'm the person who made sure that the R&D Center had a budget sustained even during the recession . . . in constant dollar terms. And, I've kept the head count the same . . . even while everything else was being cut back to accommodate our income during the recession . . . I want you to know that I am personally behind our renewal of our technological efforts."

In the ensuing years Jones strongly encouraged technological transfer between high and lower technology businesses. He initiated the practice of subsidizing transfer costs of technology between operating units so that the managers wouldn't be concerned about the effects of such costs on their profit and loss statements. He saw a need to retrain the company's electromechanical engineers in electronic technology, to hire electronic engineers, and to incorporate electronics into the organization's new operations and products. Every year he issued a series of "corporate challenges" to all the strategic business units. These annual challenges, covering issues that affected the whole organization, were characterized as "things that are bugging the Chairman." In 1977 he selected the issue of microprocessors to be addressed in their business plans for the year. "I called people together and asked what we were doing to incorporate electronic technology into our products. I arranged exhibits of microprocessors at the Belleair meetings and then took those exhibits around the country."

The New Beginning

By the close of his first year as CEO, Jones had taken initiatives on the six crises according to his "Management Style and Related Convictions." Throughout that year he accelerated the divestiture program and focused intensely on twenty of the forty-three strategic business units in the initial Executive Office reviews of the groups. He developed and implemented refined financial processes with strong warnings on cash management and imputed interest. In September he launched an intensive look at the numbers of exempt (from wage and hour law requirements) personnel across the company and a detailed review of corporate staff. Consolidations and reorganizations were part of the tightening-up process. Some consolidations flopped, and the components had to be restored to their original form.

Concurrent with fine-tuning the management system and wedding it to financial controls, Jones worked intensively with his vice-president of executive manpower, Roy Johnson, to plan for succession and manageability. They reviewed the results of interviews with fifty division general managers and some department general managers concerning their subordinates, all part of a company organization study. Jones discussed the organization and assignment of roles at the top of the company with the Management Development and Compensation Committee of the board of directors in May and September of 1974. He shared with them, and later with his officers, an objective rundown of his attributes and those of the vice-chairmen, compiled by Johnson from the interviews. "I went over these attributes—including my own as viewed by all of you—with the MDCC. Let me say that it's a very humbling experience." Apparently he had been criticized for trying to do too much himself, for he admitted he "could not continue to try to play all the roles. I have been trying to cover too much ground and several important roles have suffered. . . . The board confirmed the necessity of my continuing to try to play a strong, lead role in external relations. They and I feel this is crucial to General Electric in light of the threats we see. . . . It seemed best to try sharing the internal operations."

Jones's effectiveness was bolstered by his legendary capacity for remembering and attending to detail. No one in GE could recall a CEO with such stunning mastery of the diversified operations of that giant enterprise. Whatever aroused his interest evoked a request for details and explanation from the next person in the chain of responsibility. At one day-long midyear review of the strategic plans of a multibillion dollar, multibusiness segment, Jones took aim on a $20-million piece of a half-billion dollar business with a penetrating question about the *hows* and the *whys* of a changing market share. "It beats me," replied the senior executive in charge, "but we'll find out for you." No levity there. That subordinate knew Jones had read that plan and all the others in the inches-thick plan book. The subordinate perceived these detailed queries as a natural and spontaneous expression of Jones's way of operating. Jones didn't become upset with an "I don't know"—as long as it didn't become a habit.

Self-effacing comments about his lack of technical background ("I'm unskilled in science and advanced math. I have no physics or chemistry, which is a great shortcoming on my part.") did not deter him from religiously reading a monthly, five-page technology status report from the Research and Development Center within thirty minutes of its arrival. He would then pluck a choice item and phone an expectant executive-expert for comment. Those executives who might expect to receive such a call would instruct their secretaries to have the monthly report on their desks within minutes of its arrival, much like a physician keeping abreast of mass-media medical columns to answer querulous patients.

In November, 1974, Jones stated his management philosophy in the form of management tenets or principles. They undergirded his financial initiatives and the company's strategic approach. The first was the imperative of liquidity. The second was his intention to reinvest most heavily in those businesses that could recover that reinvestment. The strategy would be to identify product lines and businesses that were quickly susceptible to price increases and whose customers could pay their bills. The third was his determination to manage a tighter portfolio over the rest of the decade by continued pruning and avoiding "ventures where entry capital costs are just too high for short-to-moderate term return," even at the cost of diversity.

His fourth and fifth tenets dealt with some loss of autonomy and tighter control at all levels of the organization, and applying a differentiated approach to the degree of autonomy allowed. From then on, managers' authority would vary not so much by organizational echelon as by the importance of a business strategy plan to the company and by the complexity of its strategy; by issues of product safety or corporate liability; by reinvestment opportunities and requirements; by the confidence in and tenure of the executive in charge of the business; and by the need to respond to critical changes in economic and industry conditions. Finally, each higher echelon in the structure had to contribute an "added value" to the total. "The whole is greater than the sum of the parts. . . . We are not merely portfolio managers of many businesses, or a holding company, but a single enterprise. . . . Our staffs and our laboratories and our top management have a responsibility to make a special contribution that will differentiate us totally from the conglomerates."

Jones fleshed out his corporate strategy. He would pursue high quality and high technology goods and services, backed by integrity of after-sales service. A commitment to profitable, quality growth would mean developing ventures from within, with only a highly selective acquisition overlay. There would be smaller and less concentrated risk; he would not bet the company again. The international and services business "will become increasingly 'where it's at' in this decade. I fully intend for us to be 'where it's at.'" He used the vacancies created by early retirements (some the product of his encouragement) to disband the corporate executive staff. He explained its dissolution: "It was invented to do a chore. That task was finished. Now we had the strategic planning system done. . . . We had already developed, explained and reviewed and analyzed the entire previous system . . . and we really didn't need the corporate executive staff per se. We could return to the functional staff organization of before."

Touching and Caring

Reg Jones's style was not only engaging but predicated on engagement with all of the constituencies of GE. He was available by phone whenever he was in the office, or at home on a Saturday night if necessary. He or a vice-chairman spoke to every class in the GE management school. Wherever he traveled, Jones took advantage of the opportunity to stop by the local GE contingent. He prided himself on knowing more people in the organization than anyone else.

Jones was clear and open about the boundaries of that engagement process as he dealt with various groups. "There are some things I just cannot share with you collectively. These involve individuals' personal situations, their plans, my hunches, board judgments, evolving needs to move this person or that, and so forth . . . I just don't have some answers. In some situations, I don't yet know what is the best course of action. In others, I don't know enough about the problem or it isn't sharply enough defined. In still others, I haven't had—or taken—the time to study, to listen, and to decide," he told his top officers in November of 1974.

Reg ensured that his secretary brought all letters from the shop floor directly to his attention. (Workers on the shop floor also called him "Reg.") He answered some of these letters personally and other replies were drafted by a staff assistant, read and signed by Jones. Close associates noted his hand-addressed and signed Christmas and birthday cards to them. Overheard on a call to a salesman who had won a multimillion dollar turbine order: "This is Reg Jones, I just heard that you got it, and I want you to know how much this company appreciates. . . . " He complemented his appearances at the annual management meetings with addresses to the marketing, engineering, and financial technical groups, to outside audiences, and to many of the company's management school classes in Crotonville. At the company's Management Development Institute there, the struggle to implement a nonsmoking policy in the classrooms came to an ignominious end when Jones chain-smoked his way through his presentation.

Reg made it a point to meet all of the more than four hundred senior managers at the annual Belleair meetings, singling out those whose colored name tags denoted newcomer status. He was omnipresent, on the golf course, at cocktails, at the reception, and mingling while standing in line or moving through, shaking hands along the way. "You know, I think I shook almost every hand in that place." Over the three-evening period he also would address all the old-timers by name. Though outgoing, Jones preferred a handshake to laying on of hands, eschewing effusive displays of camaraderie in favor of emotional restraint. Perfectionistic people, limited in their emotional expression by severe conscience, can't readily be effusive. More often than not, despite their wish to be more informal, they must continually fight the image of being austere. (That same emotional over-control may have contributed to Reg's ulcer, for which he underwent surgery in 1968.) This becomes a particularly pressing problem when such people are high in the organizational structure and have the added aura of power to magnify their distance from others. The other side of the coin, however, is that their even brief "touching" has great significance to their subordinates or followers.

His information-gathering, echelon-penetrating calls to erstwhile colleagues raised the hackles of some who thought he was less discriminating than he might have been about the validity of the information he obtained from these sources. Similarly, some questioned whether old ties clouded his judgment on personnel selection at times, overlooking serious blemishes in some while inordinately identifying lesser warts in others. Reg's sensitivity to this issue prompted him to restrict severely his nonbusiness socialization with old comrades lest it compromise their credibility and effectiveness with colleagues. Apart from the loss of personal contact with old friends, that action caused him and Grace considerable pain because it is not easy for people to make new intimate friendships in middle age. It is even more difficult when one is in a position of power and, additionally, personally constrained. He still keeps in touch with the major life events of these old friends. A close associate noted that it appeared to be an almost compulsive act for Reg to hold on to a relationship that was relatively warm.

Jones has a reputation for being helpful and caring, another feature that characterizes each of our CEOs. He sends notes to ill family members of associates, flowers for a death in the family. "Tell your wife I'm sorry," apologized Jones to a weary staffer completing a long stint of night work on a priority project. He wrote personal notes of appreciation to some low in the hierarchy for jobs well done. During a 1979 meeting with Japanese dignitaries, his visitors had remarked on the configuration of the pastry. Reg could not explain its meaning. His guests told him it was the Japanese symbol denoting very high quality displayed by a very select group of small restaurants in their country. Jones immediately wrote a note to the chef.

"My husband, on his death bed, said I should call you," said the widow of a colleague whom Reg had visited frequently during a prolonged terminal illness. Reg cleared his calendar and had her join him and Grace for dinner. He personally did the income tax for the widow of another colleague. An associate, distraught for weeks over his son's adolescent crisis, confided his work-inhibiting predicament to Reg. Reg pitched in with his associates to structure a job consonant with the distressed adolescent's interests, abilities, and skills, and counseled the youth during an hour-long drive each way from Fairfield to Crotonville, where he was scheduled to lecture.

Jones repeatedly cautioned his executives to be concerned about their employees. At the 1979 annual management meeting he warned, "We're going to have to cut the force to fit the income if we have another recession . . . give people as much advance warning as you can. Try to make your moves when there are still jobs available. Don't wait until business slows down and nobody has any jobs to offer. . . . Do all you can through early retirements, or helping people find jobs elsewhere, or at least making layoffs when jobs are available. . . . Be as helpful as you can." Similar concerns were voiced by the other CEOs.

He was no less concerned at home. As Reg prepared to go to the office the morning after he and Grace had a Christmas party, she plaintively pointed to the shambles and asked that he help her clean up. He was on his knees scrubbing the floor when he was interrupted by a call from the White House. President Carter asked what he was doing. Fudging a bit out of embarrassment, Reg said he was relaxing after having cleaned up the house. Carter commiserated that he and Rosalynn were also resting after a hard plane trip.

Developing and Appraising

Reg carefully defined the role boundaries of subordinates. One subordinate related how Jones stated the *dos* and *don'ts* at the outset, and gradually permitted him discretion commensurate with his growing competence. Reg assigned a task in terms of goal, completion date (unless obvious), and where special handling was indicated, the *how*. He gave the newcomer continuing appraisal by referring to specific actions he deemed worthy of note, and a general laudatory comment at the end of a tacit six-month "trial" period. Reg defined his supervising practice this way: "I tell a subordinate how others are perceiving him, and tell him to take it for what it is worth."

Negative performance appraisals pained him; firing was even more difficult; neither was easy for any of our CEOs. Like most people whose consciences require them to inhibit their expressions of criticism, they are reluctant to give up on bright managers. "I gave [one former executive] four to five hours of my time at a clip, but I could not change him," Reg lamented about a brilliant but abrasive subordinate whom he had to fire. His gentle criticism relieved others. To an associate of several years who brought him an inadequate report Reg said, "This is the very first time I've ever had to do this, but . . . I just don't think I could go on with this thing. It just doesn't hold together. I just don't think it's going to work." His associate agreed immediately; he had patched the report together in a hurry from two other pieces of work and rushed it to Reg because of the pressure of assignments. Reg's quiet manner and the few minutes spent exchanging ideas allowed the aide, now freer of anxiety, to work up a revision within twenty-four hours that won accolades. The impact of his informal one-on-one exchanges surprised Reg: "I said something intuitively to a guy, and it had a tremendous impact on him as reported by a third party. I can't take credit for it."

In Reg's suggestions or revisions of subordinates' proposals there were no personal attacks or even dwelling on the negative, but rather a focus on how it might be done better and reinforcement of the positive elements. Editing an aide's draft of a speech, Reg laughed while pointing out that it was his speech and apologetically intoned, "I want to make these changes because I just feel more comfortable with this language." Reg's nonindicting style in the context of his own obvious competence and attention to detail did not always put everyone at ease. Those overconscientious subordinates who were already highly self-critical would naturally become even more so. It would have been easier for them if they could have become angry at an autocrat.

Yet Reg does not suffer slipshod work easily. His anger shows in facial tenseness and an incredulous query, devoid of expletives or show of temper—a quiet, controlled anger that was also noted by some in chairmen Cordiner and Borch. Though even muted expressions of anger are said to be few and far between, Reg has been observed by intimates on rare occasions to slam something down and say, "That was lousy," to a third party.

Businessman, Statesman

By the end of 1974, Reg Jones had reorganized the top management of the company so as to relieve himself of the chief-of-staff role and the day-to-day management of internal operations. He retained what he considered the longer-range, nondelegatable aspects of the CEO role, as well as the role of corporate statesman. The latter venture was taking about 40 percent of his time. As corporate statesman Jones first found himself literally shoulder-to-shoulder with labor leaders in the back of a large meeting room, crowded together at one of President Ford's economic summits in 1974. Reg was not very well known when he got to his feet to spell out his concept of a balanced taxation program, which included taxes on individuals as well as corporations, but his key staff members soon heard the reactive rumblings through the grapevine from one source in the White House and another in the labor movement: "Where did that man come from? A businessman suggesting public policy!" Reg took every opportunity to present his message in any forum he could find.

When the White House held a major conference on unemployment in 1974, Reg was invited to speak on the subject of the disadvantaged. "I want to do this," he told an aide. "Jesus, this is a trap," cautioned the other, proceeding to bombard Reg with all the *why nots:* "It's a loser.

I wouldn't touch it with a ten-foot pole. You're gonna get creamed. There's no way you can defend yourself with all those flakes out there and we don't want to see that happen." Reg smiled: "Every one of your reasons is correct, absolutely correct, but I'm gonna do it. Protect me from the flakes." The aide understood that Reg was doing it because President Ford wanted this White House conference to be successful. The president, he later learned, was indeed impressed with his sensitivity to the disadvantaged.

Late 1974, Jones was appointed to the Labor-Management Group sponsored by the Ford administration, composed of eight top labor leaders and eight top corporate executives. The Labor-Management Group, formed to provide a forum for informal dialogue, made recommendations on government economic policy on macroeconomic issues: unemployment, taxation, illegal aliens, international trade, health regulations, and wage and price guidelines. Areas of consensus were transmitted to the president, his cabinet, and finally to the Congress. Jones quickly became the chairman of the management subgroup. The late George Meany headed the labor contingent.

Jones and Meany hit it off from the start. Reg's penchant for detailed preparation and the trust that he had engendered allowed the "other side" to ask him to take the initiative in starting the meeting. They exchanged good-natured quips. A few of Reg's colleagues felt comfortable with his predilection for taking a broad view, talking things over, and seeing what the possible trade-offs and balance might be. Others were taken aback. Some of the labor leaders privately approached Jones for consultation about their own problems; some were shocked when Reg demonstrated a sympathetic concern for social issues. "Where did this guy come from? He's got to be something else because he isn't a typical kind of businessman we deal with," reported an insider paraphrasing the dialogue.

Reg had come from a family in which both parents worked. His father, Alfred, had been a steel mill foreman when Reg was born in Stoke-on-Trent, Staffordshire, on July 11, 1917. He and his parents had come to the United States when he was nine. The Joneses settled in Trenton, New Jersey, where his father became an electrician and eventually owned his own business. From ten to fifteen, Reg saw his parents only in the evenings and on weekends. He helped his mother, Gertrude, with dinner and housekeeping. He knew what it was to work. As it had been for many other lower-class youngsters, business was his path to upward mobility.

Working with the Kitchen Cabinet

Reg reached into the GE staff for supporting experts: Mark D'Arcangelo on labor; Paul Welch on taxation; Walter Joelson on economics; Bob Fegley on communications; and Don Watson on public policy. He affectionately called them his "kitchen cabinet" and gave them specific projects with an air of urgency. He framed the problem, allowed them time to develop a draft, and then subjected the draft to detailed screening, sometimes sitting four-hour stretches. Nor were members of the kitchen cabinet able to confine themselves to parochial specialist bailiwicks. Reg's assignments forced them to deal directly with the larger economic issues and to become minor experts in each other's areas.

The kitchen cabinet felt little concern about challenging Reg. Subordinates knew they must inform him when they saw him heading toward a precipice. Early on, associates noted that sometimes he was overly optimistic about a course of action, and they learned to reveal their disagreements bit by bit at such times. Low-key repetition would persuade him to see the traps. There were rules of the game about how one challenged—respectfully—but dissent was welcome if it was task-focused. If you did your homework, if you had a logical response to Reg's proposals, you never felt chastised for challenging a strategy or an idea. As we shall see in subsequent chapters, managing the boss is a skill all successful subordinates develop.

All his associates agree that Reg might expect something near perfection from himself, but he did not expect it from others. This perception is a paradox, for given his attention to detail, his high standards, and his underlying impatience, he necessarily had to wish others would be better than they were. Yet, he had the capacity to restrain his critical expressions. In some people this is a product of the wish to be liked or, more accurately, not to be disliked. In others it is a product of pangs of guilt for feeling hostile. In still others, it results from not wanting to hurt others. Sometimes such restraint results from a combination of these motives, as well as the influence of socially acquired manners. Whatever the case, Reg Jones's ability to balance his intense self-demands, his impatience with inadequacy and failure, and his nurturance of his subordinates was a rare capacity.

Whether reviewing collaboratively a proposed course of action or doing a postmortem of an assignment, Reg was forthright in communicating approbation but restrained in his negative comments. "Might

it not go better [or have gone better] if we did this? . . . What are we go
ing to do if [or about]. . . . What we have to do now is to keep working to tight-
en things up," he would say in his relaxed and inquiring style. Associates say
he didn't merely poke holes in others' ideas or ask questions to throw
them off balance, but offered suggestions and made resources available
for solving problems. Said one, "Reg became a participant, became part
owner of the problem. . . . You and I might say [to someone else], 'What
options do *you* have?' He would say, 'What options do *we* have? What
else might *we* do?' . . . I'd call Reg Jones for guidance at 3 A.M. or midnight
or whatever [from an overseas assignment]. That was it. 'Call me when
you need me.' . . . In my judgment, this guy is the CEO of our times."

Reg encouraged novel ideas by challenging his staff with such charges
as, "Design a tax program to top off the fat cats . . . design a tax program to
replace welfare so it will be salable," proposals that would provoke
deletable expletives in the typical Republican businessman dealing with
Washington. Reg challenged the conventional wisdom of a precept by
asking the kitchen cabinet to argue its converse. "Tell me why deficits
are bad, and I need it in three days, because I don't think they're so bad.
Give me five arguments why deficits are good!" "Well, I'm sorry, but I
studied that they're bad," countered the expert. "Go prove to me they're
good, or tell me that there is no way they're good!" To another member:
"Design for me something I can use in Washington, a Public Works
program that doesn't eat up all the money." The subordinate flew to
Washington, made the needed contacts to gather data, and developed a
proposal on time. Kitchen cabinet members understood that Reg
wanted to make his mark on public policy, to help shape policy via direct
contacts in Washington, and in addition, through his cochairmanship of
the Business Roundtable—an association of CEOs of large corporations
—and the proposals it sponsored. But if a staffer became enamored of a
social program and wanted to take it all the way, Reg would cut off the
initiative if his objectives had already been met, with, "I'm not interested in that anymore." Always pragmatic, his focus circumscribed by
the task at hand, he was not about to undertake the government's role.

Values

Reg's pragmatism is modified by a sensitivity that grew out of his
Welsh coal-mining heritage and religious convictions. He is an inveter-
ate Sunday churchgoer. His son Keith graduated from the University of

Pennsylvania and the Harvard Divinity School and is a Congregational minister, an accomplishment of which Reg is proud. Reg also has varied cultural interests. On the way to lunch in the upstairs dining room at GE headquarters, a foreign investor in a joint venture commented to Reg about the paintings along the hall, displaying considerable knowledge about antiques and art. Associates observed that Reg conversed with a depth and breadth on the subject that surprised them. Even when it came to supplying the names of obscure operas to associates stumped by esoteric crossword puzzles, Reg was there with a helping hand.

Intimates remark that Reg's straightlaced personal values about male-female relationships are not foisted upon others, consistent with his separating his own work standards from those he expects of others. Knowing Reg would hear of it shortly, a staff member told him about the office romance between a manager and his secretary, no secret in the organization. (This, too, was a problem that each CEO had to face.) Though the romance was not a breach of company regulations, Reg agreed that it reflected questionable judgment. "What's going to happen?" he inquired. Contrary to the pessimistic scenario described, the course of true love ran straight and smooth; from the outset Reg did nothing about the situation.

A different story unfurled on another occasion. Same plot, different characters, different implications. This time the manager's performance was inadequate. A staff member spoke to the man's superior about the matter to no avail, and then he appealed to Reg: "I'm going to try once more, but if I'm unsuccessful, I'm going to need you." As the staff member anticipated, the manager's boss complained to Reg. "We're not complaining about the affair," Reg replied. "We're complaining about the way the guy's conducting his job. He isn't doing a very good job. So get him off. But make it clear it's not because he's having an affair with his secretary."

Succession and Structure

Succession issues preoccupied all of our CEOs. Each had a dominating concern for the future of his organization. By the close of 1974 Reg Jones had developed and announced "Phase One" of a longer-range succession plan. That approach would provide both the organizational structure and executive staffing optimum for the company as 1980 approached. It would also leave his successor with maximum flexibility.

In preparation for the meeting with the Management Development and Compensation Committee in May, 1975, Jones began to consider possible optional organizational structures at the top of the company. He outlined several considerations involved in determining how the five prime corporate executive office roles—chairman of the board, corporate statesman, operations management, chief of staff, and CEO—should be played, and he presented the three most probable configurations of these roles. Each role was considered from the perspectives of its basic functions, significant business trends, and what it would require of the incumbent. Jones determined that all five roles had to be well played and that it was difficult, if not impossible, for any one person to play all of them well. Time, experience, and capability requirements, and the thin candidate base that would result from a "man for all seasons" search argued against that course. He planned for a multiple leadership mode with significant role differentiation at the top.

Three, possibly two people would be needed to fill these roles. The chairman and CEO roles could be augmented with at least one additional role, most probably either the corporate statesman or the operations management role. At one time Jones thought of separating staff management from operations management because of the short shrift the former received when they were mixed, but that plan was later abandoned. He felt that whatever the role(s) the CEO played, he should be titled chairman and chief executive officer, and that an individual other than the chief executive who was to play the corporate statesman role would have to have a prestigious title (that is, president) to get appropriate acceptance.

In December, 1975, Jones summarized his goals for the evolution of the GE organization between 1976 and 1980. He planned to establish sectors as organizational entities above the preexisting groups. The sector constituted a planning level above the strategic business units that would help integrate their strategies with the corporate strategy. Six or seven sectors would report, eventually, to a chief operating officer. Strategy review, resource allocation responsibility, and industry spokesmanship would be substantially delegated to sector executives, enhancing their development. Reg wanted to pilot the sector concept to allow for a "shakedown cruise" before full implementation. Both

during the succession maneuvers and in the postsuccession period he
sought to retain all contenders or key executives, without compromis-
ing sound organization design or yielding to the title proliferation game
by calling sector executives "president." He wanted to retain the one-
company image and to avoid centrifugal forces. Finally, he hoped to
leave his successor the option of choosing his own top management
team and structure.

Utah International

Then came the big dramatic move. In 1976, GE bought Utah International for the long haul, though any mention of its short-term vicissitudes, it is said, got a rise out of Reg. The largest corporate merger in
U.S. history, at the time, was the product of a serendipitous evening
discussion in the spring of 1975 between Reg and Edmund W. Litt-
lefield, the chairman and CEO of Utah International and a director of
GE.[6] The energy economics of 1974 had increased Jones's awareness of
the value of raw materials. Utah obtained 90 percent of its earnings
from metallurgical coal from Australia. That company's earnings
growth promised near-term results and a resource that could only appreciate with time. Utah also offered an opportunity to beef up GE's
international operations. The two men and selected advisers carried on
further clandestine exploratory conversations during the next six and
a half months.[7] Reg Jones followed up his intuitive leap concerning the
merger with detailed analysis of Utah by his financial vice-president,
who alone shared knowledge of the merger possibility. GE satisfied the
Justice Department's concern about antitrust implications of the
merger by relinquishing control of Utah's uranium assets until the year
2000.

The Utah International merger was proposed on December 5, 1975.
It was the first major acquisition by GE in many decades and a test of
whether the company could reverse its reputation in some quarters as
having only a growth-from-within-capability. Jones gave Utah a mora-
torium on major externally imposed management change.[8] The mining company kept its own board, with the addition of Jones, a GE
vice-chairman, and the GE vice-president of finance; Utah could be
approached only through one of these three. Jones did not want to

disrupt Utah's management team or encumber its decision-making process.

Still the External Threats

The change in the national administration in 1976 posed a threat to Reg's program to increase GE's international business. Candidate Carter had campaigned on a platform that advocated repeal of the Domestic International Sales Corporation (DISC), which provided tax incentives for exporting companies by deferring taxes indefinitely on 50 percent of export earnings that were not distributed to shareholders. The president's emotional commitment to repeal collided with Reg's commitment to preserve the concept. Called to a meeting in Washington between half a dozen business leaders and the president to discuss economic issues, Reg took the bull by the horns.

> "You are wrong," he told the president firmly. "I'm going to tell you why you're wrong. You'll be sorry if you ever do this. Here's all the data I've got. I cannot prove a one-for-one relationship. I cannot. That makes me vulnerable. But if you trust my judgment, it says that if you take this away, you have reduced the United States' competitiveness with other countries who have other incentives for their exporters that we do not have. We have nothing."
>
> "I disagree with you, I disagree with you, I disagree with you," replied the president.

DISC was not repealed. Reg's peers respected his stand. There were no hard feelings. In the years that followed, President Carter would say, "I need his judgment."

Some speculate that Reg may have contracted a mild case of Potomac fever as a result of his heady Washington contacts. Certainly he is not above noting his celebrity status. Recalling his fortieth anniversary with GE as of the previous day, Reg reminisced, "I couldn't help thinking, as I landed at Camp David, forty years ago I walked in the main gate of the Schenectady plant, and here I was, forty years later, going by helicopter to see the President." To his colleagues, that meant that Reg was human, that he was a bit awed by what he had achieved and by the realization of how far he had come.

Coping with the Pressure

Reg's breakneck pace and, at times, haggard looks invited the empathy and concern of intimates, who suggested a slower pace. His heavy speaking schedule and meetings with the president and cabinet officials spelled late hours, with midnight landings and 7:30 office appearances the next morning—sometimes for five consecutive days. "I take a week here or a week there once in a while to play golf to relax every so often. . . . I can't read what I would like, or what I want, I have no time. I'm exhausted by the time I get home. I want to escape at night, by sitting down and watching TV sports." Still, Jones insisted, "I've enjoyed my life immensely." Reg confided to an aide that the Management Development and Compensation Committee of the board told him to take at least one week a quarter off, and that he had to report back to them when he was going to take it because they were concerned about his health.

But does he ever really relax? On the golf course he fights tooth and nail, rolling the ball into the cup as he gives himself a little longer putt than others might have given him, punctuated by, "Well, that's good, isn't it?" According to associates, when he loses, he is very displeased with himself: "Wish we'd played a little better, we'd have won, you know. . . . I hated losing those two bills to that guy, just hated it."

Reg pushed hard to interest his family in the game; according to some associates, everybody had to learn it. Though his son and son-in-law (he has a daughter who is also named Grace) did not relish the sport, Reg found a willing pupil in his young grandson. "Reg will teach anybody anything whether they want it or not," an intimate observed affectionately. In the years just prior to becoming chairman, he and Grace would spend two nights a week playing bridge with GE friends or colleagues from other companies—always with much competitive spirit. That competitive spirit was nurtured in the early days at GE on Association Island. Reg loves to tell this story: "I still remember Charlie Wilson, the very epitome of the inspirational leader. He told us, in the Town Hall, how Westinghouse planned to surpass us in sales and earnings. 'They should live so long!' he roared, 'Their grandchildren should live so long!' And then he got us out behind the marching band, and they led us out to the flagpole playing 'Onward Christian Soldiers.' At that moment, I would have followed him anywhere on earth—and beyond if necessary."

Returning to Succession

For most of 1977, Jones and his executive manpower staff worked on the organization and staffing of the sectors. The secrecy surrounding that effort was reminiscent of his clandestine sculpting of the merger with Utah International. The Key Position Manning Alternatives Worksheet he presented to the board in November, 1976, contained one to three asterisked "initial (1977–1978) staffing candidates" for each of six sectors (a seventh, Utah, was unchanged). Those on the worksheet without asterisks were potential second-generation candidates in the 1979–1981 time frame.

The inauguration of the first sector was the overture to Reg Jones's three-act succession play. He had pared the hopefuls down for final tryouts and casting, and identified tiers of understudies at division and department levels. Other succession candidates would fill the new sector roles or top staff slots, replacements following from the ranks at successive levels. The second-act selection of three vice-chairmen in the summer of 1979 would provide the penultimate cut. By late July, 1977, after months of intensive work with the executive manpower staff and a review by the Corporate Executive Office, Jones completed his sector configurations and staffing plan for presentation to a special meeting of the board on November 17, 1977.

The "staffing objectives" in the reorganization sought to retain contenders by ensuring that each felt his "needs and interests were known and taken into account . . . that the organization perception of his new status is positive . . . that no other contender was given uniquely favorable treatment," and that he "see his assignment as personally challenging and beneficial." Reg wanted to balance continuity of management. He also wanted the assignments to test, expose, and develop contenders. He needed, further, to obtain the vice-chairmen's enthusiastic support of the staffing decisions so they would coach and develop these subordinates. Jones surprised many associates with his selections. He assigned many familiar faces to new areas. Four of the six sector executives were group executives on new turf, leaving two experienced group heads in place. He balanced this with seven new group executives experienced in the businesses for which they were given stewardship, and ensured continuity at the strategic business unit level by retaining forty of those forty-nine general managers in their roles. Additionally five of the seven major corporate staffs emerged with both top leadership and corporate staff officer/ manager personnel virtually intact. Topping it all off was a highly experienced, well-seasoned Corporate Executive Office. By stabilizing the echelons above and below the points of organizational "fracture" —the group and sector levels—Reg fashioned a managerial splint. Jones located sector executives and the corporate staff (excepting Utah) at company headquarters to enhance communication.

Business, Not as Usual

In 1977, GE's 17 percent increase in earnings exceeded $1 billion for the first time. That year was also a watershed for Reg's technological initiatives. He was convinced that GE's retreat from the computer field and its relinquishing the manufacture of silicon integrated circuits, a financially sound decision, had had a chilling effect on the application of microelectronics to GE products. His road show of exhibits of microprocessor technology around the country and his "corporate challenge" to use that technology had not made the hit that he wanted. In the course of individual and group discussions with top operating executives, he was dismayed to observe considerable disagreement on the extent and nature of the strategy to be pursued. He concluded that the organization had much more to learn about integrated circuits and resolved to move slowly until there was a consensus.

Following a discussion with his senior vice-president for technology in which the latter leaped at the suggestion to launch a full-scale study of the problem, Reg funded a million dollar *Corporate Technology Study* (referred to earlier) to test the validity of his concern and to amass the data that would appeal to his hard-nosed colleagues. He would pull them into the future. The inside and outside scientific/technical experts and management consultants they recruited for 1978 produced a sixty-seven-volume report, which was condensed to fifteen volumes. Between 1978 and 1979 Jones made three presentations to the board on the subject and discussed the study's findings at all management meetings. Senior technologists were appointed in each sector and comprised the Technology Council. Corporate research and development continued to present their annual strategy plan, part of the strategic planning process.

Stewardship

Given his religious background, Jones easily grafted the concept of stewardship on to his CEO role. "I spoke of 'stewardship' from Day One," he told the GE employees' Elfun Society in September, 1977. "I believe you are well aware of our philosophy of . . . responsible stewardship, and will recall that we have talked at length on this subject at Belleair meetings." The concept of stewardship included not only responsibility for the shareowners, for the economic lives of GE employees, and for the physical assets and human talent of the company but also acknowledged the "significant contribution that General Electric makes to the Gross National Product of the United States. . . . It almost goes without saying that managers of the future will have to be much more sensitive to their social responsibilities. Business is rightly expected to act not only in the Share Owners' interest, but also in the larger interests of society. . . . From its beginnings, General Electric has been very conscious of its public franchise. The public giveth, and the public taketh away when we fail to meet its exacting standards."[9] This theme will be echoed again and again in each of the subsequent chapters.

Jones also felt, and repeatedly expressed in his speeches, stewardship for "the distinctive spirit of General Electric . . . that intangible but ever-so real amalgam of enterprise and loyalty and honor . . . a distinctive set of traditions, values and beliefs." His interest in preserving company history stemmed from his concept of stewardship rather than from a sense of his own role in that history. When an employee approached him in the interest of writing a history of GE with the suggestion that those two roles overlapped—"Wouldn't it be wonderful to time this just when you retire, whenever that will be, because then the storyline could be 'The Jones Era.' "—Reg vetoed the idea. "I wouldn't want, even when I retire, to make it appear that General Electric is the Jones story, because this is an institution, and I'm a steward here. I have it for a while, and then I move on, and the whole company is doing this."

In 1979, the *New York Times* ran a feature, "America's Most Influential Jones,"[10] after 1,439 American leaders, surveyed by *U.S. News and World Report,* had voted Reg Jones the country's most influential businessman.[11] For all of that, his knees still shook.

The Sectors Appear

The coming-out party for the sector approach was held at the general management meeting in Belleair in early January, 1978. "Now, we're taking a chance here," Reg told them, "but we're going to ask everyone of you to help these fellows understand the business, and help them succeed. I know there'll be a temptation to hold back a little information, because this keeps your authority up, you know, makes you a little more important. But I want you to pitch in and help them find their footing. They're going to count on you to keep the business running. All the analysts say we're going to stumble, because I'm changing leadership so fast. . . . We're going to work together to show them that they're wrong. We're going to keep this company running. We're going to bring these fellows up to speed. You know them all. They're good executives."

In midyear 1978, there was another Belleair meeting, this time for key technical and engineering managers and specifically centered on the electronics issue. The results of the *Corporate Technology Study,* the initiatives of the sector executive responsible for the bulk of the product areas affected, and Reg's full and open support of these initiatives convinced operating people that what he was trying to accomplish was the correct thing to do. Insiders acknowledge that once the chairman hears you out and takes a different course of action, you fall into line. Somehow electronics was the exception. Reg had taken pains to persuade top executives to give it their full commitment, but there had been no significant movement toward electronic technology. Now he took matters into his own hands. Two professional employee training programs were set up to move technology forward. The Edison Engineering Program was designed to broaden and deepen an individual's technical experience by varied work assignments combined with applied engineering problem-solving studies and opportunities for graduate study for outstanding engineering and science graduates. The Professional Employee Management Course was designed to help newly appointed GE managers encourage their professional employees to pursue careers that would lead to increased achievement and personal satisfaction. Its intent was to have the managers sustain Jones's initiatives by maintaining his sense of urgency about increasing their technical, particularly electronic, proficiency.

Jones was also having trouble with nuclear power. He was disappointed and frustrated over his failure to convince various special interest groups of the value of nuclear power, an issue with which Ian MacGregor, as we shall see in chapter 4, was equally concerned. Each, of course, had a stake in that development. Though GE's monetary losses were not all that significant, the missed opportunity was. Reg's efforts to persuade the federal government to make a decision about stockpiling the waste were fruitless. He told his subordinates that GE and other nuclear power reactor manufacturers would be accused in the mid- and late 1980s of failing to forewarn the nation of impending power shortages. He held to the hope that Washington and the nation would recognize the necessity of nuclear-plant construction, making this business profitable for GE.

As spokesman for GE and the business community in the highest circles of government, Reg continued to maintain close contacts with cabinet-level people and legislators, relationships some think he could have delegated to top management. Still, there were definite indications that Reg Jones was shifting to a more selective focus in his forays outside of GE. He had refused the chairmanship of the Business Roundtable, preferring to remain as a co-chairman and sponsor younger men for the higher position. The Labor-Management Group, which had gone private after the Ford administration, met less frequently after the labor law reform. Reg began to decline invitations to testify before congressional committees or to accept other kinds of chairmanships, picking and choosing only those particularly to his liking. The kitchen cabinet met now only occasionally.

Final Selection

Early in the first week of August, 1979, the Management Development and Compensation Committee and the full board chose three new vice-chairmen. Reg Jones's 1976 plan was on schedule.

The process that led up to his selection of the finalists had begun eight months earlier, with a modified-Borch technique to maximize compatibility and mute rivalry. (Borch had met over a three-year period prior to his retirement with each of the individuals he had identified as the prime candidates to succeed him. He asked each, "If you and I were on an airplane that was about to crash, who would you say was the best person to take my place?") In January, 1979, Jones met once with each of the senior vice-presidents for staff and the sector executives. He asked each his opinion of his peers, in all respects. "How would you set up the company at the top? Would you have a president and a chairman? Would you have a Corporate Executive Office as we now have it? How would you do it differently? How may people? Who would you have in what jobs, and give me an individual-by-individual evaluation of those individuals." A second series of interviews were conducted in May and June, focusing heavily on personal compatibility. "If you were going to be on the team, who do you think you could work with? Who do you think you could work with before the next chief executive officer is chosen, and who do you think you could work with afterwards, if you were it? If you were not it?"

After making the decision and lunching with the directors, Reg called in the three new appointees as a group and told them the board's decision. Then for thirty minutes they discussed aspects of the transition plan—the retirement of the incumbent vice-chairman at year-end; the mode of interim operations between September 1 and that time; the next steps with respect to organization responsibilities as a consequence of domino-effect personnel decisions; and timetables and scheduling.

"Now I've got to go and talk to the others," he remarked at the meeting's end. He told his new team he was going to meet with all the contenders individually and explain the decisions. Then he would give them several days to think and react. He would offer to meet individually with each of them about their personal situations. Specifically, he said, he would ask what those contenders most wanted to do in the forthcoming round of reshufflings, and with whom they would prefer to work. He would give each the opportunity to be heard, but he would make no promises or commitments. Since it was especially difficult for Reg to break bad news about performance or promotion, this cut of the deck was grueling for him. Whatever wounds resulted from the narrowing of the contenders to three, the salve applied would not be at the expense of the body corporate. There would be no sinecures or honorary positions.

Between August 3 and the middle of September, when the Management Development and Compensation Committee and full board met again to review the next round of personnel decisions, Reg and the new vice-chairmen thrashed out their recommendations. It was Reg who again had to go back to inform the "losers" of the realignments. "You're going to work for ———, even though you don't want to work for him, because it is in the interest of the company to do it that way." Reg made clear to his new team that, barring major performance shortfalls or physical mishaps, the choice for his successor had been narrowed to three. On August 5 the announcement of the promotion of three sector executives to vice-chairmanships was made: international (John F. Burlingame, age fifty-six); consumer products and services (John F. Welch, Jr., age forty-three); and technical systems and materials (Edward E. Hood, Jr., age forty-eight). In the ensuing months, after the promotions had been announced, Reg repeatedly referred to the importance of being able to work together. The three new vice-chairmen understood that Reg considered it one of his absolute responsibilities to leave a team in place, devoid of divisiveness and without the residual wounds of intense political rivalry to reach the top spot.

In January, 1981, he announced his prospective retirement. In April, he passed the institution that is GE on to the next carefully chosen steward, John F. Welch, Jr., a chemical engineer, the youngest chairman in GE's eighty-eight-year corporate history. Jones left a legacy of twenty-six consecutive quarters of improved earnings through two recessions, and a sales growth of 163 percent. He tripled profits to a compound growth of 14 percent. GE's return on capital invested was consistently 50 percent more than that of major domestic competitors. GE was financially sound.

Though acknowledging Jones's financial wizardry, critics said his pursuit of financial objectives had been at the expense of major investments in technology and product quality. They alleged that bottom-line pressure on GE's cash-cow consumer products sector compromised product quality. They complained, too, that the early 1970's trading of GE's computer venture and sale of its integrated circuit operation caused the company to lose technical leadership and its edge in revamping its business.

There were criticisms, too, of the choice of Jack Welch. Welch had a reputation in some GE circles for being something of a self-indulgent playboy, constrained further by his superiors with each successive promotion, as his brilliant marketing imagination and amazing retention of detail carried him upward. Critics said the succession race had been too public and that Reg did not control Welch's allegedly hostile behavior toward his competitors. "Jack could have blown it," said one observer, "but he knew that. He said, 'I don't care if it works or not. I told them it's me or I leave.' "

Legacy

Reg Jones, as CEO of General Electric, was an executive's executive. His was a massive refocusing task. It called not only for his vaunted financial acumen but also for perceptive anticipation and the capacity to pull a giant corporation out of its traditional paths that threatened to become ruts. He vanquished self-doubt to conceive, assert, and implement a new direction for GE, leaning heavily on his phenomenal memory for detail, his wide support in GE, and on reason and persuasion to make his subordinates followers. He pointed out the reality of situations, pushed and shoved through the systematic analysis of strategic planning, invested in the coming electronic age by increasing commitment to research, and exhorted GE to become what it should be. For all of that, he was always a gentleman. Working with the grain in the stewardship role was the cadence of Jones's tenure. From the beginning he thought of the ending. He had inherited an institution, not fathered it. It belonged to the many "others." He was only a caretaker, a standard bearer until the time "for the changing of the guard."

Was Jones as good as nearly everyone who speaks of him says he was? Though he himself said he couldn't possibly be as good as the "halo effect" he stimulated, that aura has endured. How does one understand it? It was partly because of the almost encyclopedic knowledge which was the foundation of his penetrating analysis, partly because of his warm friendliness and his strict control of his angry feelings, partly because of his need and wish to be liked, partly because of his integrity and concern for doing right by all of his constituencies. At bottom, it was because he understood what it meant to be a good steward, placing the organization ahead of himself.

Coda

Under the leadership of Jack Welch, the move toward high technology in robotics and information network services gained further momentum. GE bought Calma Co. for $100 million to enter the computer graphics business. It built a $100 million facility in North Carolina to

make microelectronics parts. It established a factory automation service. By 1982, it already had 200 robots in its own plants and looked
forward to 1,000. It undertook a joint venture in robotics with Hitachi.
It acquired Intersil, a semiconductor manufacturer for $235 million and
four software companies for more than $66 million. It is constantly
rumored to be in the market for many other high-tech companies to
round out its new thrust.

In 1983 energy issues were no longer pressing. They were unlikely
to become as important as they seemed in 1976, and, since 90 percent
of Utah International's earnings came from Australian metallurgical
coal, it was perhaps not surprising that GE sold most of Utah's operations to Broken Hill Proprietary Co. for about $1.8 billion. That cash,
together with the reserves GE already held—including the $1.1 billion
it received from disposing of 118 businesses between 1981 and mid-1984
—would finance as much as $5 billion worth of expansion.

"GE is determined to become firmly positioned at the leading edge
of high technology products and the high growth segments of the industry where the company has a unique advantage," said Welch. GE was
going just where Reg Jones had pointed it.

3

Walter B. Wriston

CITICORP

WALTER B. WRISTON, a man with a global view, transformed First National Citibank into the world's leading international banking institution, and changed the banking environment as well. The foundation stones of his achievement were innovative financial instruments, commitment to logic, and an intense ideological conviction that free competition gives rise to the best in people and organizations. He became an unrelenting attacker of those governmental policies and practices that he believed threatened to undermine the U.S. banking system. That attack helped pry loose historic governmental constraints on banking.

The tall (six feet, three inches), rangy CEO of Citicorp—the parent corporation of Citibank created in 1968 to undertake businesses prohibited to banks—was known as an intellectual among executives. He leaned heavily on the carefully honed written word and critical analysis to undergird his position and that of his corporation. He tempered the intensity of his personal competitive attack by sharp witticisms, and the pressures of internal executive competition by fostering compensatory camaraderie. Despite the fact that he is a compassionate person, he believes that only a person's record, the business outcome, should be the measure of his achievement, that how a man feels and why he feels that way should have little relevance for any judgment about him. His intellectual leadership, his aggressive stance, and his capacity for sustaining long-term relationships and conceiving major deals were fundamental to his achievement. That same aggressive posture led to threatening challenges by government agencies, and, some say, to problems of succession. His will be a hard act to follow.

Wriston is an intellectual ideologue. In the tradition of John Stuart Mill, he is concerned with free, unfettered markets. His is an aggressive determination, born of that conviction. He transformed the culture of Citicorp from one of transactions to one of a modern, professionally managed, multinational corporation. He extended his free market conceptions into Citicorp itself, stimulating internal competition. He pitted people against each other and himself against the federal government. At times, however, employee fallout was severe as defeated or displaced managers were turned out and back office contraction led to threatened unionization. The force of Wriston's logic and the attacking mode it advocated subdued his sensitivity to its human costs. Wriston is an iconoclast, an aloof leader who prefers word to feeling. "You win or lose in the marketplace of ideas and your ideas have to be as well documented and thought out and articulated and reiterated as the other guy's . . . otherwise there's no way you [the organization] can survive," he said. Actions should speak for themselves; results are what count.

Wriston was born on August 3, 1919, in Middletown, Connecticut, the home of Wesleyan University, where his father, later to become president of Brown University, was a history professor. Wriston graduated from Wesleyan in 1941 and earned a master's degree at Tufts' Fletcher School of International Law and Diplomacy the following year. Wriston's was a pioneer heritage. In public addresses and private conversations he proudly recalled his grandmother's westward trek to Colorado in a Conestoga wagon train, half of whose members died fighting Indians. His father was born in North Dakota in a sod hut that had a dirt floor. "I think there is a basic feeling in Walter that he's a boy from out of Wisconsin or something like that, of simple tastes and so forth, which is all quite true," said an intimate; "He's not pretentious in any way except intellectual achievement."

Both of Wriston's parents stimulated his early intellectual bent. His mother, Ruth, had been a chemistry teacher when she married. "Anything he has ever said of his mother is of someone who was highly innovative, full of ideas, pushing for those ideas all the time . . . it's beautiful the way it comes through . . . it's just from listening to him talk about his mother, and he does this very rarely," said a close associate. That pushing certainly had a great influence on Wriston's penchant for innovation and the clash of ideas.

He and his father, Henry M. Wriston, had a close, admiring relationship until his father died in 1978 at eighty-five. A wise, organized, conceptual man of many ideas, Henry Wriston had a powerful effect on Walter's life. He was Walter's chief consultant and confidant. Walter typed his speeches on Sundays and had his father critique them. He made no secret about talking things over with him, often reporting to his associates that he had "run this one by" his father. Henry Wriston remained alert until a few months before he died, so the relationship terminated abruptly.

Walter B. Wriston walked in the door of what was then called First National City Bank in 1946. He had behind him a four-year army stint in World War II and a year as a U.S. Department of State officer. His first job at the bank was that of a junior inspector in the comptroller's division. Wriston and his postwar cohorts brought to the bank a perspective very much at odds with the then prevailing culture of the industry. "A lot of things have changed very, very dramatically. I suppose that's not due to any management skills. It's due to the fact that a lot of the people came out of the war and they were all twenty-four or twenty-five," he surmised.

"But instead of [attaining] a nice new diploma [they attained] five stars on the canopy of a P38 [or had built] the bridge at Ramagen. It was a different learning experience, to put it mildly. And so that group was not buying the black shoes and the strip collar or waiting a hundred years for a silver tray. . . . The person that . . . perceived this—and also gets a very big piece of the credit for whatever the Citibank is today—is Buzz Cuyler, who was our head of personnel. He was a colonel in the air force and he had the revolutionary idea you should pay people in the banks the same money as they did in industry. This was totally unknown [in the banking business]. Cuyler went in to see the chairman and laid this great idea on him and the chairman told him he was nuts, it was a great honor to work here. And Cuyler said, 'Farewell,' but he didn't get further than the door. . . . He hired most of the people who are in senior positions in the bank now. He inculcated them with a blend of the history of the organization, which is fabulous, and also the desire to move with the times."

Citibank had been known for its international banking position since the turn of the century. It had reached its peak in 1929 and then had become more conservative. Still, up to World War II, it had been branching more expansively overseas than any other American bank. The whole network was lost temporarily during that war. A comptroller's department study purported to show that cumulatively, from the very beginning, Citibank had not made money from those operations. At issue, therefore, in the late 1940s and early 1950s, was the wisdom of reestablishing an international presence with all of the high political and economic risks and the historical dismal financial experience.

Making It

Around 1950, Wriston, assigned to the shipping group, arranged a loan of approximately $57 million, an enormous transaction in those days, to Malcolm McLean, who had a new concept about moving goods across water. Before 1955, virtually all of the goods of the world moved by what are called break bulk ships. Crates, boxes, and bags were loaded into holds, item by item, and then unloaded the same way. The ships sat idle for days while the hold was loaded or emptied. McLean, who owned the McLean Trucking Company, conceived of the ocean as a road and of a ship as a kind of truck—rather than having to unload and reload trucks at the dock, why not just stack the back of the truck on the ship? That became containerized shipping, today the way all shipping, except bulk, is done. McLean sold his trucking company in order to become a common carrier by sea. He bought two shipping companies, Pan-Atlantic and Waterman Steamship, with money that Walter Wriston loaned to him. Walter's confidence in a man who had a good idea and the ability to manage resulted in an important loan for the bank, and even more important, a significant contribution to the world's economy.

Traditionally, ships were financed much like houses, with mortgages at a percentage of the cost of construction. This was called "tonnage financing." Aristotle Onassis approached Wriston with a new problem. Following World War II, the only ships available were second-hand. None were being built. The shipbuilding capacity of both Europe and Japan was destroyed. American shipyards were dedicated to military service and, in any event, were not building because they had built too many cargo ships during the war. Onassis had no money, but he did have several tankers, which he bought from the surplus U.S. government fleet, and he had a seven-year contract with Esso to transport oil. Since the ships had relatively little value, he could borrow even less against them. Could he borrow against the contract?

Wriston was the first to translate Onassis's question into the concept of financing a ship charter, in which the security consisted of an assignment of the contract rather than a mortgage on the ship. Of course, the mortgagee must have integrity and the ability to operate the ship. After deducting the projected operation costs, there is usually a relatively liberal margin of profit. The charter is assigned to the bank rather than to the owner of the ship. The bank takes its cut off the top. For added protection, the bank takes a mortgage on the ship and an assignment of the insurance in case the ship sinks. That concept, now commonplace, is the foundation of the giant Chinese and Greek shipping fortunes. Those shipping magnates put down virtually no money to buy their ships because, in effect, what was being financed was the credit of the company that was the obligor.

In 1954, Wriston was appointed to the legion of vice-presidents. Although Walter had never had overseas experience, George Moore—in charge of revamping the Overseas Division—was apparently impressed with his innovations, and brought the then unknown Wriston into the European Department. In 1956, Moore made Wriston head of the European Department. Both Wriston and Moore saw that the world was becoming smaller. The globe would be the marketplace and American companies were going to be more prominent factors in international operations. Together they concluded that they should establish a branch bank wherever they could get a franchise so they would be ready whenever their projected scenario developed. Other American bankers thought that the decision reflected poor judgment. It turned out to be brilliant. They expanded the network just in time to take advantage of the postwar recovery period and the emergence of the global economy. Then Moore became president of the bank and Wriston became the head of the Overseas Division in 1958. In 1982, nearly 60 percent of Citibank's net income came from abroad.

In 1961, during his tenure as Overseas Division head, Wriston pioneered another innovative thrust—the negotiable certificate of deposit (CD). This device arose from a transaction with Onassis's father-in-law, Stavros G. Livanos, a friend of Wriston's. Livanos proposed to use his large deposit as collateral for a transaction. Walter came up with the idea of a certificate that would show a deposit for a fixed time at a fixed rate, that would be fully negotiable simply by endorsement, in the same manner as a debenture or bond. That innovation suddenly made CDs the source of what is today essentially all the financing conducted in the Euro-dollar market, and banks now finance themselves through negotiable CDs.

Shipping operations were always international in character. Many of Wriston's shipping friends, world citizens, became his confidants and customers when he became head of the Overseas Division. All that made him a rising star.

Though Wriston was Moore's protégé, working with Moore was no picnic. Moore lost his temper quickly. According to several informants, he would be caustically critical one day and heap praise the next. Given his very high personal standards and the severe self-criticism such standards imply, Wriston was necessarily hypersensitive to Moore's criticism. Observers who recall those days say that Moore's cutting, temperamental outbursts left Walter with psychological bruises. In his down periods, they say, Wriston turned to his late first wife, Barbara, for counsel and support. How long should he take the punishment? How long could he take it? Yet his close personal relationship with Moore was almost like that of a father and son. Walter had had long successful experience with that kind of relationship. He stayed.

Wriston had seen that the multinational corporation was coming and that Citibank had to follow. To serve the growing multinationals required penetrating the domestic markets and being able to provide local currency, financing, and investment needs, rather than just financing short-term trade.

Turning to the managerial side of the Overseas Division, Walter observed that the absence of a uniform compensation policy so inhibited transfers within the division that, once a manager went to a country, the chances were he would spend the rest of his life there. Walter had to construct a system that would allow a manager to move with ease and equity from China to Brazil. A cost-of-living compensation plan was adapted from the State Department. Insiders surmise that Wriston's father, who had "Wristonized" the State Department by recommending the integration of the domestic and foreign services, influenced Walter's choice of system. Now the managers would expect to be transferred in order to be developed, to get a wider exposure, and to prepare for bigger jobs. A manager sent to Nicaragua no longer had to worry about spending his whole life there.

The selection and development of managers was crucial. Wriston had started recruiting people with a foreign orientation, individuals who had an interest in international affairs, who had some overseas family or business connection, who wanted to work overseas, and who, once they got there, knew how to become assimilated into the environment. As head of the Overseas Division, Walter interviewed nearly every one of them after they had been screened at successive managerial levels.

When James Stillman Rockefeller retired as chairman and CEO of First National Citibank in mid-1967, it was in the forefront of the wave of change and growth that characterized commercial banking that year, according to the *Wall Street Transcript*.[1] It was described as "a diversified giant in all phases of domestic and international banking," with "a wide-ranging spirit of venture, disciplined by adherence to sound banking principles." Its self-defined role was to supply every useful financial service permitted by law anywhere in the Free World where it could make a profit. Citibank traditionally showed the largest profits after taxes of the New York City banks. Though Bank of America and Chase Manhattan had more deposits, Citibank had a stronger capital ratio of loans and deposits. It had an outstanding position in the retail or consumer banking field, with 168 neighborhood branches in the New York City area and 215 branches and offices in sixty-three countries on six continents. It had 3,900 correspondent banks, including 97 percent of the largest banks outside of New York City. Of the top 200 corporations, 195 had accounts with Citibank. Net operating earnings had increased at a 7.5 percent compound annual rate during the previous five years. Brokerage firms viewed its stock as investment caliber.

This was the setting when Stillman Rockefeller made Walter Wriston, forty-eight years old, president and CEO, choosing him over several contenders, including George Moore. When Wriston succeeded to the top post, he established profit centers to hold managers accountable for the profits of their business segments. However, neither the restructuring into profit centers nor the system of accountability could have been executed without the Wriston-initiated transfer pricing policy. The banking business is a matter of getting money from one part of the world, or one market segment, and relending it to another market segment at a profit. That requires establishing the value of money that is transferred, or what came to be called the transfer pool rate or the marginal cost-of-funds concept. If an account manager brought in a million dollars of time deposits, that money was valued for profitability purposes at the marginal cost-of-funds in the open market, for example, according to how much interest the bank would be required to pay for a ninety-day deposit. With that, a profit center manager could generate a profit report for his business. This process was also important in determining how profitable an account was, because whether the bank made or lost money was a function of how it viewed the value of money on deposit from a client or the cost of money lent to a client. In addition to being a managerial process, this was a building block that permitted the bank to think more clearly about profitability of individual account relationships of large corporations or correspondent banks.

Walter expanded the Citibank Policy Committee, a twenty-eight-member forum for free discussion, debate, and critical analysis. To be able to tolerate their differences, people must develop personal relationships. Walter brought the group and their spouses together socially. He started the practice of offshore (Caribbean) Policy Committee meetings over long weekends. In addition to the formal agenda, these enabled people to cement working bonds.

Then the Structure

In 1967, Citibank enlisted the services of Tempo, a think-tank subsidiary of General Electric. The Tempo study opened the closed minds of many Citibank executives about banking. Talking about the world twenty years hence began to expand the dimensions of their thinking about the business. It also created an environment in which the organization began to ask how it was organized to compete best in its specific markets. Tempo clarified many issues that had been in the managerial air for a number of years, including questions about organizational structure. The study pointed out that the sources for financing were shifting from corporations to households. The bank would have to be able to tap the resources of the family unit.

The bank was organized on the basis of full-service branches. All of the customers' banking business was done through the same location. That meant that many managers were generalists, but they did not have much depth and professionalism in specific areas. Following a McKinsey study of organizational structure in 1968, Citibank was reorganized on a market concept basis. For example, instead of all branches handling corporate business, there could be a corporate bank in one location with professionals in corporate banking. Other banks followed.

Vice-chairman Howard Laeri, a blunt, honest man of long service, was perceived to be the premier commercial banker in the country. Walter put him in charge of restructuring. Laeri's credibility was so high that people went along with his decisions to change accounts, markets, people, and organizational structure. He and his task force were guided by Jack Heilshorn, vice-president of planning.

But restructuring against markets rather than against geography took a back seat to a more pressing problem—the chaos in the back office that had resulted from the avalanche of paper work caused by Citibank's dramatic expansion. Walter saw that the back-office problem threatened to choke the bank's performance. The books at the head office were out of balance with those of the branches by $70 million. The explosive growth from a relatively small bank to a major one occurred at the beginning of the computer age. The answer up to that point had been to employ more people. When George Moore was president he had tried to deal with this problem by hiring a short-interval scheduling consulting firm. That effort almost brought unionization. In Wriston's attempts to deal with the operations problem, there was a round of cutbacks in which 1,500 people were discharged. That, too, produced a union threat. Later, a Young Turk, hired from Ford Motor Company, tried too hard to get his bottom line and knocked out many thirty-five-to-forty-year people. A third union threat followed. Various other Citibank managers tried and failed to solve the problem.

After those debacles Wriston turned to Bill Spencer to clean up the back office. Some contend that the choice was also a way to resolve top-level competition, which they would not discuss openly. Why did Wriston choose him? Spencer avers that Wriston took "one of the biggest risks of his life" when putting him into the clean-up job, "because I never had anything to do with back-office work. I almost left the bank as a matter of fact. . . . I laid out all the reasons why I thought he was making a mistake and I told him I had no experience, that I might not do it. He said he wished I would do it and certainly hoped that I would stay on board and that I would do the job, which I subsequently did. . . . He indicated . . . that it wouldn't be a forever job, that it was an additional chapter of experience. . . . I took the job in 1968 . . . two years later I was made president."

Spencer justified Wriston's judgment of him and Wriston's predilection for putting good people in unfamiliar roles. Spencer brought in John Reed, who had industrial engineering experience and a reputation for innovative thinking in his planning role. Reed recognized that running the back office was an assembly-line kind of operation, not basically different from a factory. Reed recruited some people from Ford, the first to come to Citibank from the outside. The change was successful but painful. Many older managers were knowledgeable about transactions, but they knew nothing about production. Heads rolled. Only later did the new production management recognize the need for the banking professionals. The production managers reduced the 20 percent per annum cost-curve to 5 percent per annum. They brought the number of "factory" people in the domestic operation down from 15,000 to 6,000 and then to below 5,000. Wriston's initiative had begun to revolutionize the bank and bankers.

Then John Reed was given the responsibility to develop the consumer finance business, something not familiar to traditional bankers. Changing the bank into a corporation also involved massive imports of other professional manpower with no background in banking. Accountants, tax people, operations researchers, marketing people, technology types of all kinds, were brought in at significant middle-management levels. The aggressive policy of recruiting 300 to 500 young people, even when it wasn't clear that they were needed, continued. Wriston assumed that the new employees themselves would create the business that would employ them. A decade of inflow followed. The new young people moved up rapidly. At the executive vice-president and senior executive vice-president levels, most are in the mid-forties age range. Some in high-level positions are in their thirties. That fractured the old, seniority-age tradition of banking. At the other end, there was a program to induce people to retire between fifty-five and sixty. The culture of Citibank was changing.

Walter never announced a new style of management, but people knew a revolution was going on. Heated debate flared between the old-timers and the new managers. In typical and predictable fashion, the young people were critical of the old ways of doing things, and the old ones replied disdainfully that their detractors were still wet behind their ears. It didn't occur to the old-timers until later that they were going to lose. There was a great deal of animosity toward John Reed.

Wriston's style of quiet support of the army of change he had recruited also allowed him to remain above the din and heat of battle. Although he was not interested in clones, he rewarded those who represented his aggressive style. His proclivity for self-criticism made it difficult for him to face the anger of others and required him to overcontrol his own expressions of disappointment and anger. As a result, Wriston had an easygoing way with people which enabled him to keep on good terms even with the old-timers. So the old-timers thought they were still in Walter's good graces, as indeed many among them were.

The pendulum swung almost too far from rewarding banking professionalism to rewarding managerial skills. Walter was concerned about that. He expressed his concern, but had difficulty from time to time convincing the group heads to take many people whom he believed the institution needed. He would manufacture jobs to save them.

Selecting People

The style of the bank had been to hire mediocre men who would become part of the old culture and not raise problems or ask questions —good old boys. Nobody cared about their abilities as long as they came from the right places, had gone to the right schools, and had the right family backgrounds. Walter destroyed that. He never asked what a candidate's background was or what his father did.

Up to 1965, Citibank was run in an authoritarian manner. The boss wasn't interested in what the troops had to say. He said only, "This is a good credit and that's a bad credit and . . ." If a man had been around a number of years and had the title and the position, he'd make decisions by the seat of his pants. Walter completely destroyed that, too. He demanded documentation and analysis, discussion and criticism.

There was a great gap in recruitment around World War II. During the decade that followed the war, the bank hired few new people because the business wasn't growing. Wriston thought that policy was a serious mistake, so he decided to close the gap with the smartest people he could find. When he was running the Overseas Banking Group, he told one company recruiter, "I want world class people in this institution. I don't care where you find them, or what they're doing, but if you think they've got brains and they meet that test and are disposed to come, you get them in here and we'll find something for them to do." He has been doing that ever since. One executive vice-president was a Spanish major with no business background; he was first turned down by the usual personnel interviewers. Only a higher-level interview reversed that decision. Some of Citibank's brighter officers were English majors from Princeton. One had a Ph.D. in biophysics. Wriston selected people for positions of leadership who he felt had his own spirit of openness, who believed in and would promote change. He wanted executives who would give the young people a welcome working environment and who would be prepared to accept criticism from them. That's the way he believed the business must be built. He repeated his thesis time and time again that the people, the managerial skill base, was *the* asset of the corporation.

One result was that incoming young people came to think of themselves, Citibank people, as the best. Being second or third at Citibank was, they held, better than being first elsewhere. But the turnover was high and those in other banks were amused with what they viewed as Citibank's chauvinism and self-admiration.

Wriston had great trust in his own judgment of people. He kept himself well-informed. He traveled. His informality invited people to be open with him. He always had an open-door policy. All that gave him the opportunity to spot the sort of people who take the initiative when doors, exposure, and experience are open to them. If he saw such a person, usually he found a way to transfer him or her into a position to start moving. From then on, mobility was a product of performance. Every person had an opportunity to talk over with his or her immediate supervisor the year's goals, and had another opportunity at least once later to review them. A manager had to reach down two levels to get information from the second level below him rather than from his immediate subordinates alone.

A high Citibank executive recalls his own entry:

"I was at that time at the International Monetary Fund, heading [the] stabilization mission in Argentina. A Chamber of Commerce there . . . wanted me to talk to a group about the situation in Argentina. Walt happened to be visiting. He came to lunch. He had to make sure he'd get to know me a little. He had his local manager invite me to a lunch later that weekend when Walt and his wife came. He had no idea what I would do in the bank. Originally I came in to worry about central bank relations but that was just to get me in the door. And then once I came in, then it was up to me to fit into the organization and show what I could do."

The names of the top 250 people in the corporation were displayed on a big board in one of Wriston's conference rooms. The development of each one of them was the responsibility of one or another of the group heads who report to top management. Wriston's regular human resource manpower review sessions over the Corporate Property List—the 75 people who are thought to have top management

potential—were conducted with the same seriousness as budget reviews. And he was always asking the question, "What happens next
with this guy? How is he doing?" He asked repetitively, "Who are the
next guys around who are not on this chart, but that might be on this
chart?" Two backups for every position was the rule of thumb. The
personnel department scheduled visits for Wriston to see some of the
lower level people around the organization. He went to branches and
operating departments. His approach in most of these visits was not
the usual small talk about the job. He observed and listened. He
asked, "Who are you? What do you *like* to do? What don't you like to
do?" His questions were not related to the business environment.
They were about families, sports, hobbies, and activities outside the
business. He used the same kind of approach in visits abroad.

A senior executive reported, "I often followed Walt, or George, or
some of the other members of senior management around the world.
I could tell where Walt had been by the attitude and the morale and
the enthusiasm of the people. I saw a confidence level . . . a level of
enthusiasm. The CEO listened to them. They were part of his vision.
They saw where they fit, what their role was, and they felt important.
You can really see a difference in commitment and in attitude toward
the corporation."

Another executive noted Wriston's subtle style of reconnaissance:

"He relies very heavily on information that comes to him from
different parts of the organization. He gets and absorbs the feelings
of people who are not only department and group heads but always
has a wary ear open to be alert to situations, circumstances within
the shop that might not surface in the ordinary routine of the
management information flows. . . . He's got a very acute sense
. . . of the ideas as they float around the organization. Somebody
[may be] talking about his own business, perhaps, and its relation
to another one . . . he picks up a sense of dissent or difference of
opinion and works it in to his total appraisal, piling all the straws
on one pile."

When there were discussions about a manpower move, Walter was
reputed to be the one person in the room who had a suggestion that was
startling in its originality. His colleagues found his insights astonishing.
They reported a number of instances in which they were trying to find

a candidate for a key job and the individual who had the wildest idea, which turned out most of the time to be right, was Wriston. They said he had an incredible ability to break away from the more traditional approach to selecting people for a job and would spot people around the world who could in fact do it. That competence seemed to be made up of one part perspective, one part risk-taking ability, and one part ability to spot talent.

Wriston made some admittedly awful mistakes. Yet when asked what were the pitfalls for organization leaders, his immediate response was, "Pick from the wrong fellows. I do it every time. You see, people like people who are like themselves, basically. That's why clones are so popular. A lot of people don't even recognize their own clones, which is fascinating. I see this in other companies. They dislike people actually who are really their clones because they don't perceive in themselves the bad habits that their clone is reflecting. We doubtless do a lot of silly things like that. The finding and the training and the motivating of people is the whole ballgame."

Walter had a good sense of the controls necessary to keep the whole process in proper balance, but within those boundaries he liked to see people run. And he liked noise. He liked clash. He liked people bumping into each other. He let those situations work themselves through until whatever the clash was all about got resolved. It was the competitive or market principle at work.

Here is Wriston's own view of Citicorp culture:

"We sailed into a water we didn't know all that much about and we did a lot of things that worked. The skill of people in this organization is they can make something designed by a committee work if they have to. . . . When you want to change the world, you have to have the active involvement of all the people who are going to make it happen. This is a participative society at Citibank. And people might do something they perceive as dumb because somebody told them to, but it's highly doubtful. And there's a great deal of dialogue—that's a very polite word—for what goes on. I think the most important thing that we can do is to create the climate so that that continues, because nobody has the answers. People who think they have are . . . nuts. Within the group in the bank, there's a tremendous number of men and women who are smart as all get out and they have to know that somebody's listening. That doesn't mean everybody's going to buy whatever they say. It's a tough jury. The only question is will the perception be there that there is a jury? And if they give up, forget it . . . you don't ensure it except by going around and turning on your radar set all the time and listening. I go out maybe once a month for a day and wander around the branches and the warehouse and the gold vault or whatever, and talk to all the people that I run into. And if they trust you, they'll tell you. If they don't they won't. It's just that simple . . . my philosophy, for whatever it's worth, is unless you have good people in the right spots, there's absolutely nothing you can do in management to save anything. If you have the right people in the right spots, there is almost nothing you can do to screw it up, and therefore, the major amount of your perception and the time and thought should be placed on people, what makes them run and why, and trying to get a set of values that . . . are absolute integrity and then make sure that people know they're for real."

Wriston agreed that there is no way to maintain an open climate unless people know that new ideas will be heard if they have a good case and are persistent. The invention of the CD is an example. It was repeatedly turned down, but finally, with enough argument and enough documentation, accepted. The great German banker, Hermann Ops, said that the Euro-dollar market was a transient phenomenon and he wouldn't take the Deutsche Bank into it. A Citibank task force concluded that it was a permanent phenomenon and the organization bought that. Another example of going with a new idea is Citibank's investment of $160 million in the cash customer-activated terminals (CAT machines). "Conventional wisdom was people didn't want to interact with machines. Those machines now dispense 83 percent of all the cash withdrawn from Citibank, 50 million transactions a year. . . . Although it drags our earnings down, the organization knows that it's the future and they buy it," said Wriston.

"The companies that die are the ones that don't have that atmosphere . . . it [Citibank] really is an extraordinarily open society," he continued. "People say that, but [for] most people who say it, it really isn't so. But it is around here to a degree that I have never seen in any other organization because you're not going to get fired if you disagree with somebody. The guy in the gray flannel suit never came to work for the Citibank. He went to some other place. The individuals who are operating this enterprise are just about as different as human beings as you're going to find in a random sample on a subway car. They have one common denominator and that's talent. And that's about it."

On the Attack

These talented individuals compete by running their businesses as powerfully as they can, and where conflicts arise, fighting for their organization's interest. For example, a new business group—the Financial and Information Services Group—was set up in charge of business with financial institutions and governments in the U.S. market. To some extent the premises that group worked on were in conflict with the premises that some other groups were working on in the same marketplace. The new group did business through banking intermediaries in the classic sense. The consumer group went directly across the country by mail with their own direct business presence. In one state the Financial and Information Services Group was trying to work with correspondent banks, and the consumer group was trying to knock them right out of the marketplace by direct competition. Wriston said, "What the hell do I care if there's some noise. What counts is winning the game in the marketplace. And let's just see what happens." The big game is the game for the total national market. As for the correspondent banks, Wriston said: "Sure they're going to be pissed as hell at us, and they are pissed as hell at us because we're going all out for the national competitive market. But we're right because the underlying realities of the market *tell* us that we're right. These [banking] regulations *have* to come down. We're going to be out there and we're going to win. If, in the meantime, we take all sorts of gas from these guys, so be it. I'm willing to stand up and take the heat." And he was. The correspondent banks may hate Citibank, but they also respect it. They are curious about what Citibank is going to do. That was good enough for Wriston. It is said that he may even have been proud of the fact that probably nobody is quite as hard-assed as Citibank.

The managerial structure for containing the Citibank corps of entre-preneurially minded go-getters is a matrix. At Citibank this means that the bank is organized into two market areas: all of the consumer businesses worldwide, and the institutional banking business worldwide, which includes large corporations, financial institutions, governments, and the like. But that dyad doesn't cover everything. For example, Citibank manages pension funds and offers investment banking services. In England, Citibank might be trying to lend money through the institutional group to the British Oxygen Co. At the same time, the merchant banking group might be recommending that British Oxygen sell some medium-term notes and offering to market them. The two services conflict with each other. The conflicts about what is in the best interest of the corporation require a doorkeeper who makes the ultimate decision.

Wriston saw the forces of personal competition as very important for molding people and bringing out the best in them. He was quite content to see the winners win and the losers lose as a natural consequence of the competition. Some of his executives contended that with the increasingly complicated nature of the organization, Walter's loose style of management—pick good people and support them—did not allow for early awareness of problems (or progress) on a sufficiently current basis to act quickly. An associate reported, "We had a spate of financial congeneric [money market operation] acquisitions around the world, the bulk of which were essentially not successful. After it became obvious that they weren't, most of them were liquidated. One of his [Wriston's] hallmarks is a willingness to allow managers to take chances at some risk to the institution without personally dabbling in it, make their own mistakes or successes." How did Wriston decide to cut the cord? "Listening to the messages of our congenerics in Siam, Malaysia, everyplace, more by gradualism, [accumulating information until] it finally is obvious that something has to be done."

Competition and Free Enterprise

In the 1970s, Wriston sensed that inflation was going to last for a long time, so he came up with the idea of securities that had a floating interest rate, a device that was the only protection for investment in an inflationary environment. In 1974, Citibank issued a $650 million issue of floating rate note obligations. It was one of the largest issues that the public had ever been offered. An enormous outcry arose from institutions, small banks, the Federal Reserve, and others that Citibank was attempting to drain money out of the normal channels of financial intermediation because Citibank was offering a 9 percent rate on the floating rate securities. The thrust of the criticism by the thrift institutions and the small banks was that money that normally would be channeled into the housing market was being drained by a large bank. Walter immediately sensed that the appropriate counter-argument was that an institution that was taking money from financing $100,000 houses in order to pay 9 percent to 1,000 consumers should not be criticized. The equities were in favor of the small saver. While housing was important, it was not as important as giving a person a fair return on his money, irrespective of how much he had.

Walter Wriston was consistently, and some would say rabidly, for free enterprise, for management's right to manage and against interference in the marketplace by government or anyone else. He didn't like Chrysler's Lee Iacocca's "caving in" by putting a labor man on his board, which he saw as a basic mistake. He was dogmatic in his conviction that the market system would take care of all situations. He was dead set against saving Chrysler. If Chrysler couldn't make it, let it go down. He made no bones about saying so before congressional committees. In that, he was unlike most other bankers. The customary way to make your feelings known in the banking field was simply not to go along by refusing to make any loans.

For years Wriston feared government regulation was going to destroy the American banking system and hand over what had traditionally been the banker's franchise to organizations that were less regulated. He pointed out that today the transfer of money from person to person or institution to institution is by and large only electronic impulses—a computer, a telephone wire, possibly a telegraph or a telex. No longer do people carry around pieces of gold or even large amounts of currency. Today most people deal with money in the form of checks, credit cards, or computers. But the government is still dealing with banks as though they were issuers of currency and as though that currency can be exchanged literally. Sears Roebuck, RCA, American Express, Merrill Lynch, and a host of other companies that are not banks, and accordingly are not regulated as banks, deal with and transmit money in the electronic sense with complete freedom while the banks are required to have reserves, are limited on what they can pay or charge for the money they receive or lend, and until recently have been restricted from crossing state lines to establish branches. The banking system might well lose to the unregulated competitors, and the loss would be recognized too late. Wriston described his frustration in trying to gain acknowledgment of this situation:

"The whole industry is in the middle of a giant revolution. When you communicate to the world that you're in a revolution, nobody wants to listen to you. And to that extent, it was frustrating. But what we were talking about ten years ago is a commonplace today. People now know that only 35 percent of the institutions that take deposits are commercial banks. And people now know that General Electric Credit earns more money than the Wells Fargo Bank. And people now know that GMAC [General Motors Acceptance Corporation] earns more money than Manufacturers Hanover. So the whole demise of the business which is taking place is now being seen by some.

It's frustrating to me to read in the paper about banks pushing credit on people with credit cards. There are 600 million credit cards in America. Visa is as big as Mobil Oil, and yet we cannot get through to the legislature or the media or anybody else the simple facts about this. So we . . . write a book every twelve to eighteen months here, and that's the way you change the world—you launch an idea into the market place. That's why we spend so much time doing it, and it works over time. You've got to believe that or you wouldn't be doing it. . . . But you know, if you're going to do anything worthwhile, you're frustrated at least half the time . . . a sense of humor helps."

Wriston fought government attempts to regulate business morality. The Federal Corrupt Practice Act grew out of Lockheed's payoff to Japanese government officials. It declares it to be a violation of American law for an American corporation to pay a bribe to a foreign government official. No one disagrees with that in principle, although there continues to be a good deal of discussion about the exportation of American morality. Another requirement of the law is that a publicly traded company must establish a system of internal financial controls that is able to catch accounting falsifications. But in an organization the size and complexity of Citicorp, with 2,437 places of business in 95 countries, $130 billion in assets, and 59,000 employees, catching all accounting errors, intentional and unintentional, is impossible. The law failed to establish a standard of materiality. Wriston wrote to Harold Williams, then chairman of the Securities Exchange Commission, complaining bitterly. When no corporation could possibly obey the law, corporations automatically would be lawbreakers and their integrity impugned. Furthermore, the integrity of the law would be called into question, undermining the respect for law which should be part of the American economic system.

These convictions and that leadership style scare some people, as do the tough and forceful executives who flourished under Wriston's leadership. But Wriston's position was Darwinian. It's a tough world out there. You've got to take it as it is and not bullshit or minimize the fact that life is tough.

Calling the Shots

Walter did not order subordinates to accept his choices. He would not say, "Okay, now it is agreed that we're going to do this," but rather, "I really think that this will work." It was perfectly apparent that that's what he wanted to do. One associate reports, "He puts an awful lot of his energies into the major policy pronouncements that he makes internal to the organization, and he has a tendency to feel that once he's said something in this sort of definitive, tightly argued, elegant way, that suffices to deal with the question. The administrative mechanism is to track it. He feels that's basically the responsibility of the operating structure. He stays informed but he doesn't typically structure his own routine for tight follow-up."

As would be expected of a sensitive, perfectionistic person, Walter is thin-skinned and does not suffer criticism lightly, according to those close to him. Down the line, people were careful about being critical of Walter to his face. Although the atmosphere was open to expressing opinions and to intellectual conflict, overt criticism was scarce. Disagreements were demonstrated by building a case of facts that he had to accept, and that case was then presented as if it were something new.

Sometimes Wriston could not sell his viewpoint to his cohorts, even when it was a question of persuading them to scratch one of their initiatives. In his opening talk at one of the offshore policy meetings, he laid out the issues for the meeting and what he thought ought to be done. One issue had to do with the fact that Citibank had developed its own unique credit card technology, which was different from the so-called "mag-stripe" technology of all the other cards and required the development of a special terminal to read that unique card. There was a proposal to manufacture the terminal so that Citibank could build its own network, which it has subsequently done. At that meeting, Walter said:

"I think we're kidding ourselves when we, as a banking enterprise, suddenly get ourselves into this terminal business. We're not a communications company or a technology company like IBM. It seems to me that it's beyond our resources and probably our competence to try to develop this terminal to the point where we can use it ourselves on a large scale or commercially exploit it. I would like us therefore to approach somebody like IBM. You decide who. I would like you to say that we would like to license them and have them manufacture it, because what the hell do we know about putting together electronic devices?"

He spoke, they listened. The proponents did not follow his suggestion because the people in the group that developed the terminal wanted to go ahead on their own. Walter continued to push his point of view in follow-up efforts, but his subordinates were equally adamant in their argument that the project was too good to do his way and that they could handle it. In the course of discussions around budget reviews, performance reviews, and policy meetings, the issue arose several times. Finally, Walter gave in to the consensus. He seemed to operate on the maxim, "I've put that out, but the people working with it came to a different view. And consistent with my conviction about decentralized responsibilities and giving people their heads, I won't challenge that, even though I might not agree with it."

Sometimes, Walter admitted, he became obsessed by an issue, fixed on a particular point of view. That obsessiveness seemed to contradict the cool, machinelike analytic posture he conveyed. It seemed as if his inability to win his case with purely analytical, logical means frustrated him. It was as if he were trapped in a zero-sum game. Walter is the kind of man who doesn't agree easily. Sometimes when he was unsure of the success of a potential action or when he was tired of an issue, he would say, "Oh, the hell with it. I really don't think you can get it done that way. I think we ought to sell the whole thing to get out of this," or make some similar statement that reflected his frustration. Eventually he might buy a reasonable solution, especially when the presenter was persistent, and apparently without feelings of anger for having been pressured to agree to that solution.

But Wriston didn't hesitate to make a difficult decision straightfor-wardly. Once he and Bill Spencer were engaged in a series of two-hour annual reviews with members of senior management. This annual cycle is important at Citibank because executives are told what their salaries will be for the coming year, what their bonus is, and how their perform-ance is being judged. At the same moment, time was running out on a decision about how and when Citibank should settle important litiga-tion arising from the New York City financial crisis of 1975, and whether Citibank should go along with Morgan Guaranty and Chase Manhattan or go it alone in reaching a settlement. A colleague who needed that decision to guide his action left a note with Wriston's secretary and said, "When he's finished, could he give me a ring because I would like to discuss with him how we should dispose of this situation." Within about fifteen minutes of the subordinate's request to discuss the matter, Wal-ter interrupted the interviews, showed up unannounced in the subordi-nate's office, sat down, and quickly concluded: "The decision is we'll go it alone. We've given the other banks an opportunity. They haven't chosen to avail themselves of it. Go settle the case."

Citibank lives day by day with Morgan and Chase. Should Wriston call the heads of those banks and tell them of this decision, asked the subordinate, or should Citibank just go ahead? Wriston responded, "You call up the number two guy at each of the banks, tell them what our decision is, and if they want to call me they can call me. I've got to get back to interviews." In the space of four minutes he had inter-rupted a highly important part of the annual management cycle and resolved a crisis with a firm, forthright position.

In times of crisis, when push comes to shove, Wriston takes charge. In the New York City financial crisis there was a risk that the city would default on its bonds. The news media were saying that the crisis might affect the solvency of some of the big banks. Like all the money center banks, Citibank had a big block of New York City paper. Walter just stepped in and said, "I'm in charge." He called the shots. He had several meetings with the mayor and the controller of the city. He said Citibank was not going to underwrite any more city bonds until the city had a financial plan and could show that it could balance its budget. Citibank was part of an ongoing underwriting syndicate for city securities. The staff was gearing up to handle the next issue, although they knew that the situation was getting sticky. Walter said, "We're stopping right here and we're going to take the heat." His staff debated the pros and cons, but he cut off the debate saying, "No, somebody's got to say 'Stop,' and we're saying it, that's all."

Barbed Wit

At Policy Committee offshore meetings, after the business was over, there were always set dinners. An important part of the routine was the telling of jokes and the trading of insults among the group. For Walter, it was a way of testing and toughening the people, and preparing them to keep their composure under difficult circumstances, but he also just thoroughly enjoyed it. The laughter and noise volume got higher and higher. By the time it was over, as one participant described it, "People are just kind of . . . flushed out. When you go through it for the first time, you just wonder what the hell's going on and if somebody hasn't lost his marbles. But I guess you get accustomed to it." For some, that process did not come easily. It might take two or three years before they could muster the comfort to tell the few necessary dirty jokes.

In those sessions members of the Policy Committee who might be in professional conflict with one another found themselves sitting next to each other, or playing tennis as doubles partners, or playing golf together. There was a compelling cohesion that echoed that of a military combat group. The same group met every Thursday morning. Then the agenda was business so the talk was about serious matters, but the joking and the same tone generally prevailed.

People enjoyed Walter's brilliance and his sarcasm. He always laughed as much at himself as he did at anybody else. But he wouldn't use his sarcastic wit on a person he didn't care about, reported a colleague, because he might hurt that person. Board relationships, though muted to some extent, reflected the same kinds of behavior—the give-and-take, the jousting and kidding around.

All humor is tempered aggression. Somebody or something is the butt of a joke, but humor blunts attack. In effect, to make a joke of a remark is to deny its hostile or critical import. If the object of the joke is offended, the wit can always say, "It was only a joke." Yet everyone knows that there is much truth in humor. From the court jesters of old to contemporary comedians, one *pokes* fun. For Walter, humor apparently helped him avoid the feeling of attacking others. Such a talent serves also to temper the formidability of the big boss and simultaneously fosters the sense that he is a likeable person.

Humor is also a device for lightening the load of obligation one puts on oneself. "Walter," a close observer notes, " . . . likes very much to give the impression that he's carrying the whole goddam load on his own shoulders. If [Bill] Spencer [then president] is away for a while and Ed Palmer is someplace else traveling, and Walter is here a week by himself, he'll let it be known that it was a tough week, a lot of things got done, but it was tough. And he says, 'Well, you know, while you're out in the north woods, here I am slaving away.' [When he says] that, then the two or three different men, who know that tactic, will look knowingly at each other. Walt's not aware that others sense that in him."

Wriston's witty barbs were known in Citicorp as "Wristonisms." The *New York Times* was a preferred target. In the early 1970s the *New York Times* was viewed by the business as being opposed to it. Wriston commented that, "The *Times* can say that there are no calories in a Clark bar and get away with it." In 1975 regulatory efforts became so complicated that he commented, "We started out with a mouse and now we're winding up with a zebra." Walter used to worry about what he perceived as the nonsense that came out of the regulatory authorities with the question, "How do you nail that jelly to the wall?" Another Wristonism: "It's not the tree bending that makes the wind blow."

Jack Hanley invited the Citicorp board to hold its first meeting outside of New York in St. Louis. Fifty St. Louis business heads had joined the board for dinner the night before. A top Citicorp executive reported: "Walt wrote a clever speech. He talked about his grandmother going down the Mississippi in a boat at the time St. Louis was an outpost of civilization . . . he said, 'When the bank was formed in 1812, Napoleon stood at the gates of Moscow.' The next day I said, 'Walt, geez, I couldn't believe that you came up with that gates of Moscow jazz. When I read it I didn't believe that you would include that sort of hokum in your speech.' He laughed like hell. And every once in a while I say, 'Well, why don't you give them Napoleon at the gates of Moscow?' as an example of pretension."

The Intellectual

Skill with words became Wriston's trademark. "He's fascinated with the written and spoken word and the depiction of events in words," said a close associate. "I think that's how he makes more of his impact on all of his publics, whether they're within the institution or outside, by his ability to use words to describe and catch the meat of situations. I think he's miscast in this [chairman's role]. I think he should have been a lawyer or an editor of the world's greatest newspaper because he does have these smarts. [Employees] continue to refer to what he said in his speech at the Hominy Eaters Convention or what he said in the State of the Nation message to the bank."

Wriston's intellectual orientation is heavily historical, no doubt a legacy of his father. He usually approached a subject by thinking back through the historical record to find a precedent or a situation that was comparable or provided insight into the problem he was addressing. Often in his speeches and in informal commentary, he drew on history. From the start he came across as someone quite different from the conventional business leader. That difference also added to his distance from other CEOs. His CEO peers tended to see him as not quite cut from the same cloth that they were, but they respected him and particularly his intellect and his achievement. If Wriston wanted to make a point, he said everything that he had to say about the subject. He was dedicated to putting his best foot forward at all times. According to an intimate,

"His expression of his intellect comes principally through his speeches. Once in a while he's done a very short article but his basic contribution to the intellectual domain is really through his formal speeches, and secondarily . . . through the power of his person. . . . A part of his power as an intellect and as a presence, particularly in this informal stuff—business meetings, meetings of the Federal Reserve Advisory Board or the Clearinghouse—is that he just comes to those meetings with a very finely honed sense of the issue, the facts surrounding the issue, the history of the issue, and what should be done about it . . . and he's usually three or four notches ahead of everybody else at the table. That's how he can be so very effective. But the other side of it is, because he's so well prepared, he often turns them off because they can't keep up with him . . . he takes them off guard. He does so by virtue of putting an intellectual formulation on the thing that is not in the customary lingo, so to speak, of business. So therefore he stands apart. Then, as the elegance of his oratory and his phraseology unfolds, and the tightness of his argument, they listen . . . get very absorbed, follow very closely, and they become sort of respectful. But when he finishes, it's almost too powerful in the sense that they have trouble relating to it and arguing about it or challenging it. The typical response is a very heavy round of applause, admiration for what he said, and yet it's as though he operated on a plane that they can't work with in terms of ongoing communications. It's almost as though the effect is something for the historical record.

"To give you an example, he made a speech to about 300 or 400 of our [correspondent] bankers.[2] His basic thesis was and has been for some time that the industry is too wrapped up in its own internal competitive problems between big banks and small banks . . . and the real issue is that a whole new range of competitors outside of the industry per se are taking business away from the banking industry as an industry. He led into that by quoting from Winston Churchill's memoirs, specifically the one, *The Ring of Fate,* where he was talking about the fall of Singapore and the Maginot Line mentality that prevailed then. . . . And he developed that theme into a theme of what he called 'fortress banking.' And he used it to illustrate that we're looking at each other as the enemy comes over the wall and we don't perceive it. He used Churchillian quotations brilliantly, and it came off as a very powerful speech. But who in the hell would expect the head of a major bank talking to a bread-and-butter meeting with correspondent banks to be quoting Churchill and talking about fortress Singapore? Well, he just takes them right off balance when he comes across that way."

Wriston himself said, "I'm almost always in some kind of dialogue with CEOs, and I'm not too sure they buy very much of what we're selling. . . . If you represent an organization like this that's constantly generating ideas, and these men and women in this store do, they're upsetting to the conventional wisdom. You don't get many flowers."

Wriston's speeches were written to have powerful impact. He sweated them out. Sometimes he went through ten or fifteen drafts. He took them home at night and worked on them on the weekends in the country. He spread out his thesaurus and Columbia Encyclopedia and other books for quotes. He edited and refashioned and reworked. Then he rehearsed. In many of his presentations he used slides. If he was to make a presentation to the directors, he would rehearse in the boardroom, just himself with the projectionist.

Every January Wriston made a major internal speech, which he called "The State of the Bank" or "The State of the Corporation," modeled after the presidential addresses to Congress. It was a time for summing up how the previous year had gone—the successes and failures—and for handing out a few congratulations, making some criticisms, and then setting out the priorities for the coming year. Wriston wrote that speech as though every person in the corporation was going to take it seriously and find some meaning in it. He generally started working on it during the week between Christmas and New Year. He liked to have a first draft about the time the New Year break ended, and then he had two or three weeks to fuss with it. Speeches for him were major expenditures of energy and time and emotion. He shrank in anticipation of the task, but then he plunged ahead. He had an enormous faith in the ability of ideas, over time, to make a difference. He understood that it takes time, that you have to plant seeds, let them gestate in the public domain, and that whatever you plant will ripen four or five years thereafter.

Wriston initiated Citibank publication of major studies on topics of the day which were critical to the bank: regulatory issues, bank capital adequacy, credit controls, marginal pricing, restrictions on the prime lending rate, and so forth. He nominated a person to write a study on each subject. In the case of regulations, he wanted to destroy what to him was a fallacious argument on the part of the regulators and to put an alternative in the public domain. The studies had to hold up in scholarly terms and make an intellectual contribution to the debate. On some of the subjects, the studies made a difference. As Wriston stated his point: "I don't want anybody to write or think about this subject that we're writing on without having to refer to our study, because that's the standard that we will aspire to."

On such topics, Wriston had the data and a position, and he knew what the other position was. He felt that the opposing position could be defeated by a proper marshaling of the facts, the evidence, and the logic. The studies have had a significant impact. For example, the concept of the marginal cost of funds is basic in the management of financial business. It is now much better understood because of a study that Charles Kelley did at Wriston's insistence. One Citibank executive made the case for these studies:

> "It's about ten years from the time a Harvard professor writes a paper until the law is passed mandating it. Unless you have a competing idea in the marketplace, you're dead over time. We believe that very strongly and can prove it, but you can't convince an academic or a legislature of anything unless your scholarship is impeccable. . . . The regulators didn't like George Vojta's book on bank capital adequacy because we showed that every bank that failed since 1900 exceeded the ratios they themselves had set, and

therefore that wasn't the critical item, but today that is the starting
point of any argument. For the first time there's a competing force
in the marketplace of ideas. And we'll keep on doing that."

The same principle applies to Wriston's attempt to embed his own
vision in the organization. Said Wriston, "A great book written by a fine
historian said at the end of the day the British Empire is run by a man
sitting at a table writing on a piece of paper with a pencil. Nobody's ever
learned anything more than that. So you can sit at a table and write on
a piece of paper with a pencil and get up on your feet and read what
you've written. I started giving the State of the Bank messages to all
senior officers as an oral presentation and then it went around the
world."

Wriston's intellectual incisiveness wedded to his communication
skills made him a forceful spokesman for business on complex issues.
Part of Wriston's management style was the ability to get to the essence
of a problem and reduce it to simple, understandable terms. That ability
proved to be enormously helpful in calming down a lot of people
throughout the world at a critical time.

When President Carter froze all Iranian bank accounts in the United
States and in American banks overseas, 8:00 A.M. on November 14, 1979,
that unprecedented move required Citibank to act. There was an end-
less stream of calls from the communications media. The bank had been
in touch with the Treasury Department all morning. A press conference was called right after lunch to let the media know what was
happening and what impact this would have on the international
money market, so that nobody would panic. The Treasury was extremely grateful that a leading banker, if not *the* leading banker, was
to explain the situation to the media.

Because of a luncheon appointment with New York State Senator
Warren Anderson, which could not be broken, Wriston didn't have
much time to discuss what the nature of his remarks should be. At 2:15
P.M., some sixty reporters and three television network crews were
waiting. Wriston still hadn't figured out what he was going to say. He
went into his office with his top associates, who quickly recapitulated the
mass of events that had occurred during the morning. In five minutes he
reviewed them in his own mind. He talked with his staff briefly about the
theory of the president's action and the rationale behind some of the
actions that bank officials had taken, concretizing the issue by using the
analogy that a receiver had been appointed for the assets of Iran to
permit an orderly settlement of their debts. With only that briefing, he

said, "Okay, I've got it." He walked out to the podium. The floodlights glowed. Cameras began to roll. The reporters got out their pads. His colleagues worried, "What in God's name is he going to say?" And it all flowed out in the most coherent fashion, totally rational, totally calming. The reporters who were disposed to try to create crises couldn't get a rise out of him. He reiterated that the president's action was a perfectly rational act in response to an irrational act on the part of the Iranians. Not to worry. The world's markets would open tomorrow just as they had opened today. The press conference ended about forty-five minutes later and appeared on the evening television news. The next morning everything went along as usual. Wriston had absorbed an enormous amount of diverse material, some of it unprecedented, made it all seem coherent, and calmly answered questions with great facility.

The Future

Citibank formed the holding company Citicorp in 1968 under Wriston's leadership. The original dream of building, under Citicorp, a business that was banking in its traditional sense plus the insurance business and the information services business did not materialize because the law and the banking regulations insisted that a bank is a bank is a bank, and bankers should stick to accepting deposits and lending money. However, other banks soon followed Citibank into the holding company structure. In the eyes of some Citicorp executives, the man who put the final nail in the coffin of that expansionistic concept was John R. Bunting, then president of the First Pennsylvania Bank and Trust Company, who, in testimony before Congressman Wright Patman's committee said, "I may even go into the used car business." Patman went on the attack, and the advantages Citicorp had in the holding company form were swept away by subsequent legislation. The first move that Citicorp was to make in the holding company was to buy a trucking company, a George Moore idea. The effort got all the way up to the altar, and the Justice Department said no.

Of Patman, Wriston said, "There they are, the Patmans of the world. They stand there and they command the sun not to come out." The objective of diversification is still a major theme of the organization, although it may take years to achieve. The holding company was able to buy a finance company and the Acceptance Mortgage Company. It now has a national distribution system for finance company products and mortgage company products, but the original dream or strategy was much more dramatic. Citicorp says it is not a bank but a financial services institution. The notion in Washington is that a bank has very limited powers, but the regulators have finally agreed that banks are required to be competitive. Breaking down the barriers and the preconceived notions of what the financial services business is all about continues to be a force that drives Citicorp.

When he became president, Wriston challenged Citibank with a major financial objective. Although a premier bank, Citibank had been earning at about 7 percent per annum. Wriston wanted to make it 15 percent per annum. No one on the Policy Committee believed the corporation could grow at twice its current growth rate. Sherman Adams, who was then the chief planning officer for George Moore and theoretically the ultimate guru of the bank, said that 8 to 9 percent was all that could be expected. He failed to recognize that the financial institution that Wriston was going to manage was to be very different from the run-of-the-mill bank. In the 1970s Citicorp came close: 14.5 percent.

Walter's commitment to 15 percent reinforced the importance of profit center managers knowing what their profits were, as opposed to having them aggregated at the corporate level. It was clear to every profit manager that Wriston meant 15 percent. Not all did well with what was experienced as 15 percent pressure across-the-board, compounded year after year. Sometimes staffs were decimated or costs cut in the wrong place. Sometimes the bottom line became all-preoccupying for Young Turks driving to make their marks by increasing the pressure on subordinates who could not be speeded up further. Sometimes nothing more could be squeezed from a given function or operation. When problems erupted, Walter changed the policy on staff reductions. Retraining, attrition, opportunities for other jobs, and pay outs became the preferred order of the day. Those whose practices conflicted with his own values did not last.

About those values in leadership Wriston said: "Some people like to have confrontational management. Other people like to build consensus. . . . There are things that I would not do . . . ITT has a meeting every month and has all the managers come in and then they rain all over their parade on a public basis. That is alien to my nature. . . . Everybody's human and they bleed when you stick 'em. They get colds and their feet hurt. So these people who don't have any [compassion] I don't really want working around here."

Wriston's second challenge after increased earnings was to build an actuarial base, which meant that no significant piece of the corporation's assets or risks or earnings would be put in any one industry, any one country, or any one operation. The third challenge was to develop the best people. Walter said to the Policy Committee, "Look . . . there are four of us at the top that are going to be leaving in the next few years, and it'd be stupid as hell for us to leave you with a plan you're stuck with. It would make sense, since you guys are going to have to live with it in the longer term [to work out a plan]." Arthur D. Little consultants helped forecast the managerial needs over the next ten years. Walter bent over backward at times to suppress his own views and probably went along with some choices that he personally did not fully agree with.

Humanist

Despite his convictions about competition hardening winners, Wriston's concern for people permeated his managerial effort. Said a senior executive:

"I don't think I've ever had a business review with Walt where the people side of the equation hasn't been an issue. We do have separate manpower planning reviews. But . . . the human dimension and the human fabric of the organization is very important to Walt. . . . Walt will not sit down with you and line-by-line go over your numbers. He will not want to know why there's a $10,000 increase in one line item. Walt's style is more directed toward the really key, fundamental, overwhelming issues in the business, as opposed to the nitty-gritty detail on a line-by-line basis. . . . And on a number of occasions Walt will come in and say, 'Why haven't we tried this idea?' . . . If you've done a reorganization and you've moved a senior person around, he'll ask, 'How's he doing? How do you feel about him at this stage of the game? Is he back on board, or is he still a problem?' . . . Walt might just come right off the wall and say, 'Well, you know, maybe we ought to transfer that person to someplace else.' "

Walter is the kind of man who puts his arm around others affection-ately. If a colleague is standing in a crowd at a cocktail party, he'll put his arm around the person and say, "What do you think this old bastard did today?" His display of affection to a handful of intimates earned him the appellation "Big Bear," a term of endearment coined by his wife, Kathy, who is a prominent attorney with the prestigious firm of Shear-man and Sterling.

Wriston was typically informal with close associates. "He sits right there and I sit at my desk," one reported. "He respects my chair. He comes, pulls up a chair. It depends whether I've got my briefcase on it. If it's not there, then he sits on the easy chair. When I walk into his office, which I do without announcement or a telephone call, after four o'clock on a Friday [when top management gets the problems others couldn't solve], his typical reaction is, 'Oh my God. I've already gone home. What is it now?' But he's prepared for it and we usually dispose of the matter quickly. The ability to move back and forth without announcement makes my life a lot easier."

Some thought Wriston was too easy-going when it came to terminat-ing people:

> "He's tough in his management position, in his management con-cepts, but he's also chickenhearted and kindhearted. We've got a problem with an officer that we have wanted to get rid of for the last couple of years who's not serving a very useful purpose. And yet Walter doesn't know how to do that without hurting the person. Can't fire him. He can't look him in the eye and say, 'You've had it. That's it. We'll find you a better position someplace else.' He can't quite take that one. He tried to figure out how he can do it and save the fellow, which I think is commendable. On the other hand, some guys are not [salvageable]. They've obtained such high positions, anything else would be meaningless . . . the thing you have to do is try to figure out how you can make him whole some-place else. . . . I think he finds that difficult to do. He'll acknowledge the incompetence, or some major shortcoming, but he doesn't get into saying, 'Look, do something with that man. Get him out of that organization'."

A long-term executive who had once made an important contribution was having severe personal problems that made him distraught and influenced his performance at work. Wriston remembered that he had done a good job for the bank and therefore Citibank owed him a lot.

He felt compassion for the man's deep personal problems and believed that the business issue should be secondary to the human issue. He supported the man in his role for about eighteen months. When the executive began to work out his personal problems, he was moved aside, and then he ultimately left the bank. That was said to be typical of Wriston's loyalty to people.

As a consequence of Walter's not stepping in firmly enough, however, some people seemed to move past their potential and stumble. Others may have been measured in ways that put them below not only their potential but also below their actual performance. That makes for career problems and discharge. Walter would say, "Well, you know, it never worked out with that guy. But what are you going to do?" Although he has great compassion for people, if a manager got to be just a person with a problem, then Walter readily said, "Well, you know, I've got a hell of a lot of other things to do." He has the ability to turn himself off so he doesn't worry about everyone's problems. He is willing to say, "Well, I guess you can't pursue that forever. It didn't work out. The guy's got to go."

Wriston has had his own share of personal pain, which, colleagues say, increases his sensitivity to that of others. In 1965, his first wife was found dead in her bed; she had been getting ready for a luncheon with the wives of some other bank officials. Her death was a severe blow to Walter. He seemed to be the first to know of the personal tragedies in his colleagues' lives. A senior colleague reports: "Fifty percent of the time he'll ask you how your wife is. If you've got some problems at home, he'll come in to make sure that she's all right. He'll send flowers to her. He'll call her up . . . my wife had an operation . . . the very first plant she got was from Kathy Wriston. . . . And he's very upset when people get ill. He's very touchy about that. He'll make telephone calls to the house of these people. . . . Mostly the Policy Committee, the people he works intimately with."

Despite his sensitivity to the pain of others and his informal manner, Walter regulated the distance between himself and others carefully. He was said to be very difficult to engage in exchanges unless *he* wanted them, and unless there was a purpose. If he wanted to bring a person closer, he would do so, then push him or her back again by not responding to a question or statement. He would just go on talking. To some, he seemed to make a conscious decision about whether he would respond to a question, or even respond to a statement that didn't necessarily have a "What do you think?" at the end of it, de-

pending on whether he had the time and whether he thought it pertinent or interesting. Sometimes subordinates could go to Walter with a
problem about which they had an opinion, and he would let them lay
out the whole issue. He would listen to everything, but he would not
necessarily reveal his position or his answer on every issue as quickly
as others might have wanted. He would do so when it suited *his* purpose. In effect, he would not permit himself to be bogged down by
issues and events that he might not have initiated. He could be very
selective so that the issues that would take his future attention were
the ones that he thought the most critical, interesting, or valuable.

One of the reasons subordinates said they could work with Walter
without feeling necessarily affronted by this behavior is that he was not
consistent in these attitudes. He would change pace, now accepting and
responding, later rejecting. Either he had already recognized the issue
as important and intended to deal with it, or, on a relative scale, it was
not as important as the person presenting the idea believed. It seemed
to be a matter of discernment and control, the ability to measure and
judge issues. Of course, another reason such behavior was accepted was
because Walter was king. People accept more from their boss than they
do from their peers. But Walter had the ability to keep things from
becoming unpleasant.

When Walter did become angry, he tightened up on himself. He
became studious in his negative replies. He grew quieter. Some said you
could almost see the hackles rising on the back of his neck. His subordinates could tell by this attitude and by the way he cleared his throat that
they had scratched his surface and that he was going to prove that his
concept was right and theirs was not. He would methodically create a
case to establish that someone was incorrect in his appraisal. "When he's
uptight you can see it in his face," a colleague said. "He becomes more
of a Satan. His eyebrows kind of look like Satan's . . . or he wrinkles his
forehead when he's uptight. . . . His eyes will go up and he will blink
spasmodically."

Bill Spencer outlined his tandem black hat–white hat relationship
with Wriston:

"We, as a matter of corporate practice, spent a lot of time with
different groups looking in depth at their operations. . . . I was
always the person who led when we were together . . . perhaps
it's an identification of our roles that I was the operating manager
and he's the chief executive. But in terms of interactions where

we had joint visits with staff members or others, I did 90 percent of the stuff, but he obviously threw in his own questions . . . he is much less direct . . . I'm the guy that always carries the stick and hits people over the head. He's back there smoothing the ground . . . remaking the flower bed after we tear it up."

Another insider concurred with Spencer's view: "I don't think he can be quite as direct as [Spencer]. [Spencer could] look you in the eye and punch you in the nose. It's very easy. You know, that's the way the gentleman is. I don't think Walter can. I think Walter has more tender spots in him." Apparently it was that very complement that led Wriston to choose Spencer as his chief operating officer.

Walter is essentially a private, self-contained, self-controlled person. He has a farm in Connecticut and gets deeply involved fussing with the machinery and wiring the house and other manual activities—that got him away from banking and protected his private life. In effect, he locked himself in for a weekend or several weeks of a vacation and depended very little on outside social contact. Wriston got involved in business association meetings and similar activities, but he pulled back when those activities became more social or cronylike. Although he is widely known, to some of his colleagues he did not seem to have as many close personal friends as might have been expected from all of his contacts.

A colleague described Wriston's vacations and associates:

"He tends to organize his life in a pattern. As long as I've known him, he's always done the same thing. He goes away for ten days to two weeks in February to Antigua, where he plays tennis and likes to sun. And then he takes the month of August off and he usually goes to Bermuda for about a half of that, and spends the other half of that at his country home . . . he seems to be sustained by the repetition of that . . . pattern. . . . I think there's a pattern in [his friends]. They tend to be very intelligent people, people who are very cosmopolitan in their thinking, and they tend to be people who have the temperament that he has—sort of a wit, and ability to exchange friendly insults constantly, but who are very decent. . . . A lot of his buddies are people that he plays tennis with regularly. . . . He keeps himself in great physical condition. . . . One of his good friends is Billy Talbert."

Outside Man

Around 1976, Bill Spencer encouraged Wriston to devote more time to the external aspects of his role as CEO. His external activity continued to grow. He was in Washington almost weekly because, as a leading member of one of the most heavily regulated businesses, he had a crucial interest in the regulatory and legislative activities that affected the bank. Wriston brought that external arena into the managerial process. At the Policy Committee, he usually started off with a recitation of things that he had done in connection with Washington or the Business Roundtable or a call from the president. Some of his associates thought he had a slight case of Potomac fever. He would mention having had dinner with Secretary of State George Shultz or having talked with the president, or he would comment, "Last night I was with Kissinger and his wife . . . in this nice little apartment," and drop a few names, which he did freely. Walter would talk about being called to talk with Paul Volcker, chairman of the Federal Reserve Board, about banks dropping out of the Federal Reserve system. He might have been called down to a special Labor-Management Group. He was on the policy committee of the Business Roundtable. He was chairman of the President's Economic Policy Advisory Board. He liked to deal with the important people of the world. Walter enjoyed the sense of being able to influence public policy and legislation on taxes, foreign policy, and other matters. He was ambitious to be a useful, important American. Citicorp got credit for being above average because Wriston was identified as an unusual spokesman and an original thinker.

Wriston's sense of the importance of the social and political climate in which organizations are imbedded was a recurring theme. "In the practical world you're going to live and die on what the society accepts of what you do. It's just that simple," he pointed out. "And if the society believes that whatever business you're in is no damn good and doesn't make a constructive contribution to this society, you can be the greatest managerial genius since Sloan, and your company's going down the chute. . . . All CEOs basically try to make their organizations congruent with the society in which they live, and produce some goods and services that can be sold. . . . Well, sometimes we do something right . . . in the World Series if you hit .302 you're a ruddy hero. That makes it less than half the time that you're right. Business people want you to bat .800. Nobody's ever done that except in their own biographies."

Ebb Tide

Where did it all lead—the perfectionistic standards, the selection of world-class people, the intense competitiveness along with freedom to make mistakes, the satisfaction from having those he had chosen and cultivated achieve new heights, the wish to be liked by those close to him coupled with challenges that risked the hostility of those more distant, the faith in the eventual potency of written and spoken ideas? In Wriston's perception, the outcome is an innovative institution, constantly pressing against the frontiers of knowledge and evolving new ways of doing things—occasionally brash but of the highest integrity.

What managerial monument did Wriston want to leave behind? According to him, the next generation of managers:

"The thing I would like most is obviously not to make too many mistakes in putting our next team in place. That's the only one I want. This is a continuing outfit. It's been here since 1812 and my monument will be that we didn't total it. It's still around. . . . We're spending a lot of time looking at the tides that run in history, structuring the organization to ride with them. So our successors are going to have to deal with contemporary sociohistorical trends. If I knew what those were, I'd have a bestseller on my hands. . . . the greatest professor I ever had is dead a lot of years, Sigmund Neumann, who wrote maybe the best book I ever read called *The Future in Perspective*. . . . He had a seminar on the tides of world history and politics. He might have thought that we went with the flow recently. Well, I don't know that, but I hope he'd think we were able to do that."

Wriston's awareness of history told him much about how the bank had arrived at where it was when he took over. He sought to combine the continuity of its vital assets with innovation when the environment indicated that innovation was necessary. His colleagues say he has a good sense of those trade-offs between tradition and innovation. The history of the bank from 1812 reflects four alternating cycles of innovation and expansion or retrenchment and consolidation. The cycles of innovation were always triggered by a leadership group that was innovative and entrepreneurial. It is deeply ingrained in Wriston's thinking that at critical points, when the environment changed in a decisive way, the bank survived and prospered because it was able to innovate. "But," said Wriston, "I doubt very seriously that I thought of all of those things [innovations] when I took over. Most people rationalize their lives when they get old enough and make believe they planned it that way. It's almost totally untrue. . . . The vision of a global marketplace, I might have brought something to that."

As of January 1, 1980, another process was unfolding—the dance of succession. It was imbedded in a reorganization dictated by a new strategic plan for the 1980s: Hans Angermueller assumed responsibility for Citicorp's legal and external affairs; John Reed took charge of individual banking; Thomas Theobald became head of institutional banking. Hans Angermueller was an engineer before he turned lawyer. He has a reputation for being "fantastic" at solving specific, intricate individual situations, but it is said he doesn't have the larger perspective of the other two men. There is an intense affinity between Walter and Angermueller. To Walter, Reed is a dramatic change agent. He has a wide-ranging interest in science. He is a student of systems and econometric modeling. Theobald is an investor. He reduces everything to the simplest possible set of denominations and works very hard at those. He is interested in the big economic picture. In him, Walter saw wisdom. The 1980 order of battle reorganized all of Citicorp's services around four generic customer groups on a global basis—private corporations worldwide, individual consumers, governments, and financial institutions—thereby consolidating these core businesses and having them report to Reed or Theobald.

To agree with Wriston that his achievement represented the compelling power of ideas is to underestimate the rest of the configuration—the high level of intelligence and the commitment to that intelligence at considerable risk; the confidence that the best will win; and the recognition of the need for bonding to contain the hostility that critical cross-examination engenders. He demonstrated that ideas without fight are mere platitudes, and fight without convictions is merely hassle. To attack vigorously represents the flowering, the translation, of values into action.

Coda

By the end of 1982, net operating earnings had risen 35 percent to $747 million over the $535 million of 1981, and problem loans in the last quarter of 1982 had risen 60 percent to $1.04 billion from the same period a year earlier, primarily because of private sector borrowers in Mexico and other Latin American countries. Yet, interest rate margins increased and costs were down. Together with the rest of the major banks, Citicorp was under attack for loans to foreign governments that threatened to default. Some feared the whole international banking system would collapse.

As a result of the earning loss of 1980, employees did not get their anticipated 10 to 15 percent bonuses that were tied to year-end profitability. They complained that they didn't have much to do with whether the bank made a profit. That ended a twenty-nine-year policy. Instead, beginning in 1982, all employees with two years' service received an automatic 6 percent increase and flat 13 percent bonuses at year end.

In 1982, Wriston got Federal Reserve Board permission to create a new wholesale bank in Wilmington, Delaware. Meanwhile, bank regulators were rapidly implementing 1980 legislation that allowed them to eliminate the interest rate ceilings on bank and thrifts by 1986. Then the Federal Reserve Board gave Citicorp permission to acquire Fidelity Savings and Loan in San Francisco. For the first time a New York bank could take consumer deposits in California—and by extension, across all state lines. That breakthrough was followed by Citicorp Net Asset Network Account, which combined brokerage services, money market funds, checking, credit cards, and credit tied to deposits. At long last, Citicorp was fully in the financial business. In the same year, Citicorp won a three-year battle with computer services companies. The Federal Reserve Board authorized Citicorp to operate a subsidiary called Citishare, which offered banking at home on computer terminals and electronic publishing of financial data.

Essentially Wriston had won, but he was not yet out of the woods. In 1982, the Securities Exchange Commission (SEC) staff found that Citicorp violated other countries' tax and currency laws, allegedly transferring trading profits from high-tax countries to low-tax ones. But the commission overruled its staff and declined to initiate civil action, its enforcement chief contending that what Citicorp did overseas was none of the SEC's business. John Feders, the comptroller of the currency, expressed his concern about some of the bank's trading in foreign currency and raised questions about Citicorp's safety and soundness. Citicorp asked its law firm, Shearman and Sterling, to investigate. The *Wall Street Journal* questioned whether Shearman and Sterling's investigation of those matters was a whitewash because of the close relationship between the bank and its lawyers. All that came on top of Harvard University's sale of $50.9 million worth of Citicorp's bonds and CDs because the bank was part of a consortium that had lent money to the South African government. The loan, its defenders argued, was to finance construction of schools, housing, and hospitals for the nation's black population.

Bill Spencer, president, and Ed L. Palmer, chairman of the executive committee, retired in 1982. Angermueller, Reed, and Theobald were named vice-chairmen. Banking circles were favoring Theobald to be Wriston's successor as head of what now had become the world's dominant banking institution.

In 1983, Citicorp attained a 16 percent return on equity, earning $860 million, twice as much as any other bank holding company, which made it the most profitable of money center banks. It had 2,000 corporate lending offices in 300 U.S. cities, 800 consumer finance offices in 44 states, and 12 million credit card customers. It had acquired 3 savings and loan associations with 190 branches, and 22 industrial banks in 7 states. It had $141.8 billion in net assets. It was the world's biggest private lender. Walter Wriston was named the country's most influential financier in the 1984 *U.S. News and World Report* survey.

Citicorp's consumer, electronics, and management development momentum had paid off. After the $300 million cost of getting its consumer business going, Citicorp was doing profitable business with one out of every seven U.S. households. Others would have a hard time catching up with its technical resources and management depth.

In June, 1984 Wriston announced that John Reed would be his successor.

4

Ian K. MacGregor

AMAX INC.

SOME might say Ian K. MacGregor was a consummate gambler. He bet big stakes on the future. But that was only after careful sociopolitical and financial analysis—and only after hedging his bets. He was also a consummate deal-maker, for most of his ventures required partners. But that label doesn't do justice to him either. His deal-making was more accurately the forging of long-term alliances, both personal and financial.

MacGregor's deals were costly and left AMAX with a massive financial burden when his successor failed to follow through on MacGregor's plan to be acquired, and recession and inflation wreaked havoc with the minerals market. Nevertheless, he built a collection of mining holdings into a major corporation with worldwide interests, interrelated with other companies around the globe. He is an international citizen, widely and highly regarded in the world's capitals and in its backwoods as well.

MacGregor had a rare capacity to think years ahead, to think big, and to think of the best way to do things, that is, to spare no expense for quality. As we shall see over and over in this chapter, MacGregor was a man who liked to see connections. As a colleague described him, "Ian could pick out an incident or an event and connect it in his mind with half a dozen other things and relate them together somehow into a whole." He was also secure. The same colleague said: "Ian struck me as a man who must have been brought up with a great sense of his own worth. He never seemed to exhibit many doubts. If he had doubts, or suffered a defeat, he seemed to be able to internalize the lesson, recover quickly, and go on to a bigger and better victory. He did not make the same mistake twice. . . . that extreme curiosity and high-energy level combined with this inner sense of mission seemed in his case to blend into an unbeatable combination."

Reg Jones was noted for his political sensibilities and his capacity for compromise. Walter Wriston sought to move the political corpus by logical argument and political challenge. Ian MacGregor was more the take-charge actor. Like John Foster Dulles, he circled the globe, constructing partnerships, maneuvering around political thickets, and all the while maintaining the respect and regard that accrued to a powerful person who remained sensitive to the self-images of those with whom he interacted.

Like Wriston, MacGregor was a combatant, but his most important fights were within his company. Earlier on, this quiet, dignified, well-mannered man fought the interests of a faction on his board who, he thought, would hold his company back. But he did not translate that fierce adversarial posture into a generalized attitude toward labor, conservationists, or—later—the workers of British Steel and British Coal. He did, indeed, often take a firm, tough stand with rivals and both British steel and coal unions. But he preferred to prevail through subtle means—persuasion, negotiation, or horse trading. All the while, with quiet demeanor, great personal control, and unrelenting, but not rigid, determination, he remained the modest Scotsman whose customary lunch was a hamburger.

Ian K. MacGregor was CEO of AMAX for a decade until his retirement in September, 1977; he then became successively the chief executive of British Steel, and, since September 1, 1983, chairman of Britain's National Coal Board. His philosophy: "Managing a company is a little like playing gin rummy. You know what the long-term objective is. To a certain extent the short-time circumstances are outside of your control, and you really have to play your hand in accordance with what happens, how the cards turn out, so that you have to have a degree of flexibility within the framework of trying to achieve certain objectives."

MacGregor was always mechanically minded, a talent that was to serve him well in mining. As a boy, he used to tinker with automobiles. At one time in his career, he sold automobile equipment. Cars were one of his passions. MacGregor earned degrees in metallurgy from the universities of Glasgow and Strathclyde. After college, he got a job as a management trainee at British Aluminum, where his father was an officer, but MacGregor quit when his superiors insisted that he work in a research laboratory. On being selected for the Fortune Hall of Fame in 1979, he recollected, "In a lab I would be working by myself. I felt more at home in a factory, working with people." He did just that. Never thereafter was he without a small coterie of people he trusted. By his late twenties he was in charge of a 2,500-employee defense plant, while advising the British government on tank design. After the 1940 Dunkirk debacle, he was one of a small group of experts sent to Washington to deal with the technical aspects of arms purchasing. With the entry of the United States into the war, he helped develop joint U.S.-British war production policies. Armed with extensive knowledge of American industry, he chose to remain in the United States after the war.

After holding executive positions at Manning, Maxwell and Moore, Inc., a Connecticut manufacturer of industrial instruments and control equipment, and the Campbell, Wyant and Cannon Foundry Company of Muskegon, Michigan, MacGregor joined Climax Molybdenum Co. in 1957 as a vice-president in charge of Eastern operations. That same year Arthur H. Bunker, president and head of the company, put him in charge of its diversification program.

On December 30, 1957, the American Metal Company, Ltd. (Amco), seventy years old, merged with thirty-nine-year-old Climax Molybdenum Company to form American Metal Climax, Inc., later abbreviated to AMAX. Amco was one of the world's largest traders of nonferrous metals (copper, lead, zinc, tin, silver, and gold), as agents for others as well as for itself. MacGregor and the other vice-presidents of the merged parties continued as vice-presidents of the new entity.

During the integration process, some attempted to abbreviate MacGregor's career. Following lunch after the merger, MacGregor went back to his office. Three senior executives walked together to theirs. Another walked ahead of them, but close enough to overhear. According to the eavesdropper:

"In the few months after having joined the company [MacGregor] displayed so much intelligence, so much spirit of undertakings, and . . . for the established members of the system, so much dangerous ambition, that when the merger came, the first thing that the Climax traditional group was interested in was to discharge Ian. But the two factions, Climax Molybdenum and Amco, were more interested in fighting each other than bothering with the brilliant, disturbing MacGregor, so they put him in charge of new enterprises, where presumably he would be harmless because nobody wanted to undertake anything new anyway."

MacGregor's assignment to a minor aspect of AMAX's business activities may have spared him from becoming a casualty of the intense jockeying for power that raged between the Amco and Climax factions from 1958 to 1967. AMAX had a lot of cash in those days, and MacGregor had nothing else to do, so he took his new assignment seriously. He started on a path that changed the scope and character of AMAX.

Entering Aluminum

Pierre Gousseland, later MacGregor's successor but then based in Paris, met him while MacGregor was on assignment. The two took long walks together in Paris, spinning out their fantasies about what they could do in and with the company. In those days, 1958, MacGregor had identified aluminum, nickel, timber and paper, and fertilizers as the four big areas in which he thought the company should expand. They fitted the abilities of AMAX. Also, they were capital intensive. MacGregor's view was that the company must have an important component of its costs in depreciating dollars. As inflation escalated, that concept of investment against depreciating dollars would be the basis of his later strategy for AMAX.

Building the aluminum business was an evolutionary process. Extensive research convinced MacGregor that to enter the aluminum business one had to have a market. On August 31, 1962, a year that marked the seventy-fifth anniversary of AMAX (really of Amco), he executed mergers with Kawneer Company and with Apex Smelting Company. Kawneer manufactured architectural aluminum products and appliance parts. Apex was a converter of aluminum scrap and primary metal into foundry alloys. In May, 1963, AMAX purchased Hunter Engineering Company, a producer of aluminum sheet and other mill products, semifinished building products, and a leading designer of production equipment for the aluminum industry. These three companies, which consumed aluminum, had combined annual sales of more than $100 million.

MacGregor wanted to continue the vertical integration process from mine to consumer by acquiring a smelter. He tried to assemble a primary smelting venture in Tennessee with Swiss Aluminum Company. They liked his idea but joined with Phelps Dodge instead. Undaunted, MacGregor continued to shop for a partner with the requisite technology and people, one that shared his optimistic vision of the development of the aluminum market and was looking to enter the aluminum business in the United States or to expand its holdings. Foreign companies best fit the bill because AMAX could offer them an American passport to its banking connections. AMAX's track record of successful projects in the United States could give financial support to a partner in a joint project.

These advantages had little appeal to the Swiss, who had a strong currency and knew how to manage money in the United States. It was a different story for the French. Their complex regulations made investment abroad difficult. MacGregor approached Pechiney Compagnie de Produits Chimiques et Electrometallurgiques, the leading French aluminum producer. Pechiney's founder had invented the aluminum smelting process and mined his first ore in Les Baux, France, the village that gave bauxite its name. Pechiney had developed an excellent ingot technology and was fabricating aluminum in the United States but not producing ingots. One associate recalled the day of decision:

"There is a famous day when we were sitting in Paris and we had finished a day of long, painful, difficult, discussion with Pechiney . . . and at the end of that particular day Ian had come to the conclusion that Pechiney would bring in what he wanted, and we had to do it. So we put down a memorandum of understanding, and at midnight he called Walter Hochschild, chairman of the board and chief executive officer, and he said, 'Walter, there's this, and this and this. Here's the agreement.' And Walter, who was keen on the deal but always was nervous when it came to the decision time and preferred to have options, said, 'Ian, you know this is just too much money. This is too big a project. Come back and we'll discuss it, and tell the French we're going to come back in a month or so and pursue discussions.' Ian said, 'Too bad, I have signed.' And Walter said, 'You come back immediately.' . . . today our business is the seventh largest aluminum company in the world. In terms of profitability it is the number one company."

Whether bold or brash, MacGregor had taken the initiative. As he
would from time to time, he forced the decision. AMAX would never
be the same again.

In 1964, a joint venture with Pechiney gave AMAX 50 percent ownership of the Intalco Aluminum Corporation, whose new primary reduction plant on Puget Sound at Bellingham, Washington, would begin
operations in 1966. Some years later AMAX built its third smelter, this
time without Pechiney.

. . . And Iron

In 1963, AMAX learned of high-grade iron ore deposits in the Mount
Newman area of Western Australia, a country whose probusiness economic policy attracted foreign investors. That year AMAX formed a
new wholly owned subsidiary, Mt. Newman Iron Ore Company, Ltd.,
to do the exploration work. Responsibility for this project was in the
hands of Elmer N. Funkhouser, Jr., who joined the company in 1961 as
executive vice-president, became a director, and was being groomed
for president.

The project ran into escalating costs that indicated the need to increase the project's scale so that unit costs could be brought down by
higher output. But the Japanese steel mills that had signed purchasing
contracts were unwilling to accept stepped-up shipments. Despite
great effort, Funkhouser could not put the floundering project together.
It was given to MacGregor, whose gift for figuring out who might be
interested in a deal moved the project. He was able to bring in the
Broken Hill Proprietary Company, Ltd. (BHP), a steel producer and the
largest company in Australia (which in 1983 acquired most of GE's Utah
International Australian coal properties). Later, in 1967, BHP became
a partner and a purchaser of ore (8 million out of 40 million tons in 1980),
manager of the project, and owner of a 30 percent interest. MacGregor
negotiated the sale of 5 percent of the project to Roan Selection Trust,
Ltd., (in which AMAX had a large minority equity position) and 10
percent to Mitsui and Company, Ltd., and C. Itoh and Company, Ltd.,
two major Japanese trading companies, because Japan was a big market

for the ore. MacGregor dealt AMAX 25 percent of the project and Selection Trust came to own 30 percent.

One associate observed:

"He [Ian] believed in thinking on a very large scale. Often in a new mining situation, if the ore reserve was large enough but the predicted economics of the project looked thin, his solution would be to scale it up. . . . The original [Mt. Newman] plan centered on starting at a 2-million-ton annual production rate, scaling up to 5 million after a few years. Well, by the time the mine opened it was ready to produce at the 5 million rate and today it has a capacity of 40 million tons. He sensed this might happen. The ore reserves are virtually limitless. He insisted on building the best possible railroad and the largest possible port in anticipation of the tonnage exceeding all expectations. . . . Typically, in mining, the incremental cost of expansion is small compared to the basic facility cost, especially if there's a major infrastructure component such as a railroad, a port, a town. Doubling the size of the output by no means doubles the expenditure on infrastructure."

Within a few years, MacGregor's initiative had changed the course of AMAX. AMAX had acquired Canadian Tungsten Mining Corporation, Ltd. MacGregor had doubled the size of the Australian iron ore project. He had constructed aluminum primary metal and fabricating plants. He had expanded AMAX's Missouri lead mine into a mill-smelter complex. Though in the beginning finance had been his weakest suit, he had become a maker of mining deals. Assigned to an organizational backwater, he had turned that assignment into a new organizational frontier. MacGregor's impending success with the Mt. Newman venture was the final card that enabled him to cash in on a top management post. He was elected president of AMAX in March, 1966, succeeding Frank Coolbaugh, who had moved up to chairman of the board and CEO on January 1 when Walter Hochschild retired. Coolbaugh resigned that role in May, 1967, according to the *Wall Street Journal*, "after a bitter power struggle that lasted for nearly five years."[1]

MacGregor's accession to president was as much a product of Funkhouser's misfortunes as it was of MacGregor's adroit dealings. Enmeshed in the Mt. Newman project, Funkhouser went off to Australia for six weeks during the very period when important work was being done on his plan to acquire the Southern Nitrogen Company. Upon his return he made a poor presentation to the board and was unable to answer critical questions about his proposal. It has been said that the embarrassing questions asked at the board meeting were stimulated by discussions MacGregor had with members of the Climax faction on the board about the pitfalls of the proposal. MacGregor was shrewd at corporate infighting, too.

In the Saddle

When MacGregor joined the top management of the company in early 1966, AMAX was in a comfortable financial position. Earnings increases for 1963 through 1965 had been 34.5 percent, 21 percent, and 32 percent, respectively. The company had earned $60 million on sales of $475 million in 1965, and its stock had hit a high of 65 3/8. Although the earnings gain for 1966 was only 9 percent, the AMAX board apparently had other concerns that led them to tap MacGregor for the top rung. Yet, "There was no charge from the board at all," he said later.

"Nothing. There was no indication from the board as to what strategy they wanted me to follow. Perhaps the reason for that stems from the fact that my predecessors left a fair number of unfinished projects which they had been working on over the years and one of the board's concerns was that something happen to these things, one way or another.... All that the board sought was someone from inside the company who had been identified with and at least reasonably familiar with the business, and who had done something that was reasonably constructive and who had gone ahead and operated successfully.

"The company had a history of board domination in the previous five years.... Part of the reason for the collapse of the management was the interference from previous, retired executives, still important shareholders and active every day within the company. This tended to undermine the management, as consultations took place with their subordinates, and indication of opinions and judgments of the management were made. They were literally evaluating the management hour by hour. This brought great stress on the management. My first task was to try to find ways to run the company without as much interference as had been going on. . . .

"I think that part of the climate arose from uncertainty, lack of understanding of the objectives. So, I outlined the things I thought we should try . . . and more or less always attempted to deliver to the board what I had projected."

MacGregor tried to cope with opponents on the board by persuading the board to adopt a retirement policy that mandated retirement at age seventy. But he was unable to get the policy to apply to incumbent board members. The conflicts with the coterie of board members who gathered around retired CEO Walter Hochschild, and their intrusion into management, meant that the company, though public, was still being run as if it were private. MacGregor felt that part of his task was to help the company emerge as truly public by broadening the owner-ship of the company and, when possible, using stock for acquisitions. Meantime, he tried to mitigate board conflict in order to maintain as much support for management as possible.

Mining companies traditionally generate most of the cash they need through internally generated funds. MacGregor introduced a historic change by persuading AMAX to accept the enormous increase in the amount of debt the company had to have in order to finance projects and become a manufacturing company. The Hochschild faction, remembering the Great Depression, was worried that he was getting the company over its head in debt.

The dissident issue came to a head over the aluminum business, which MacGregor had built from nearly nothing to a half-billion dollar business in seven years. Many of the AMAX people, including Donald J. Donahue, the president, didn't like the aluminum business because it is more a manufacturing business than a mining one. MacGregor suspected that Donahue would have been happy to take over from him.

Donahue enjoyed a close connection with the Hochschilds. He was a more traditional manager than MacGregor, given to close financial control, wanting to run a tight ship and to focus on internal productivity and profitability. MacGregor was more expansive and creative, inter-ested in future growth, in combinations of properties and markets, in financings and partnerships and technology. "About a year and a half later when we had the final showdown, I suggested that he should think of doing other things," MacGregor recalled. Usually one to avoid direct confrontations, nevertheless MacGregor could take a firm stand when necessary. Pierre Gousseland succeeded Donahue as president.

The issue was not the aluminum business alone. Some AMAX execu-tives thought Ian was not going to let what he had built be destroyed by someone who would put the brakes on expansion and slim down the organization. He opted for an internationalist and expansionist who was similar in mental capacity and imagination to himself, who was at heart optimistic rather than cautious. It became clear as succession approached that Ian had been grooming Pierre for many years.

"Most of our major businesses require political skills that far exceed those that are applicable in the world outside because you are dealing with the motivation of people to take on the responsibility," said MacGregor. "I worked on the theory that it was better to evolve things than to go in for any revolutions. The temper of the whole enterprise, including not only the people in the management but people in this group of shareholders who had major influence in previous decades, was such that I had a feeling that if we were to succeed, we would have to work on an evolutionary system." Shades of Reg Jones's "working with the grain"!

Notwithstanding his professed desire to avoid confrontation with the board, in many respects Ian is combative. Some say at times he may have purposely irritated the Hochschild faction. Ian made an investment in a company and didn't tell them. That created a fracas. It also resulted in a vote of confidence. The board met on Thursday before the Fourth of July weekend in 1974. Ian had done his homework with the other directors, convincing them of the value of the investment. He also made it clear he would stick to his guns and threatened to resign. Most people don't want conflict. Not too many wanted to talk to the press about Ian MacGregor's resignation. Besides, he might have other corporate tidbits to offer the press. Ian made them stew. (He had another job waiting at Lehman Brothers.) He went off to Scotland for the Fourth of July weekend. When the board met again, he won 15 to 3.

Here's MacGregor on MacGregor's style:

"There were many areas where my actions were less than satisfactory. But by and large I sort of keep my head down and keep working away, hoping for the best. That seems to be a pretty good formula. . . . I suppose that I get in people's way now and again, get some people all stirred up. Every now and then I get some convictions which don't agree with everyone else's, usually feel fairly strongly about it. I hate to see things where a situation is sort of drifting along without somebody coming up with a plan of action. I wouldn't say that I necessarily am good at executing these . . . any set of circumstances where there seems to be a crowd of people milling around on some problem, I usually try to contribute some

course of action. My wife says I try to boss all the people around.
. . . She says it isn't always successful."

Another AMAX insider sized up MacGregor's style: "He didn't want
to run everybody's business. He's not a business runner, he is a putter
together. . . . AMAX has always been a group of things rather than one.
It isn't like everything is run out of New York. The mine . . . runs itself
as much as possible. When I went to New York . . . they didn't have
anything there except central accounting and benefits plans and stuff
like that. The various divisions are pretty autonomous. . . . We don't
write books for our people."

CEO

In 1967, MacGregor became CEO of AMAX. At that time, the company produced half the world's molybdenum supply, which accounted for half of its profits on 21 percent of its sales. It had a thirty-
year proven reserve of molybdenum. It was molybdenum that gave
strength to steel, which, in turn, made the automobile a reliable vehicle. Aluminum mining, processing, and manufacturing accounted for
38 percent of AMAX's sales; it was the seventh largest aluminum company and the most profitable. It had worked out a major deal with
Japanese and Australian interests for massive long-term production of
metallurgical coal. According to Wall Street, selling at eleven times
earnings and having raised its dividend each successive year since
1963, its financial position was strong, and its long-term outlook was
promising.[2] It had a solid base in copper, lead, zinc, molybdenum, and
potash, with developing markets in tungsten, vanadium, zirconium,
titanium, and cobalt. MacGregor had defeated his corporate enemies
in what had sometimes been bitter battles. Although he himself was
not an operator—a general manager in the Reg Jones sense—and
AMAX was never held out like GE as a managerial model, he was an
outstanding delegator, and his managers were free to operate. He had
transformed a mining company into an operating company.

In the 1967 Annual Report, MacGregor's title remained president
without formal mention in his Report to Shareholders that he was also
CEO. The cover of that report, however, sported an embossed white-

on-white, flattened-at-the-poles, oval-shaped projection of the globe, a departure from the staid white covers that were sometimes adorned with gold and silver bands. The globe signaled a new perspective at AMAX and in the mining industry. Frank Coolbaugh reportedly had kept a pair of rubber mining boots in the trunk of his car, a comforting reminder of his days as a mining engineer. The generations of mining engineers who had dominated the industry with insular perspectives had yielded to the vanguard of a peripatetic breed, passport in hand.

. . . And Coal

"I made the observation in the late 1960s," MacGregor recalled, "that . . . you might not be able to run the U.S. transportation system on unlimited cheap petroleum forever and that, like Boss Kettering of GM, we should be making plans to use less and perhaps something else . . . that brought me to look at the future of the coal business." In the fall of 1969, MacGregor acquired Ayrshire Collieries Corporation, the eleventh-ranking bituminous coal producer in the United States. By 1980, AMAX was the third largest U.S. producer of coal, producing 40.5 million net tons, behind Peabody Coal Company (59.1) and Consolidation Coal (49).[3]

The original deal seemed almost to fall through. AMAX was puzzled about how Ashland Oil could offer a higher price in the form of a deal structure involving tax treatment only recently outlawed by the courts. Ian just said, "Let us wait at the mousehole like a cat waiting for a mouse, for the mouse is bound to come out again." A few weeks later the deal collapsed. At that point Lovett Peters, the broker, called, extremely upset. His strategy had become unraveled. Peters needed a deal, then and there. AMAX offered him slightly less than its previous proposal but in a hard currency: AMAX preferred stock. The deal was closed that night.

Still, the coal business did not take off as predicted. AMAX had too many small mines. The industry had been in the doldrums for twenty years or more. There were too few experienced managers and coal engineers. It took six or seven years until AMAX could say that it knew how to run its coal mines.

Labor Relations

Climax mine, AMAX's largest molybdenum mine in Colorado, had a history of severe strikes before MacGregor was involved. It has had none since. Mining was traditionally a feast and famine business. Mac-Gregor concluded that the layoffs when times were bad and the heavy demands when times were good had resulted in insecurity that was reflected in poor labor relations. He decided that he was going to run Climax on a predictable, uniform basis. In hard times, as he was later to do in aluminum, he would stockpile. "The employees could see that the company wasn't selling its products and they still had their jobs. That was a new experience for them," he said.

Despite his penny-pinching Scottish heritage, MacGregor felt that haggling over a few cents an hour was silly because those differences averaged out in time. "But I did take the view that labor relations should fight very strongly any attempts to breach the management's right to run the place efficiently; that's where the survival of all concerned comes from."

Political Insights

The historic root of much of AMAX's fortune prior to MacGregor's succession lay in the rich copper ore bodies operated by Roan Selection Trust (RST) in Northern Rhodesia, now Zambia. It was clear to Ian and his predecessors that the political conflicts rising in Africa would shorten their days as investors there. Despite high profitability in the last colonial years of the 1950s and 1960s, AMAX sought to divest its African positions, but no one was interested in buying. When Zambia achieved independence in 1964, it promptly limited dividends to 50 percent of profits. The rest had to be retained in the country. As a result, a large amount of cash piled up in those companies' treasuries. Suddenly and unexpectedly, in 1969 the president of Zambia announced that 51 percent of the shares of the mining companies must be sold to the national government, for which it would pay fair compensation. He meant book value, which was a small fraction of the real value of those mines. Ian quickly perceived that Zambia wanted control of the mines and did not assign as high a value to external assets as AMAX did. By being cooperative and friendly, showing no criticism of Zambia's arbitrary actions, and willingly selling the mines, he asked as a quid pro quo that the $200 million of cash tied up in the copper that was already en route from the mines in Zambia to the markets, along with a London metal trading company and some newly discovered nickel ore reserves in Botswana, be distributed to the shareholders. If Zambia would relinquish those assets, he would gracefully sell the mines at a bit more than book value. Zambia wished to project a statesmanlike image. The mines were divested, and AMAX acquired the remainder of the shares of RST.

MacGregor's firsthand knowledge of the people involved and his reputation helped in all these negotiations. "He's made a life's work of knowing people," reported one observer, who also described MacGregor's extraordinary breadth of knowledge:

"He's always interested in operational details. I've been to shipyards with him, and he has demonstrated by the nature of his questions that he knows a great deal about metallurgy, steel-rolling, whatever. . . . He understands the business. He understands its operation. He has one of the broadest knowledge of the details of the mining and metallurgical business of anyone I've ever experienced. We were having dinner one night with a group of people who were railroad chief executives. A discussion developed on brakebands and the metallurgy of brakebands on steam locomotives. Ian knew a great deal more about the whole brakeband problem on steam locomotives than any of the guys on the railroad did, who were financial types or whatever. . . . You can give him a sheet of figures and he has enough operational sense of the business to determine to his own satisfaction whether the figures are correct or overstated or understated or whatever. He's a remarkable technical person, not a guy who can have the wool pulled over his eyes by some mad scientist. . . . Because of his encyclopedic knowledge of business throughout the world, he knows who needs what, who might like to sell what. He has a marvelous understanding of where raw materials are, who has need for raw materials, who might swap this for that."

Notwithstanding all of MacGregor's preparation in the Zambian copper deal, a wild card appeared. Although 85.5 percent of the shareholders participating in the voting approved the sale and reorganization whereby RST became a wholly owned subsidiary of AMAX, and though the deal was also approved by the RST shareholders other than AMAX in a separate vote, a class action suit was brought against AMAX and RST by an RST shareholder. Three years of litigation prevented AMAX from managing its interests in Botswana. Meanwhile the rapid escalation of capital costs and unforeseen problems developing a high technology smelter in a rather primitive African setting escalated the cost of the project beyond what he had estimated. Ian then revealed another master stroke. He called upon Sir Harry Oppenheimer of the Anglo-American Corporation, in South Africa, and negotiated a joint venture of the mine in Botswana, which borders South Africa. The Botswana government was given 15 percent and the remainder split evenly between AMAX and Anglo.

However, the classic MacGregor structure turned into a debacle. High inflation in the mid-1970s distorted the investment projections. As the banks limited themselves to their original loans (and the Germans had theirs denominated in appreciating Deutsche-marks), all the additional capital had to be supplied by AMAX and Anglo. But the most serious problem of all was the decline of the price of nickel. A splendid business controlled by a dominant producer, Inco, suddenly became a snarling pit of aggressively competing producers. AMAX took a write-off of $170 million in 1977, and the losses continued until 1979. By 1980, AMAX had repaid more in interest than the capital that was still owing. There was no way out except by taking a big write-off. MacGregor did not want to do that. Within three weeks of taking over from MacGregor, Pierre Gousseland took the write-off. "I think that was probably his biggest setback," concluded an associate.

What was MacGregor's behavior when he realized he had no more cards to play, or when he experienced adversity? According to one associate:

"I had a sense that he believed a man learned more from his adverse experiences—from his failures—than he did from his successes. Ian had a great ability to take a setback, and to learn from it, and after a fairly short interval to come back with a different tack, a solution. He was flexible, willing to change, willing to learn. Almost all the time this stood him in good stead. He didn't have many failures, but I think he probably had a point at which an accumulation of setbacks in the same endeavor brought him to a breaking point on a few occasions. I believe he could reach a stage when he was unwilling really to try one more time to salvage a failure. At such times his mind would turn away from the subject.

He would talk about only peripheral or minute aspects of the situation, or perhaps just as a sort of mental game, in a half-bantering, half-serious way, spin out a solution to turn the situation around. . . . in the year and a half preceding the write-off, he spent an undue amount of time in imagining all kinds of fantastic solutions to the problems that had no justification. You know, like selling to the German government the idea that nickel was so strategic that the German steel companies would buy us out. . . . Another time, trying to get the Mercedes-Benz people to buy the nickel mine in Botswana just because he happened to know Mr. Flick. . . . I knew he wasn't serious, it was sort of a mental game.

"Contrast this, for example, to his reaction in the aluminum situation. He had spent ten years creating from small elements a major, fully competitive aluminum corporation and was then told his directors didn't look kindly on expanding it. His solution was almost petulant, it had an 'I'll show them' flavor. He went out and arranged the joint venture with Mitsui. It was a splendid deal, under the circumstances an excellent solution."

To the small failures, the same associate said, MacGregor "tended to respond by sort of shrugging and forgetting about it, and leaving somebody else to clean up the situation. He simply went on to other things. Sometimes a part of this business would be salvaged into a reasonably respectable business, sometimes not."

Time Strategy

MacGregor's peripatetic travels took him to the world's major cities and the far-flung outposts of new mining ventures. Increasingly, like all of the other CEOs in this book except Sulzberger, he shuttled to Washington to influence legislation. He evolved a technique that mitigated the rigors of his breakneck travels and enabled him to function with little jet lag effect. When he got on an airplane, he put on an eyeshade on which was printed "Don't disturb for anything," and went to sleep. He reasoned that aircraft cabins are pressurized to a 7,000-foot level. That means rarefied atmosphere with less oxygen. What requires oxygen? Eating and drinking. So he didn't eat, didn't drink. He just slept. When he arrived at his destination, he ate whatever meal was due in that time zone. He entered that zone and lived on its schedule until it was time to leave. He then started that process all over again. Often he would go around the world in a few days with little disturbance.

That pattern was part of MacGregor's general mode of maximizing his use of time. He programmed his time tightly, blocked off in fifteen-minute segments. Says an associate, "If he has ten minutes, he knows how to make maximum effect of those ten minutes, by avoiding details, by entering for one or two critical moments, making his mark and then withdrawing. . . . He has an extraordinary energy level. He has the stamina of a man twenty years his junior. He gets by with very little sleep."

Despite his travels, like Reg Jones, he was always available for the business. Any of his senior people could call him day or night or week-ends. Although Ian spoke of AMAX as a decentralized company, his thirst for being involved in everything, coupled with the wish of people to talk to the boss, stimulated traveling executives to call him every night. Some would not make decisions because they knew Ian (like Jones, Wriston, and Hanley) had the fantastic ability to be up-to-date on almost everything and, like all the CEOs in this book, was both able and willing to make decisions.

Besides work, there was golf and fishing. But for Ian, golf was part of business. He played with executives who wanted to talk business. He almost always fished with other businessmen. Ian's reading was primarily business papers, journals, and publications. He was a quick scanner. He had the ability to let his eye run down a page and immediately pick up the gist of items. He was vitally interested in virtually all of the productive and power processes in all spheres of human endeavor, and in every phase of industry, commerce, and finance. He was a student of the technological as well as the business and management aspects. He was interested in social structures and customs of peoples ranging from primitive tribes up to complex modern parliamentary societies. But he had little interest in the artistic; he did not read much for pleasure.

The hours in the office and the incessant traveling left little time for the family. His wife, Sibyl, frequently traveled with him. Once in a while he took a vacation for a week or ten days, sometimes with his family (he has a son and a daughter). Now and then he took a few days off in his Scottish haven near the village of Crinan, where he loved to walk the moors and drink with the townspeople in the local pub. But there were telephone calls even there. An executive reports, "One time Isabelle Morrison [MacGregor's executive secretary] called me up . . . there was a question. And I gave her the answer. She suggested I

call him there in an inn where he was going to eat dinner. I said, 'I really
don't want to do that, now that he once is on his own, having dinner
in a Scottish inn, I don't want to bother him.' She said, 'He'd love to hear
from you.' And, well, he did. I was on the phone for quite a while with
him."

Dealing with Environmentalists

MacGregor saw environmentalism coming. He felt the company
could not win in confrontations with the movement. He thought it was
just good business sense to work to solve the problems that the environmentalists identified. For the company to stay in the mining business
in a big way, it had to have a good reputation. In developing AMAX
properties, MacGregor took environmental considerations into account
before other companies did, even when that concern was not required.
AMAX became a proud leader in assuming responsibility for the impact
of its properties on the environment.

Work on the Henderson mine—50 miles west of Denver and 10,400
feet above sea level—presented an ecological problem: What was
AMAX to do with the 1,991 pounds of waste from each tone of ore? It
wasn't until two years after the ore body was found that work could
begin. Before giving the go-ahead to mine, the engineering, environmental, and logistical problems were ironed out. AMAX organized a
joint committee with a local citizens' group, the Colorado Open Space
Coordinating Council, to study the ecological aspects of the project.[4]
Additionally, a variety of local and government organizations were
involved from the beginning. After a review of thirty-six sites within a
25-mile radius of the ore body, AMAX found a location 14 air miles away
that met engineering prerequisites and was out of the public view in
a terrain that would eliminate the pollution potential. The site would
have to be reached by tunneling 10 miles through and under the Continental Divide—at a cost of $40 million.[5] But there were snags to even
the best negotiated plans. "The decision was made to buy the transportation system for the new mine . . . from the Swedish ASEA Company,
which had built similar successful mine transportation systems with
presumed Swedish quality," an executive reported. "It didn't work.
Even they hadn't experienced the conditions of the mine. The mine is
deep underground, and hot and moist. The locomotives became per-

meated with moisture. Then they went up through a tunnel which emerged at 10,000 feet on the Continental Divide, where the temperature was twenty-five degrees below zero. The moisture froze." It took time to resolve all of the problems.

Ecological considerations played a part in another decision, that involving the Blackwell, Oklahoma, zinc smelter. The smelter used powdered coal; it was ancient and filthy and required a lot of labor in an obsolete process technique. On a clear day airline passengers, 25,000 feet up and 200 miles away, could see a cloud of smoke. It did not seem to be feasible to change to a new technology in that location, so the problem was to get out of Blackwell and to have a new plant at minimum cost. But environmentalists everywhere would fight a new smelter. About the same time that the Blackwell problem was being considered, the American Zinc Company went bankrupt. Its East St. Louis plant had used an electrolytic process, theoretically much cleaner than the process used in Blackwell. But the ore had to be roasted before it went to the electrolytic plant, and that process yielded sulfur dioxide fumes, which had to be collected and formed into sulfuric acid. That by-product could be used by many plants in the area. MacGregor took an option to buy it for $3 million. The plant had a bad labor situation with an exaggerated wage scale. MacGregor instructed his labor relations people to tell the union that AMAX would rebuild the plant if the union agreed to give up featherbedding and let management manage it. The proposition worked. AMAX put about $30 million into rebuilding and rehabilitating the plant.

A similar venture that failed nevertheless shows MacGregor's far-sighted vision. Copper Range was a medium-sized copper-producing company in Michigan which had only rarely been profitable. The mine was difficult to operate. It had relatively thin seams trending ever deeper. Ian saw something else. Environmental laws had by then become a serious problem to the mining and smelting industry. He reasoned that it would be virtually impossible to build a new copper smelter anywhere in the United States because of political and social opposition and because of the extraordinarily costly fume-control mechanism needed. When Ian looked at Copper Range he saw not a difficult mine that would always be marginal but a smelter in a remote corner of the United States operating on relatively pure ores that did not pose difficult pollution problems, located in a depressed area where employment was important. The whole Copper Range Company could be acquired for substantially less than the cost of replacing that smelter alone. He could get the ore body for free. Ian alone saw past the obvious problems of the mine to the hidden value of the smelter. However, the government brought suit and stopped the merger.

Stockpiling and Responsibility

MacGregor credits his predecessor, Arthur Bunker, with selling the government the idea of stockpiling strategic metals, a policy that was pursued during the late 1940s and 1950s. When the government decided that the stockpiles were unnecessary and were to be sold, MacGregor faced the risk that an enormous supply of molybdenum would come on the market and the price would drop precipitously. His foes on the board had their whipping boy in a whipping position. MacGregor offered to buy the whole of the government's molybdenum stockpile. Some of his directors thought he must have rocks in his head. But then, other companies, learning that AMAX was willing to buy the stockpile, concluded that they were missing something. They, too, made bids. AMAX got only a modest portion at a low price. Then the famous MacGregor foresight came into play. MacGregor reasoned that when AMAX sold the molybdenum at a profit even five, ten, or fifteen years later, the company might be investigated for making windfall profits out of an error on the part of the government. He worked out a deal with the government. AMAX would buy the stockpile material at the current market price. It would share with the government any incremental profit on an ascending scale from 50–50 to 90–10 (90 percent to the government). No one could say AMAX exploited the government's innocence in the marketplace.

. . . And Now Oil

MacGregor decided that the oil companies in the decade to follow would enjoy a fantastic cash flow and at the same time would become more aware of the fact that their cash flow would be of limited duration and related to their abilities to find oil, an increasingly difficult exercise.

The oil companies would embark on a process of liquidation unless they could switch their investments to long-term mineral resources. He anticipated that the big oil companies would try to take over mining companies. To protect AMAX early enough in the game, he would take the initiative with an oil company. AMAX would go into a reverse takeover situation, identifying an oil company that had large resources but not enough talented executives. That company would be allowed to take AMAX over and yet, in fact, be taken over. In Cities Service he saw an opportunity to acquire a company that he thought had a good asset base but was poorly managed. In addition, given his competence and the strong shareholder proxy he would have because of the concentrated ownership in AMAX, he would ultimately achieve the power in the new organization. But it didn't come off. There was a similar scenario with Union Oil Company, which at the time was about 30 percent larger than AMAX. MacGregor was prepared to sacrifice his personal pride by agreeing to be "number two" in the reverse merger. AMAX wanted a 1-to-1 share exchange, Union a 1.2-to-1. The AMAX board refused to compromise. The deal fell through. Some within AMAX saw MacGregor as a Jonah trying to swallow a whale.

Could MacGregor have done any more at the time? "I don't think so," said an insider. "I think he went really out of his way in trying. . . . The deal was very good. . . . He did his homework with the directors. . . . He was just too far ahead of the guys as far as the normal understanding of people was concerned. . . . Ian sees further away than many people do. It was his most disappointing failure but one which I think is to his great credit."

But MacGregor would not be denied his thesis. He would toy with the cash of an oil company. According to its own criteria, AMAX needed capital. Following the business cycle, every six years or so the debt/equity ratio rose above the board's preferred 30–35 percent figure. Then the company acquired some assets by merger or sold some. After both the Cities Service and Union deals failed, selling assets was next. That led to selling 20 percent of AMAX to Standard Oil of California (SOCAL). In order to keep the negotiations moving along, MacGregor felt that AMAX should continue with a registration of a projected public stock offering so that AMAX would have a backup means of financing, while simultaneously SOCAL would be confronted with a real-time deadline. As a result the $300 million transaction jelled in a few weeks, unusually rapidly for a transaction of that size. An associate who watched MacGregor, the deal-maker, close up, remembered vividly the negotiations with SOCAL:

"It is a perfect example of a deal that had died. It had been worked on by people at various levels and everybody had folded up their briefcases and gone home. And over Memorial Day weekend (Ian had been out of the country) he called me, I think, on Saturday morning, and said, 'Can you arrange for us to go out there?' And I got the Standard California people, and we flew out there on Memorial Day and put the deal together Monday night, Memorial Day, in San Francisco. . . . We got to San Francisco, I guess, about 5:00 P.M. and met for dinner . . . we'd shaken hands by 10:00, and closed the next Friday. Remarkable transaction."

Dealing with the Board

MacGregor's preparation of his board characteristically followed a pattern. He would never speak of the target company, but for three to six months before the board meeting at which he would propose the acquisition, he would make remarks and speeches about why a given industry was desirable and say that AMAX was studying several possibilities. When a specific move was proposed, the directors already had a predigested idea that the direction was desirable for the company. Then he distributed to the directors a blue booklet of forty to fifty pages presenting the general conditions in the target industry. He focused his lobbying on the receptive directors. He was always building. A key factor in MacGregor's initiatives was the support of Gabriel Hauge, then president of Manufacturers Hanover Trust Company, and Harold J. Szold, a Lehman Brothers partner. Both directors were respected by the Hochschild faction.

Ian was a champion of the soft sell. He would usually not make a proposal that, if rejected by the board, would get him into trouble. Whenever he felt that the wind was not blowing in the right direction, he had an unequaled ability to shift his behavior early enough so that the defeat of an idea would not be a personal failure for him. However, in the twilight of his tenure, MacGregor departed from the soft sell in his haste to crowd in as many deals as he could in the short time remaining. Said one colleague:

"He acted as if being conscious that the runway was getting short he wanted to put more gas on the airplane, faster, so that he could do more things—at which point, for the first time, he lost his patience in spending the necessary time to prepare the board for some of these things, and he tried to act quickly and bulldoze them in a way, into situations. . . . the less homework he has been able to do on something, because he has had no time . . . the more abrupt his final position would be, by telling people, 'Look, you have to trust me because that's what you are supposed to do.' He felt that this was natural. It's only human for a man who has built a company as he did for such a long time, no matter how much personal confidence he may have in the next team, to feel that the more you can do before you leave, the easier the task will be for the newcomers."

Guiding the Ship

How did MacGregor see his method for embedding his operating conceptions in the organization? "Well, I suppose working with people and imbuing them with the same kind of thinking; trying to outline why and how you arrive at conclusions. . . . A scenario is sketched out and you try to get enough people to believe in it and after a while, if you are reasonably logical and consistent, people will start believing. I think I erred on the side of never giving the impression that I didn't clearly understand where I thought we should go. But still, I was willing to say, if you don't agree, you let me know what you think is wrong with my view."

"Ian could let people take liberties with his status if he trusted and liked them," said an AMAX executive:

"You could tell him he was wrong or that he had to do something differently; he might shake his head and grumble a little, but he knew you were thinking of his needs. There was no trouble getting along if one was in that inner group, but woe to the person who presumed on him and didn't have that inner connection. . . . He could turn frosty and let it be known he was displeased. Generally, there would be subtle messages; such persons might be disinvited to key events. He was not vindictive, he didn't overreact, but he would signal with varying degrees of gentleness that he had been presumed on. Then he would usually forget it. However, Ian did sometimes carry a grudge. If someone really crossed him, if he thought he had been treated one way and then behind his back another way, [if he thought someone] had bad-mouthed him, he could be fairly hard about it. His grudge then wouldn't die for a long time. But for a minor business or social gaffe, he'd simply deliver the message and then forget about it. . . . I can remember the look as a sort of stern stone-faced look. He shifted from a chatty, loquacious manner to a silent manner and a few cryptic words such as, 'Well, we'll see,' or 'We'll deal with that later,' or some statement fraught with meaning but which could be interpreted almost any way. He could always engineer the moment so that his feelings could be interpreted in several ways. He was very good at both oral and written statements that could be interpreted in more than one way and didn't pin him down. He could speak platitudes that were appropriate to the occasion. He liked to retain flexibility and even on the rare occasions when he allowed himself to show petulance or annoyance, he never lost control."

Ian was always an extremely thoughtful person about the niceties. Colleagues report that they never saw him shout at anyone, or show strong anger overtly. He could evidence a certain frosty politeness in the British way when he had to. The lower in the organization a person was, the more cordial and civil Ian was to him or her. He made great efforts to be friendly, accessible, and easygoing with the juniors and secretaries.

Sometimes he was too subtle. One AMAX comment was, "Ian will fire you and you won't realize that you're fired." He was like Reg Jones in that respect. There is a story that he fired someone who didn't know he was fired and was still on the payroll ten years later. Sometimes rather than forbidding some action, he would raise questions: "Have you considered this and have you considered that?" These left subordinates to infer that he would rather not have them act or that he disagreed with them.

If Ian had only a vague notion about a particular course of action, he would characteristically set a lot of ideas in motion on slightly divergent tracks. By launching several efforts in several directions simultaneously, he retained flexibility with a high probability of getting a winner. Events would overtake the various ideas. When the best one emerged, he would be perceived as brilliant for having chosen that course of action. If, for example, he was thinking of entering the coal mining business, he might launch various people in different inquiries: an exploration program, an acquisition program, a discussion with another company about a venture. These inquiries were not mutually exclusive, so he greatly increased the odds that one of these tactics would lead to a way into the coal business. His associates saw his method as brilliant strategy. To them it meant that he had the good sense to know that the best laid plans go awry and that he greatly increased his chances by launching competent people in promising directions simultaneously. They also saw him as explicit in his long-term objectives but extremely flexible in how he got there.

Ian operated on the concept that he was responsible. If something worked, he was entitled to the credit, and if it didn't, he was also responsible for the blame. He never did anything unless he believed it should be done, as distinguished from receiving a recommendation from someone and executing the recommendation because he thought the person had superior knowledge and understanding. Nor, in most cases, would he execute anything unless he had done sufficient homework to feel reasonably comfortable that he was making the right decision. He had to know all the answers.

Dealing with People

Ian had two major modes of control. First, like Reg Jones, he understood the use of purse strings, particularly the allocation of capital. He made sure that was in his hands. He was not much interested in the more formal systems of control—audit, management by objectives, self-rating of employees, or other more bureaucratic procedures. He would go along if someone in the organization promoted a new system for ranking personnel or salary administration or a new form of financial budgeting and planning. He wasn't a great believer in comparing month-to-month performance against budget. He understood the vagaries and vicissitudes of the market place, and he knew that no amount of formal planning was going to lead to predictable results. He didn't want to be fettered. He wanted to be free to wheel and deal, particularly on external matters, such as mergers, divestitures, ventures, and financings, and on important internal transaction decisions, such as labor settlements, major price changes, and matters having the nature of single events with a beginning and an end, as distinct from ongoing day-to-day management issues.

The second control mechanism was Ian's informal network of contacts and relationships that kept him informed about what was going on. As with Jones, his network was comprised largely of people who had worked with him at one time or another. He could call any of them for a "What's new?" conversation. Like Wriston, he visited the properties of the company throughout the world as often as he could. If he were in an area, he would try to contact all the company units and trusted long-time employees in the area and especially on the telephone. Addressing the person by his first name in a soft-spoken, easygoing way, he'd say, "This is Ian MacGregor." "How're you feeling? What's going on?" Working such long hours, he had an enormous amount of time to do so. That, together with his ability to reach through to lower levels of the management, to talk to those people directly, gave him detailed information about people and what was going on in the organization.

His capacity to relate to people informally was based on what a close associate described as "... a great sensitivity.... He'd sort of figure out what was on your mind without you even saying it. . . . When I was disturbed or something was bothering me, he was able to sense it. I think he was . . . receptive to the wavelengths or the body movements . . . that people may emit. . . . He would give you the opportunity to unload or bare your problems if you were prepared to do so. He would give you the opening . . . 'Is everything okay? Do you have everything right? Are you satisfied?' . . . On the other hand, if he did not want to give you the opportunity to open up . . . he just wouldn't say anything."

MacGregor's way of going through to the middle managers undoubtedly helped him to get the results he wanted, without his being particularly visible. If a middle manager knew exactly what Ian MacGregor wanted, undoubtedly Ian would have considerable power to pursue that objective. Sometimes he got to the subordinate as a way of lighting a fire under the subordinate's boss. That method worked for Ian because he had enough information coming in to enable him to read the variances and determine pretty well the accuracy of what he was hearing. That method would not work for someone who was not willing to devote the time to the job or who did not have the range of contacts.

Ian let it be known when he wanted to be engaged in a specific issue. For example, in labor relations he was by and large content to let the division managers settle contracts. But when a strike possibility arose in one of the major divisions, no settlement was made unless Ian was consulted. Similarly, he allowed the product pricing strategy of most of the businesses to be set by the general manager, except in molybdenum, which was absolutely critical to the company's destiny. He was

deeply involved in any decision about changing the price of molybdenum.

Reflecting on his manner of working with his subordinates, and how
he understood them and the key executives with whom he had to
negotiate, MacGregor recalled:

"Our organization, during the twelve years I was around, was reasonably free from tension. People were reasonably at ease. I believe
the bulk of the people were reasonably satisfied, and they were
encouraged to do their own thing and come up with their own
solutions to problems. . . . I imagined myself as a very low-key
operator with people. I always made myself available. Anyone who
had a problem, I told them not to hesitate to come and sit down
with me and see if we could figure out what the answer was. I think
it is important to encourage people on the one hand to go out and
do their own thing, but on the other hand to say that I'm always
your backstop. . . . It may not be popular to do that. It tends perhaps
to encourage the nursemaid theory. People vary. Some people
need counseling all the time, others are happy to charge ahead
whether they are right or wrong, so I don't think there is any simple
principle. I always encouraged my associates with problems by
saying, 'Look, if you've made a mistake, we've made a mistake; let's
sit down and talk about it and see what we can do to resolve it.' One
of the tricks in this as I perceived it was that you must never force
people to do something they don't agree to. . . . Very seldom did
I issue orders. I remember reading one of Mr. Alfred Sloan's dicta
. . . during the famous antitrust case in which DuPont was asked to
divest itself of its holding in GM. Someone in court said, 'But Mr.
Sloan, you were chairman of GM. You could have ordered anything
you wanted done in this business and presumably, as chairman, you
did just that.' Mr. Sloan thought for a while and said, 'You know,
I've never ordered anyone to do anything in all my life.'

"From that I learned an important principle in management. We
don't have much opportunity for absolute authoritarian management. Therefore, you have to work on the basic principle of the
consent of the governed. And that goes with a reasonable success
in the things you try to advocate and reasonable knowledge of what
you're doing. . . . In many situations there are people who are not
necessarily in agreement with what the course of action should be
and I frequently worked to try to convince them . . . but I was
always willing to accept that maybe we shouldn't do something

because there weren't enough people in agreement with me. You have to learn over a period of time to analyze very carefully the motivations of people who come to you with various things . . . [when] people come tearing in with wonderful gifts for you, you wonder what's going on. . . . Some people have a high degree of honesty and principle, others scheme and so on. . . . I worked on the theory that no matter how hard you try, you end up with a cross-section of humanity with all sorts of individual idiosyncracies and the thing to do is to see what you can do with the ones you've got. You also have to be reasonably aware of people's motivations in the things they do and the things they tell you because sitting at the top of a pile of people, to a large extent, you are very dependent on what they tell you to understand what's going on. So, you have to be able to interpret what you are being told. One has to be a bit of a cynic.

"In any kind of a negotiation an assessment of the other side's motivation and viewpoint of the factors . . . is extremely important. And I think I always used to feel that a very, very important dimension in negotiations was to really have done a lot of reconnaissance of the other side . . . I always used to insist that before you go into a negotiation you must understand fully what are the motivations in the other side of the table. What are the things that limit them? If we do this, are we going to in any way challenge their judgment, embarrass them among their peers, or force them into a situation which, in the public view of what they have done, is completely untenable? In other words, the other man invariably has some kind of face to save."

AMAX is significantly a business of partnership. To make partnerships work requires careful maintenance effort. That takes time and sensitivity. The alternative is conflict. When Australian partners suggested an action that would have been destructive, MacGregor understood that their motivation was related to growing xenophobic developments in Australia. They seemed to find it difficult to have an American partner who was in a dominant position. They wanted to appear to the Australian public as dominant. MacGregor suggested a series of meetings with them to redress their grievances. The solution was to create a joint Australian company in which they would assume some of the marketing chores. MacGregor followed these principles in acquisitions and mergers as well. In such circumstances he considered himself as much a seller as a buyer. He made certain that the principals of the other company

were escorted around AMAX's properties and met many of its manag-
ers. He tried to co-opt their feelings into a sense of identity with AMAX.
A colleague reported, "He would always say, 'You're not selling out.
You're buying in.' In almost everything he did, there were rarely losers.
In a MacGregor deal everybody won something."

The force of MacGregor's personality must be evaluated in terms of
his effectiveness. To meet Ian for the first time is to experience him as
a mild, soft-spoken person. Nevertheless, he invariably ends up dominating a meeting, his associates report. He doesn't do so by raising his
voice. He occasionally does it by not pausing (if someone is trying to
interrupt) to allow that interruption. They say he dominates in a meeting by the facts he marshals and the information he brings to bear on
the subject. He uses all the illustrations he needs to make his particular
point. There's dialogue, give and take, but he makes sure that he has
time to communicate his point, and if he feels it's necessary, he doesn't
hesitate to make it two or three times, using his dry sense of humor.

Despite Ian's mild manner, some of his colleagues think he thrives on
conflict, partly because most people don't have his intestinal stamina or
his tolerance for conflict and risk. They suspect that he may even generate conflict in order to achieve an objective. They think also that since
he is intellectually superior to most people, works harder than most,
and has a supreme command of the facts applicable to any situation, the
aura he creates becomes intimidating. Sometimes in a meeting a manager would make a presentation, perhaps about the demand and supply
outlook over the next five years, and the someone might ask the presenter about a specific figure. Before the manager could answer the
questions, Ian would do so. One executive offered his own explanation:
"I think that could be chalked up as inability to restrain himself from
seizing the limelight all the time . . . he must feel it's necessary, and I
think he does, to constantly prove that he's good. . . . [He] gives the
impression of the only child syndrome or the syndrome of having a
bigger brother, which he has, and always being in the shadow of the
bigger brother at home . . . and therefore he has to exhibit his knowledge." Another AMAX associate offered this observation:

> "Even though some people probably feared him because they said
> there's no room for disagreement, I never encountered that. I
> recall specifically that one time I went on a much discussed case.
> A pretty big one. People said, 'Here's what MacGregor thinks.' And
> I said, 'That can't be done.' A couple of people responded, 'You
> know, he won't buy that.' I said, 'I'll tell him.' I *made* myself go over

there early one morning. He got in earlier than anyone, I think 7:30, 7:45. He almost always had time for you, a real empathic trait of his. After we'd talked [about] rather routine subjects, I brought up the matter at hand and told him that, in my opinion, it was not workable even though I understood he wanted it done.

"His answer was something like this: 'I don't give edicts. You're the expert in this field. If you tell me it can't be done, it can't be done.' That's how MacGregor was, usually. . . . Incidentally, there is no question MacGregor is one of the most ambitious men I have ever met. . . . He tries hard to get the most of what he wants. In spite of all his success, he's still as ambitious as he ever was, now, in his current endeavors. I'm sure he's also financially oriented. . . . I'm not implying that Ian would sell his soul to some clowny outfit for double the money. That doesn't apply. But as far as this company is concerned, Ian MacGregor deserved every penny he got from it. . . . And then some, quite likely."

. . . And the Public

MacGregor made it his business to meet the right people. He likes to mingle with the rich and famous. He derives a special pleasure out of the feeling of being an insider. He likes rubbing elbows with the political leaders of all countries, and he feels quite at home with them. He is friendly with former Chancellor Helmut Schmidt of Germany. In his role as head of British Steel and now of the British National Coal Board, he sees a lot of Margaret Thatcher. In his younger days he knew Gerald Ford when Ford was a congressman from Michigan. After Ford left the presidency, Ian recruited him as an AMAX director. Although he didn't flaunt them, he got a particular delight out of letting it be known that he had these contacts. He would let the word slip out in a subtle way or, better yet, just let it be noticed that he was hobnobbing with them. He often didn't even mention to his colleagues that he was going to see the president of the United States or a major captain of industry. It would come out later through a press report or through a casual statement.

"When you were with MacGregor," an associate reported with admiration, "he knew all the players. Chances were," he said, "you would be introduced to them and you broadened your own horizons. . . . He would introduce subordinates to them as 'my colleagues,' or he would say, 'Hello, Charlie, you know [name], of course.' The subordinate often wouldn't know who Charlie was. Charlie might well be the chairman of a major corporation."

MacGregor often hit the newspapers. He had directorships in a number of major corporations. They built up the MacGregor image and, at the same time, gave AMAX a whole different image. The chairman had become a world figure. "If it were known that he was coming to a meeting it would be easier to get the right people together. If proceedings started before he arrived, there would be a sense of anticipation preceding him," a colleague said:

"Many businessmen were flattered to be associating with Ian, it was a high point of the event. Ian understood the use of his power.

"On a couple of occasions the final stroke in closing a major deal occurred when Ian and the leader of the other company would wander out of the room, arm-in-arm, and settle among them the last few millions that were needed to reach a handshake. There was one famous transaction that actually closed in the men's room outside the meeting room. He loved to tell that story. They split the difference of the last $10 million there. He got a kick out of little, offbeat, human solutions to a particularly intractable problem."

Another story is told in AMAX about a negotiation with Dr. Armand Hammer of Occidental Petroleum, himself a highly regarded trader, in a hotel in California. A few minutes before Dr. Hammer's arrival, MacGregor went out for a walk. Dr. Hammer arrived, but MacGregor didn't return. The junior members of the negotiating team had talked around the subject. Dr. Hammer fidgeted and was getting increasingly annoyed. Sandwiches were ordered. About an hour later, Ian wandered in with a package of shirts under his arm, smiling as if nothing had happened. Dr. Hammer, who perhaps was losing face among his subordinates, at that point brightened up visibly and his anger disappeared. Ian had one-upped the situation. The deal then proceeded quickly to a conclusion.

As viewed by some around him, MacGregor rarely did anything without premeditation. Judging from some of his failures with the board, that was an idealized aura. But it was exactly that idealized aura that became powerful charisma. He used to chuckle at himself as being a bit of a salesman and at being able to charm people into doing his will. Both skills are frequently found in second children who early on must learn to maneuver around the older first child to win the attention of the parents.

Communication

Although Ian is not an outstanding speechmaker (as is Jack Hanley, who we discuss in the next chapter), he is something of a ham actor and has great rapport with his audiences. Those who have observed him say that he knows how to raise his eyes at the right time, use his hands, and move his body. His wide vocabulary and forceful imagery have to be heard to be appreciated. He is reputed to have rewritten prepared speeches in the middle of the night, a perfectionistic propensity he shares with Walter Wriston. But he can also ad lib answers to tricky questions with good humor.

An executive offered this anecdote: AMAX had investments in South Africa and Namibia. At a shareholders' meeting, an Episcopal clergyman rose to criticize MacGregor's alleged failure to respond to his previous objections to those investments. He complained also that MacGregor had never given his bishop an appointment to discuss the matter. With a gesture that implied "What more can I do? Have pity on me, I'm trying to do the right thing," MacGregor said he had tried to reach the bishop. He added that he would be happy to meet the clergymen in their estate (in a nearby wealthy residential area) and have the hamburger with them he usually had for lunch. The house broke down. The clergyman conceded, "You won that one, Mr. MacGregor." A close associate notes, "He's very direct and straightforward. He doesn't hesitate to tell you what he thinks. The fact that he's done so for forty-five or fifty years means he has a reputation for credibility. He personally inspires a great deal of confidence."

MacGregor wasn't always soft-spoken. A group composed of representatives from different governmental departments were asking him questions. Some were obviously not up to the level MacGregor was accustomed to. When one brought up an issue that he didn't like, MacGregor snapped, "My company will not spend another red cent on this, until I have specifics [he spelled out the details] in black and white from the Secretary, and I mean that literally and you can tell him I said so. I hope you tell him today." Suddenly the group sat up straight. They knew he was right. There wasn't any room for anyone to say anything, because if he did, he might be in deep trouble.

His wish to avoid confrontation sometimes gave way to battle, as when he was challenged by Dick Lamm, then the governor of Colorado. The governor's problem was raising revenue. He hit upon a normal solution: raise taxes on the largest industries. He came up with a tax on mining. That would have meant a serious cost problem for AMAX. In the hands of less well-intentioned politicians it could be disastrous. MacGregor decided to fight. AMAX organized a dinner in Denver for the purpose of thanking the people of Colorado for their contribution to the construction of its new mine. Twelve hundred people and the governor were invited, so the dinner got wide public attention. At the dinner, MacGregor pointed out that the new mine was a product of the work of all of the union people who were involved in the construction, all of the small contractors and other suppliers, all of the state regulatory people, and even the people from the educational system who were supplying the company with trained employees. He said that AMAX was betting half a billion dollars on the good sense of the people of Colorado, on the future of the mineral industry, and on his confidence that Colorado, was going to remain a competitor among mineral-producing states. His statement hit all the Sunday papers. The tax was voted down. In the process, the governor lost some of his legislative supporters and the legislature shifted from Democratic to Republican. The governor made peace, and he and MacGregor have been good friends since.

Developing Assistants

AMAX had no problem getting the best technical people in the industry. One reason, said Ian, was that AMAX had never been in a financial position in which it couldn't give its people the best, most modern, most expensive equipment. They took it for granted that the function of the head office was to provide them with everything they wanted. In a sense, that assumption was dangerous, but it was also uniquely attractive. It made working in an AMAX mine a privilege as compared to many other mines.

Ian liked to surround himself with three or four active, bright, people, usually younger men with a strong grounding in a field such as science, finance, or law. They would become a sort of inner circle, something like Reg Jones's kitchen cabinet, people with whom he felt relaxed and comfortable. He could communicate with them in a form of verbal shorthand, encapsulating a complicated situation and his viewpoint on it in a few words. This small coterie would immediately sense what he was thinking and share his excitement. He let his hair down with them, but there was never any doubt about who was the boss. They weren't formally a group because their relationships, which tended to be long-lived, were one-on-one with Ian. If one of them moved on, Ian continued to take an interest in his career. He would light up when he ran across a former junior comrade who had gone on to other things.

Ian's joking with his comrades was lighthearted bantering about the business issue of the day. This bantering was never cruel or malicious. The participants derived a warm, close feeling, a sense of being an insider with a powerful sponsor or mentor. "Ian's magnetism was like a light source," said one insider. "It fell off as the square of the distance." He rarely sponsored a second-rate executive or pushed one into water over his head. Once or twice one of his bright young men got into a situation that was beyond his abilities, and Ian perhaps should have provided more support than he did. In that situation, the young executive was seen as Ian's protégé, and other officers were reluctant to interfere. Ian never promoted a second-rate mind or person of inferior competence. There were no flunkies. An intimate commented on MacGregor's informal management development activities: "Sometimes MacGregor dropped by the division's New York office. He knew some of the people there, including some of the 'youngsters.' He would ask them, 'What do you think about copper?' He might have been talking to a thirty-year-old man who's been three or four years in the business. Sure as hell, MacGregor can do better than that. But how do you think that young fellow felt as a result of a talk with the chairman?" And, conversely, MacGregor, like Wriston, picked up grains of knowledge from most of those conversations. Besides, the attention from the boss enhanced the self-image of the junior. That attention would become even more stimulating when, for example, the junior was invited to MacGregor's house for dinner. There he would find himself with ten or twelve other people, all of them extremely successful, whose knowledgeable conversation revolved around politics, international business, and finance.

Despite his tremendous schedule, Ian would say, off and on, to those

young executives, "Why don't you drop by?" Most were cautious, concerned about conserving Ian's time. If they did not follow through,
often he would say, "Why haven't you dropped by? Do you have some
time? Come over. We'll talk." Sometimes he would stop them as they
passed his office and insist that they talk with him about things that
ranged far beyond the business and about which the younger person
had neither experience nor insight. The younger person might then
make a determined effort to learn what he had not known. The result
was that he made the junior feel a part of AMAX as a whole.

Ian drafted bright young people into his own service as soon as he
discovered them. (In the subsequent chapters, we will see John Hanley
and Thomas J. Watson, Jr., do the same thing.) Another associate told
this story: Ian said that he was going to Brazil for two or three weeks.
His colleague told him that he had a young man in his group who was
born in Brazil, spoke Portuguese, was well educated, well mannered,
physically attractive, and widely acquainted at senior government and
business levels. MacGregor promptly agreed to take the aide. "So I
called in this young man," the colleague continued, and said:

"In three weeks you're going to go to Brazil as an aide to Ian
MacGregor. I want you to know that either way, I'm going to get
screwed. If you do well, he'll come back to me and say, 'Well, that's
a nice young fellow, he did all right, now what are we going to do
with him from there?' If you do badly, he will say, 'What did you
do that for?' . . . Within the next three weeks you will know everything about the population of every village, the oil production in
every town; you will know how much is earned per capita in Brazil.
What you know is insufficient, even though it may be a lot. You will
know everything out of the almanacs that you can find.' . . . Later,
MacGregor took me into a corner. I knew what was coming. 'Very
nice young man you sent over with me. Very smart. He was very
helpful.' (That's a word he uses often: 'helpful.') 'Now, what are we
going to do with this young man? I think he should come work with
me for a while, sort of like an intern, seeing how the surgeons
perform their operations.' I said, 'That's fine . . . how about January
first?' (It was now October.) He said, 'Oh, I don't know, let's say six
months, starting Monday.' I said, 'Ian, this guy's performing a function.' He said, 'I think Monday's a good day.' So I called this kid's
boss in New York. I had to hold the phone far away because he was
furious. He went. Did very well. Came back to my group after it
was decided to offer him a bigger position in the group."

Looking Back

AMAX grew faster than any other mining company due, undoubtedly, to the relentless energies, the intelligence, and the qualities that Ian put in it. In a world in which mining companies have periodic doubts about their independence and future, with recurrent problems of finding money for larger and larger investments, AMAX appeared to be one of the few companies that had nerves and strength.

Although MacGregor said he got used to living with the tension of his position, like living with a toothache, that tension was unrelenting. "I never got into the position when I felt totally comfortable, [I] always felt that there was a certain amount of static in some part of the business for one reason or another . . . I was always upset anytime that I was looking at our figures in the down market and margins were being dwindled and I wasn't able to push the cost down to maintain margins. I always felt inadequate, concerned and worried about that. You must have good health to be able to concentrate on the business day in and day out."

It was the scale of those multimillion dollar burdens that would have given MacGregor's parents the greatest pride in his accomplishments:

"I doubt if they would understand the consequences of actions, but they would be concerned about the scale, and the responsibilities involved. . . . The iron ore business that we went into in Australia, we were looking at a veritable investment of about $350 million. When we started the Henderson Mine, the minimum investment was something of the same order. Every time we built an aluminum smelter it was a $150 million to $200 million bet. And when I acquired half of the Twin Buttes mining operation, it was a $200 million plus bet. You know they're not exactly fail-safe operations. Somebody has to believe and to bet on some assumptions about projected course of events."

How did MacGregor assess the fruits of his labor and the opinion of his peers of his accomplishments? "I think that as I understand from the few that do communicate with me about me, they generally take the view that it was a fairly substantial job of building, of taking a company and converting it from just a small, relatively small operation with limited activity into a fairly broad-gauge company that seemed to work

. . . and as it grew it seemed to establish a reputation which was constantly growing and not in a disadvantageous way. I think that when I started with the company it was just a minor league player, and today it's perhaps the world's major mining company."

Notwithstanding all of that growth, there were necessarily disappointments. When asked to describe significant disappointments in his years at AMAX, MacGregor expressed frustration at being unable to pursue even bigger fish.

"My inability to do things that I thought were opportunities, in which I just felt the organization wasn't capable of taking on. I just didn't feel that I had the ability to generate a new organization. You know, I banked on that I would always be in the mining business. I am reasonably familiar with other industries, but never able to have the conviction that I could weld this into the AMAX context. The reason for this is that I just felt that unless we had a group of people who could be reasonably conversant with these alternative industries that it would have been foolish to start. . . . I was tempted from time to time to take a whack at some of these things that seemed obvious opportunities, but never did screw up enough courage to do it. I doubt whether I would have been able to convince the board on any of these things. I was always running with the brakes on and the anchors down. The board had sort of developed the syndrome, I think, that the bigger problem was to make sure that they kept MacGregor from getting involved in too many new angles and running the financial capability of the company up against the stops.

"I always felt inhibited from moving into areas with which the bulk of the organization wasn't familiar. . . . I took the easy course, which was to diversify within the framework of things which seemed to be reasonably compatible with the experience of the organization as a whole. . . . The great problem in all of these situations has been how to manage them at the top. Are there people sufficiently familiar with the diversity of these companies to be able to keep track of them? At least I had the advantage in AMAX of being reasonably familiar with all the things we were engaged in and I think built up a crew of people who had similar familiarities."

What managerial monument would MacGregor like to leave behind?

"Well, I would hope that the business had a reasonable chance to go ahead and continue to succeed. Many of the things that I decided will not show up for good or for bad for years after I left the business. Some of the results of decisions I made are still surfacing. Some of them are good; some of them are bad. . . . I think that I am kind of a cynic about the individual in an organization. He leaves no real enduring mark. Perhaps creation of some of the properties, new mines, acquisitions, job appointments. . . . I would say that there's nothing deader than yesterday's chief executive . . . within an organization there is nothing with less influence over the average person than the holder of yesterday's authority and as long as you realize that, you will not cry tears for the past. This is one of the things you have to get used to and be able to understand that it happens. Once you hand in the gold ring, your authority in that organization is zero."

What would he do differently if he had it to do over again?

"Oh, I would perhaps waste less time trying to convince people. I might have been more courageous and taken issue earlier on some of the things, even at the expense of changing my career I suppose. You know, one gets lazy. We tend to do the things that we are accustomed to and even, in situations that are very trying, there is a strong effort to retain the status quo ante rather than take off into some wild, new unknown. I suppose that maybe perhaps one of the defects of my quasi-engineering training [is] I tend to like to look along straight lines and see what are the consequences of things, rather than taking emotional decisions. Maybe if I were a little more emotional about things, I wouldn't have had to suffer at all of these areas of uncertainty and delay in getting things done."

Moving On

Some were puzzled that in 1980 MacGregor took the chairmanship of British Steel, which looked like a no-win situation. In what ought to be his emeritus years, he assumed one of the world's most difficult industrial situations, in which he had to fire tens of thousands of individuals and become subject to enormous political abuse. He had to do at British Steel the things he had always shuddered to do at AMAX. AMAX never had an arbitrary reduction in force in the years he was in charge. His method was to go forward, not backward. Both British Steel and the National Coal Board are running nationalized industries. For all of his prior professional life, he had aggressively championed private enterprise. The position of British Steel depends heavily on the success of the European steel cartel, which is the antithesis of fighting in free markets. Ian may have wanted to go back to the old country—the country boy who made good, particularly the Scotsman who made good in London. Whatever his reasons, as a star in an almost impossible situation, he was a "natural" for that role if there ever was one. He was the rescuer, the rebuilder, and at the top of business, social, and political pyramids. His shrewd, tough, yet sensitive, intelligence found its most difficult challenge—until he moved on to the British Coal Board in 1983.

According to Ian, "Some people at my age go fishing, others take up golf . . . I still feel active and business people like myself often like doing what they do. I have no strong urge to give up work, and there are few opportunities for overage mining engineers. I am concerned about Britain's place as an industrial nation because an improvement in its efficiency is essential for its survival. I thought that a start could be made in the country's steel industry. Here is a society that has access to the technology of the day, in fact, has created much of it. It seems reasonable to assume that we could again harness that knowledge. There is nothing impossible about the task. The only imponderable is how soon."

MacGregor was a master builder. Some build massive cathedrals, some great skyscrapers. He built combinations of resources into major commercial institutions that are simultaneously good for society. They take into account society's needs and wishes and social costs. To an industry that had a history of exploitation of both people and natural

resources, he brought a value system that undergirded business states-
manship. Even in his difficult subsequent British assignments, his task
was one of regeneration. He presents reality, then brings people around
to seeing the possibilities. Once they grasp his vision, they are willing
to work out the sometimes painful steps of getting there. He is strong
yet gentle, a fighter yet a gentleman. He exemplifies the quiet yet
imaginative use of leadership power.

Coda

After his retirement as CEO, MacGregor remained on the AMAX
board for five years until 1982. As he had planned, SOCAL offered to
buy the remaining 80 percent of AMAX stock it did not already own for
$78.50 per share. But Pierre Gousseland wanted to be his own man, to
head his own independent company. MacGregor's protégé did not follow his mentor's script. MacGregor complained that Gousseland had
gotten bad advice and exercised poor judgment.[6] Critics said that the
error was MacGregor's, that in choosing Gousseland he had picked a
low-profile successor who did not challenge him, but who, once on his
own, would not be able to follow the same strategy. But then, who could
follow such an act? "It's almost enough to make me cry," said MacGreg-
or of the SOCAL fiasco. Earnings and assets continued to increase year
after year. Then, in mid-1981, the bottom fell out of the mining market
along with that of other businesses. AMAX had a 57 percent plunge in
net profits to $230.8 million. Gousseland, following the usual practice,
sought partners for the coal reserves. Interest rates skyrocketed, pre-
cluding borrowing. The historic cash cow, molybdenum, was also down.
The worst recession since World War II sapped AMAX's financial
strength. At the end of 1982, AMAX faced a loss of approximately $250
million. It had a massive debt of $1.7 billion, which in 1982 cost about
$300 million in interest. Twenty-five percent of its 21,000 employees
were laid off permanently. A number of mines were closed. The stock
plummeted to $21 and dividends from $2.40 per share to 20 cents.
Capital spending dropped from $1.3 billion in 1980 to $300 million.
AMAX swapped more than 1.9 million common shares for $16.6 million
face amount of its debt. Only as the recession bottomed out did AMAX,
too, begin its slow climb back to profitability. Critics faulted MacGregor
for diversifying too widely and argued that most of AMAX's mineral

resources faced a bleak future. Gousseland did not agree.

MacGregor meanwhile ran into hard resistance to further drastic cuts in British Steel's overmanned, obsolete mills. He had reduced the employees from 166,000 to 85,000. Already labeled "Mac the Knife" because of those cost-cutting efforts, he faced greater hostility from coal union leadership. Arthur Scargall, president of the National Union of Mineworkers, called his appointment "an unmitigated disaster" and MacGregor a "hatchet man" and "the American butcher of British industry."[7] MacGregor said he wasn't a "butcher" but rather a plastic surgeon trying to redeem the features of aged properties that needed some kind of face lift.

In March, 1984, the miners struck against MacGregor's intention to cut coal production by 4 percent, reduce manpower by 20,000, and limit 1984 raises to 5.2 percent. MacGregor projected that by investing $1 billion a year in modernization, the mines might break even in 1988, saving Great Britain $600 million in annual subsidies; in fact, they might even pay a dividend.

John W. Hanley

MONSANTO COMPANY

ACCORDING TO the security analysts, in 1972 Monsanto's stock, sell-ing in the range of 34 to 56 1/4 at a 14.7 earnings ratio to its average $50 price, was paying a $1.80 dividend.[1] With sales of approximately $2 billion, 23.5 percent came from plastics, resins, and coatings; 23 percent from synthetic fibers. The analysts expected that Monsanto's industrial chemical output would grow at a compounded 8 percent growth rate; it had grown 6 percent in 1971 and would, they said, grow 11 to 12 percent in 1972. The company had had a poor year in 1970, but it had begun to recover in 1971 because of improvements in the synthetic fibers and plastics markets. It would probably return $3.40 a share, the analysts predicted, approaching the all-time high for Monsanto. They expressed confidence in the underlying trends that suggested that com-pany's specialty—crop protection chemicals—would gain an increasing share of the market, as would Monsanto's many specialty products. It had developed methods to increase the fire-retarding qualities of cel-lulose carpeting and strengthened that product's competitive position. Its widely diversified products were to be found everywhere in the economy. While its earnings were still price-controlled, the stock was recommended to those seeking a high quality turn-around situation, partly because of Monsanto's heavy capital expenditure in recent years.

As had been the case at GE, the true picture wasn't all that rosy. As a matter of fact, Monsanto was becoming a moribund, self-satisfied chemical company. John W. Hanley was the hired gun, the shaker and doer who was to turn it around. Unlike Reg Jones, Walter Wriston, and Ian MacGregor, who had grown up in their companies, he was an outsider who didn't even know the technology of the business he was to rebuild. He had no established organizational constituency. He was at heart a self-described peddler, who had to establish his authority as a leader of an organization that hardly wanted to follow—until he could demonstrate strength and competence. This he set about doing with a vigor that shook and startled Monsanto—and the rest of the industry.

Hanley saw that fundamental changes had to be made and that to make them he had to take charge. He had to take multimillion dollar risks without adequate information and establish aggressive organizational leadership where passivity had been the rule. Some of his decisions resulted in failure, and some of his take-charge behavior left a wake that disturbed those unaccustomed to directness. He was direct and heavy-handed until he reinvigorated the sluggish ship that was Monsanto, setting it on a competitive course with major investment in research and development and a plan for succession. His task was to make an offensive team of a defensive one and to create the model of an attacking leader. He freed up people's energy and broke down their complacency. He attacked and changed their organization—and after years of invigoration, he gave it back to them.

Hanley was the kind of leader who leaned heavily on himself, and on some of his ideas. He brought to Monsanto new analytic techniques, a preoccupation with development of subordinates, and a conviction that research was the way to go. Sometimes abrupt and often controlling and insensitive to his impact on others, he nevertheless established himself in an authoritative role. He convinced his subordinates that he knew how to revive Monsanto, reinforcing that conviction by the allocation of heavy commitments to research, even when his business was in down periods. His single-handed turn-around of Monsanto raised questions about how well those who succeeded him could carry on in his image and in his shadow.

"I've been damn lucky, I tell my friends, and I really mean it. As a matter of fact, a candid associate said that I'm no super guy. And he's right. I'm the guy who had the good fortune to be in the right place at the right time, several times. And so, I'm a little surprised to find myself

doing reasonably well with the responsibilities that are assigned to me
—surprised, an honest word!"

As he described his good fortune, Jack Hanley sat beneath a large oil
painting of a charging bull elephant. On his left, the translucent drapes
of a curtained glass window wall masked the office from the outside, yet
provided a screened view. To his right, facing the door, was a massive
desk. From that desk he could control the sliding panel entry doors. He
had ordered both the desk and the doors built the first day of his arrival,
from plans he had brought with him. Angled forward and catty-corner
on his left was a sofa for guests, comprising an informal alcove in a
mammoth groundfloor office.

Six-feet-three-inches tall, athletically built, tanned and trim in a characteristic dark three-piece business suit, ebullient Jack Hanley looked
anything but the passive beneficiary of dumb luck.

As he told it, his father was the youngest national sales manager
Toledo Scale Company ever had. James P. Hanley was a turn-around
expert who reorganized faltering branches. The Hanley family (Jack
was an only child) moved twenty-one times before Jack was twenty. The
continuity of Jack's early life was in his cohesive family, not in the
locales. Philadelphia, Wilkes-Barre, Detroit, Baltimore—these and others were his stops. Jack Hanley matched the pace of each new school,
in a day when textbooks and curricula were relatively standardized.
Usually such a pattern of moving, with the frequent disruption of relationships, leads young people to inhibit their investments in others and
to become prematurely self-sufficient. Their yearning to be close to
others must be buried beneath their independent manner. For Jack
Hanley, a by-product was a well-developed adaptive skill, and, in turn,
a generally sanguine outlook. With the model of his persuasive father
as an important constant in his life, Jack Hanley's odd jobs during high
school and college were selling. "Peddling," he says. Beer mugs, dance
corsages, and men's clothing were his products. Anything, including
taking bets for a bookie, to work his way thorugh Penn State—and to
support his Taylorcraft 65 airplane. He graduated as a metallurgical
engineer in the top 15 percent of his class, having been elected to two
honorary scholastic societies.[2]

Poor eyesight hadn't stopped Hanley from flying his primitive airplane, but it squashed his plans for wartime fighter aircraft flying. Instead, Lieutenant Hanley became a radar-intercept officer on a cruiser
in the Pacific. When World War II ended, he sought a sales position at
Allegheny Ludlum Steel, but following the process of steel making to
understand the product required a long run through the mill, which

held little attraction for him. He opted instead for the two-year Harvard MBA program. While at Harvard, he and his father agreed to team up as manufacturers' representatives after Jack had acquired significant sales experience.

When he completed his degree, Hanley followed his father's recommendation and signed up with Procter and Gamble (P&G) because of its vaunted training program. The postwar baby boom created a demand for diapers. Diapers (in those days) had to be washed. Soap salesman Hanley rode the crest of P&G's heavy-duty detergent Tide. The right place at the right time.

A portent of his management style surfaced after five months in his first assignment in Los Angeles. He had been sent there to help sell another detergent, Dreft. To win a sales contest, he undertook to sell to mom-and-pop stores on a Saturday. To help do that, he recruited his prospective bride, Mary Jane Reel, whom he had met five days after his arrival. Half teasing, he stated the objective and the conditions: sell four out of every six stores on your side of the street, or there will be no lunch. She got lunch, he won the contest, and they married a month later.[3] They have three children, two boys and a girl.

In 1951, four years into a career that brought him to district manager for the southern half of Chicago, Jack Hanley's aspirations for his own business collapsed with his father's death. Four years later, thirty-three-year-old Hanley vaulted over six senior managers to head national sales for P&G's soap and detergent division, which accounted for 70 percent of U.S. sales and 85 percent of U.S. profits.

The Charging Bull Elephant

By the mid-sixties, Hanley was responsible for the Hewitt Soap Company, a $20 million P&G subsidiary. He proposed a pilot project to P&G president, Howard Morgens, to test the concept of motivating managers by tying bonuses to individual performances. That experiment, Hanley believed, could have relevance for P&G as a whole. Morgens demurred.

There had been other heated Hanley-Morgens discussions. (The charging bull elephant picture in his office was not merely decoration.) "I was a bull in a china shop. I used to stomp around Morgens's office and press my arguments too hard . . . when I get a conviction, I fight for it until a decision is made; but then I get in the same boat and row."

In 1970, Jack Hanley became one of two P&G executive vice-presidents, having been elected to the board the previous year. But in 1971, Hanley's twenty-five-year career hit a shoal. Neil H. McElroy, chairman, CEO, and Jack's mentor, fell ill with cancer and retired. Howard Morgens succeeded him, and Hanley knew Morgens would be more comfortable with Edward Harness—the other executive vice-president —as CEO. Competitive consumer product companies leapt at the opportunity of recruiting a top P&G man. But Hanley stuck to his credo of "Never jump ship for a competitor."

The Opening Door

In early March, 1972, Monsanto opened its pavilion at Disney World. Jack and Mary Hanley were among the sixty business leaders and their wives invited to the affair. It was the articulate Hanley who took the initiative and thanked his hosts on behalf of the assembled group. This act, and his command of the pricing and availability of phosphates, impressed Charles Sommer, Monsanto's chairman.

Monsanto's president and CEO, Edward J. Bock, had suddenly resigned in February under pressure from the outside directors. Later in March, after the Disney World affair, the Monsanto board designated Sommer to head a search committee. Sommer was being pressed by the four managing directors of the Monsanto operating companies to choose from among them. Sommer and a board majority opted for more careful consideration. When informed of Hanley's possible availability, recalling his impressions of their earlier meetings, Sommer's interest flared, despite his concern about jeopardizing the $50 million yearly business Monsanto did with P&G, and about Morgens's probably explosive response to his "courtesy call." Meanwhile Hanley had boned up on Monsanto's problems and opportunities, asking people in the know. "Good people, without a common direction, in need of a professional manager," was the reply.

On September 12, Sommer phoned Jack and Mary Hanley, who were on a golfing holiday at their summer vacation cottage at the Highlands Country Club in North Carolina. He suggested a chat—there, the next day. Hanley got the green light to try his management development-compensation ideas, and to be "the boss and chief planning officer."[4]

Hanley was the highest ranking P&G officer ever to leave before retirement. He became the first outsider to captain seventy-one-year-old Monsanto, which had been rudderless for eight months.

The opportunity came at the right time; midlife is a good age to be concerned with developing others. And it echoed history. The elder Hanley had enjoyed hiring and training new salesmen while turning around floundering sales operations. Now Jack would be to younger managers what his father had been to him.

As had happened with MacGregor, the board hadn't given specifics when he asked what they wanted from him. He would have to define needs and propose actions. Compared to Mother Procter, growth in earnings per share was modest. Capital investment had been $200 million to $300 million per year. That might have looked good to the security analysts, but it was anemic by Hanley's reckoning.

D-Day

At eight o'clock in the morning of Day One, Jack Hanley, briefcase in hand, walked briskly into D Building (executive headquarters since 1955) on the 300-acre campuslike complex of long, low structures in the suburban St. Louis County community of Creve Coeur. He strode directly to his office, sat at his desk, opened his case, and began to work —as of old, a stranger in a foreign culture. Hanley dug into the long-range plans for the previous five years. The plans would predict that the next year's business was going to be flat and then business would go straight up. Said a disdainful Hanley, "It's like a porcupine's back . . . hockey stick is another word that I use . . . each year the point at which the damn thing turns up is moved back another year. The projections just weren't worth the powder to blow them up." Furthermore, it was openly admitted that "analyses" for investment proposals provided whatever conclusions were needed to justify investments. The business "misses" were as large as 50 percent.

Later that day, Hanley gathered the top eleven executives in his office, including past rivals for his job, and charged them: "You guys have the responsibility for training J. W. Hanley. I don't even know whether you spell chemistry with a k or c. I make mistakes every day, and you have to catch them."[5]

Hanley quickly commandeered a Harvard Business School professor and Monsanto veteran, Dr. Robert Stobaugh, for a seven-week crash course in petrochemical technology. He invited interested associates who also didn't understand how a barrel of oil, entering the front end of an ethylene cracker, was broken down into various products. "I've got to go to school. You want to go to school with me?" he asked in his dissembling way. The weekly two-hour class continued informally into a two-hour group dinner.

Hanley's learning blitz included assimilating complex financial data. At the next monthly board meeting, it was Hanley, already in the executive saddle, who presented the operating facts and figures of the company. "By Friday nights I used to be like this," he remarked to a reporter, holding a clenched fist to his midsection.[6] Hanley broke the tension with twice-daily, twenty-minute meditation periods.

He defined these priorities: (1) to complete the transition from a familial style of instinctive, unstructured management to contemporary professional management; (2) to upgrade the management development program; (3) to take the longer-term view of developing growth in both sales and profits. As with Jones, Wriston, and Watson, succession and research were paramount issues.

Building a Legend

Being on top and in control of himself and those around him is the dominating thrust of Hanley's activity. "Off and running" about 5:30 A.M., Hanley got to his office by 7:50 A.M., dictated to two secretaries until 8:30 A.M., and handed them mail with his appended handwritten responses. He then raced off to a series of meetings. Unlike other Monsanto presidents who tarried a few minutes during chance hallway encounters to chat with a senior executive, Hanley interrupted his whirlwind pace only when it served some business need.

At first, people were amused. Soon, according to one executive, it was, "Bing, you go in, the door flies open, you sit down. 'Okay, let me tell you what I want. I want . . . and you've got it. Can you give me an answer?' And you give him an answer. His reply to that in all likelihood is, 'Thank you,' and that's it. Bing . . . he'll turn around and do something else." Hanley favored an equally succint style in his written communications—a legacy of P&G. His memos at Monsanto came to be called "zingers."

Jack allotted one executive fifty-two minutes to make a presentation in a meeting. Jack needed eight minutes to get to another appointment. The executive tried to say much too much. At the fifty-two-minute point, Jack closed his notebook and said, "Thank you, gentlemen." The executive tried to make another point. Jack said, "I must leave." The executive persisted. Jack said, "I thought I made it very clear to you that I had fifty-two minutes to spend with you. If you need more time, call my secretary."

But another reported a different experience. "I've never seen him dismiss anybody or say, 'You're taking too much of my time.' He would never do that . . . he's just not as relaxed as he is when I've got his full attention. . . . You cannot overstay your welcome in Hanley's office. If you start doing that, then he'll come to your office. . . . He's got his notebook . . . he'll just turn the notebook over and sort of push it aside, and that's just sort of a signal. But not overt. You've got to be sensitive to pick it up."

To the "bing" of the door, Hanley added the beep of an alarm wrist-watch that punctuated many a meeting. Reactions ranged from "He's made the people around him much more conscious and sensitive to the value of time" to an intimate's blunt rebellious "Get rid of the damn watch, because it bothers people. It bothers me, and it just isn't helping the situation any. What the hell does it achieve?" Hanley grinned "okay" and got rid of it.

Though less of a problem for those who reported directly to him, Hanley's clipped style intimidated some. The predictable result: "I think people tend to be somewhat reluctant to raise issues with him . . . save only the ones they've kind of got to go in on. . . . They don't like that atmosphere. They can understand it. They can live with it. But they don't enjoy it. . . . The bad part is, he probably doesn't hear some things he ought to hear."

Later, in 1977, Hanley would further streamline communications by connecting his top forty executives on a "green line" that bypassed secretaries. Executives made a beeline for the green line when its green light and distinctive tone were activated on the telephone console. Hanley's subordinates used this line to communicate with their subordinates. The latter frequently called their bosses on this circuit, too. But not those who reported directly to Hanley. They thought hard and long before invading his time preserve.

Hanley's notebook, which he has been keeping all his adult life, is his follow-up system. "Once I write down a few notes, several purposes are served. First of all, I have learned to condense and summarize—in cryptic notes which usually only I can decipher. Also, when I write something down, it sticks pretty well. In addition, I use those notes as a follow-up. My pending file is an active one. When someone tells me he'll have something ready on the 18th, I write it down and I look for it on the 18th—and begin asking questions if the commitment isn't met." During a technical review, Jack pulled out from his notebook entries made a year earlier, awing and flattering the presenter with his careful listening skills.

Hanley socialized warmly not only at parties he gave for top management and their spouses, but also at parties for thirty to sixty lower echelon managers and their spouses in those early years of his tenure. He prepared himself before each party, memorizing the names of spouses, and even their children, so that he could greet each couple with a "Hello, ———! How are you? How are———?" That performance in the entrance hallway frequently startled the spouse. It is said he could recall her name if they met three days later.

Hanley's legendary time boundaries were sometimes perceived as controlling or discourteous. Others found it helpful, even when social events were involved, to be able to get home early and on time. Guests invited to a Hanley dinner party learned that he was adamantly punctual at home: cocktails at 7:00 P.M., dinner at 7:30. No unobtrusive coaxing with subdued tones on the half-hour, but a shrill whistle from two fingers planted in Jack's mouth followed by, "It's dinner time."

When Jack was the guest instead of the host, he was usually the first to leave the party. He skipped the cocktail hour, arriving fifteen minutes before dinner. As the leading personage at these parties, his nine o'clock departure often created an exodus that ended the festivities prematurely, behavior that some say removed Jack and Mary from some dinner lists. Associates infer that Jack followed the early-to-rise-early-to-bed philosophy.

The first two years of Jack Hanley's learning experience included flying 200,000 miles to Monsanto's far-flung outposts. He carried his work pattern into the air. Immediately upon boarding a 747 jumbo jet for the first leg of a nine-hour trip, Jack turned to one senior executive who was accompanying him and said, "Okay, it's 12:15. I'll see you . . . at 4:15 up in the top of the 747." Then he turned to the other and said, "I'll see you at 6:30." After each meeting he offered a perfunctory "Thank you very much" and returned to a document-laden briefcase. There was no time for trivia, reported one executive.

Embarking upon the traditional whirlwind worldwide tour of company facilities by an incoming president, Jack Hanley and a group of subordinates boarded a corporate jet for a plant visit. No sooner were they airborne than one of the executives reached over to open the bar, tilted his head toward Hanley, and asked, "What can I get for you?" Hanley briskly shot back, "Any fool that wants to have a drink on working hours can, but I'm not one of them." There were no further rounds between eight and five. (Hanley picked up wastepapers on the floor of the company airplane, threw them in a wastebasket, and said, "This is my house.")

Returning Monday mornings from weekend interludes at his Palm Beach winter home, Hanley waded into two briefcases of mail waiting on the corporate jet flown in Sunday night. If his breakneck pace prompted subordinates' quips about reading business reports in the bathtub, it wouldn't have surprised him. He did. "I have an arthritic back and so I take an hour's tub every night. And I take an hour's reading material in there with me. Once in a while it drops in and I have to get a dry copy of it."

Periodically, Jack relieved his arthritic back by getting out from behind his massive desk and making the rounds of the office of close associates in the mausoleum calm of D Building. He shattered that calm when he burst through an associate's door, dropped a sheaf of papers on his desk, and said, "How about reading this and giving me your opinion. . . . I've just talked to———and he told me———and I thought you ought to know about it." Then Jack whirled around and bustled back out as abruptly as he had entered.

Jack's frantic pace on the golf greens required a sense of humor and a stout heart. Trying to keep pace with Jack as he hurried to the next tee after finishing a putt or jumped into the cart to track his ball down the fairway, the angina-plagued spouse of a golfing partner popped a nitroglycerine tablet by the sixteenth hole.

What did Jack Hanley say about Jack Hanley?

"Hyperthyroid. I had dinner last night with the retired medical director of Monsanto, and he told me I'm hyperthyroid. I'm very high energy level, well, with blood pressure very low. . . . Not a workaholic in the sense that some people seem to get masochistic enjoyment out of it. I'm not that bad, although I do enjoy work. I enjoy what I do and I work long hours. I am a very well-disciplined person. I set reasonably high standards for myself and don't waste a lot of time in rationalization of why they did come true or why they didn't come true. I picture myself as being beloved by my associates, but I'm not sure that I am . . . my personnel fellow and confidant [Robert Berra] comes in here periodically and tells me off, and tells me I'm too goddamned tough, and urges me to try to behave in such a way as people will see the real me, whatever that is. I have a reasonably good mind, not super, but reasonably good. I meet people easily, and therefore am very good with customers and important people. God, this self-aggrandizement is embarrassing!

"I think I have reasonable courage. I don't shirk responsibility. I have a, maybe, overly developed sense of personal obligation to others. [A quality shared with all the other executives in this book.] For a long time I had kind of a sense of guilt, because I was having such a good time in life. I found a biblical quotation, in the second chapter of Ecclesiastes, which resolved that for all time for me . . . it says in effect that, if you work like hell for something, you ought to go ahead and enjoy it, that's part of the Lord's plan. I'd never read that before. It was a great help to me."

No Wine, No Roses

While Hanley stimulated initiatives to transform and rejuvenate Monsanto for the long haul, he sallied conspicuously against entrenched practices and attitudes he thought inimical to professional management. Moreover, these sorties raised blips and echoes on Monsanto's early warning sensors that unequivocally heralded a change in command, course, and speed.

Although Hanley signed his interoffice memos "Jack," he eschewed the practice of subordinates signing memos with nicknames or first names, which was a previous Monsanto style. He indicated that it would be more appropriate to use "Mr." One associate used initials to satisfy him. Hanley addressed people by their surnames in business memos and at meetings, a practice that gave such meetings a solemn ambience. That mode exacerbated the unsettling effects of some of his other initiatives.

The plethora of rules and regulations Hanley unveiled on June 11, 1973, to his senior management group sought to rein in the "perks," to bridle costs, and to bring consistency to Monsanto practices. It was called "Project Equity." "It was just a bunch of chicken shit," an observer laughed. The new order limited support to one country club membership (and extended this perk from twelve to seventy managers), abolished first-class plane travel and previously acceptable weekday golf games, and prohibited off-campus employee lunches (which squashed the plans of one department head to fete a retiring twenty-five-year Monsanto veteran at an outside luncheon). Company-paid entertainment, attendance at business meetings, Christmas parties, parking privileges, expense account systems, vacations, and numerous other fringe matters were affected. A long stem rose adorning each secretary's desk on National Secretaries Day was traditional in one department, until the practice fell victim to "Project Equity." Many dubbed it "Project Uniformity," faulting its egalitarian tone for sapping incentive from managers striving to join a merit-elite that had previously enjoyed these badges of achievement. The grapevine had it that one general manager who balked at "Project Equity" was terminated.

"It was a disaster," a chastened Hanley recalled. "It was formulated during meetings of the CAC [Corporate Administrative Committee], but I take full responsibility. It was a real bomb!" He publicly buried it at a global management conference in the summer of 1973. "To the degree that nagging and nit-picking have existed, to the same degree I declare that era is ended—tonight! I wanted to go on record against *all* nit-picking—by me or anyone else. Nit-picking is debilitating," he said.[7] Yet a person given to meticulous attention to detail will always be viewed as nit-picking. And that very trait, exemplified also by Reg Jones and Tom Watson, though sometimes experienced by subordinates as degrading, is required to maintain high standards.

Hanley's standards had to do with decor as well as decorum. "I'm a guy who's interested in everything. The cafeteria had a toothpick dispenser in a fairly prominent location, which I thought was out of character with the kind of society we are. So I had it removed." Yet it was hard to predict where and when his standards would apply. "When I first came, they just assumed a lot of things. They assumed that there was going to be a dress code. So, to disabuse them of that, I wore a green suit and a red tie, and wore it all through the cafeteria for a couple of days. That took care of that." However, an observer re-collects that a few weeks after arriving, Hanley issued a memo critical of the sport coat and slacks attire frequently seen, even on most lawyers, at Monsanto.

Direction

In formulating his plans for long-term investment and programs, following the course set by his predecessors on the basis of inadequate planning did not make sense. Hanley set about being more rational.

Nineteen seventy-two was the first full year of operation under a new organizational structure implemented in September of 1971, in which four operating companies were created: Monsanto Industrial Chemicals, Monsanto Textiles, Monsanto Polymers and Petrochemicals, and Monsanto Commercial Products. In 1973, Hanley increased capital expenditures to $205.3 million. Of even greater import was the fact that the company's financial vitality had increased despite the U.S. Economic Stabilization Program, which had frozen domestic prices for virtually all of the company's products from June 8, 1973, and the higher prices for petroleum resulting from OPEC in late 1972.

Jack Hanley's reputation as a super soap salesman raised speculation he might steer Monsanto into consumer products. He denied the speculation,[8] but that didn't mean he would be satisfied with Monsanto's emphasis on commodity businesses. He looked forward to moves into more high-margin proprietary products, downstream toward the consumer and away from commodity-type businesses tied to the vagaries of economic cycles.

An early Hanley question was, "What kind of a company do we want to be?" As Jones did at Belleair, and Wriston at his offshore meetings, Hanley took the CAC off-campus to think about that. A major conclusion was that their fate really was in their hands, regulatory bodies momentarily aside. Hanley recalled the first CAC meeting:

"The top dozen or two guys . . . saw that I was absolutely sincere in asking what otherwise might have been a rhetorical question. And when together we hammered out—and I really do mean together—we hammered out a set of specifications on the kind of company we want to be . . . they got an ownership position in our remodeling, if you will. And as long as what I was proposing was thought through sufficiently well to answer their reasonably pointed questions, they were prepared to help me. Now, don't misunderstand me, I'm not suggesting that all of them had instantaneously the courage to challenge the validity of everything I asked. But there were enough of them around here who not only had the courage but who are instinctively hair shirts. . . . I'm a salesman, and I did have to sell them the programs, but they had a stake in it from a fairly early date."

Gaining commitment for his program meant selling it by using classic sales techniques. "Jack's been selling for a long time," noted an intimate," . . . he does it very well, very skillfully . . . he leaves room for discovery, for identification, for all the stuff that's in Salesman 101. . . . Discovery is I allow you to discover a benefit that's there, and you discover it rather than me beating you over the head with it. You discover it, and therefore you're part of it, and therefore you accept it. . . . The man has a very strong personality, he has a very strong way of doing things." Some have contended that given Hanley's formidable power, few would really challenge him and that he might well have mistaken acquiescence for acceptance. Selling is by definition a vanquishing activity.

That first CAC meeting, at which long-range goals were set, had another theme—the "Corporate Hat." Before Hanley, there was substantial competition among the operating companies. Some observers thought Hanley exaggerated the importance of those competitive differences. One associate recalled Hanley's solution:

"So we went out to that first meeting at a lodge out here in the country, and at everybody's place that morning was a golf cap with the Monsanto logo. And in walked Jack, and in a very dramatic sort of way—everybody was assembled in the meeting room, and he was kind of the last one to come in to this meeting room, and he's wearing this hat. He said, 'Now, I want you all to put on that hat. That is a corporate hat. And when we're in this room you're wearing the corporate hat.' . . . He said, 'I want you to pick up that cap and put it on your head.' And everybody picked up his cap and put it on his head, feeling and looking like a damned fool . . . let's say strange. . . . But, it was designed to register. I didn't forget it, and nobody in that room forgot it. To this day we still laugh about putting on the corporate hat. . . . He dramatizes it, and I think that tells you a little bit about the guy's approach to things. If he has a point to make, he's going to work hard at trying to figure out a way to make that point and make it register."

Thereafter the CAC met weekly on Mondays in what was called its operating mode. Every other month it met for two days as the planning committee of the company. Operating executives were expected to doff their Monday operating hats and don corporate ones. Some thought a conflict of interest existed in such an arrangement, doubting that an operating executive would decide against the interests of his particular company, even if he were capable of shifting gears twelve days a year to long-term corporate planning.

Jack Hanley's flair for the dramatic did not always win applause. When, at another CAC meeting, he decided to try the same dramatic technique in support of President Ford's WIN campaign against inflation, it became apparent that there were a number of people in the room who thought the whole idea was stupid. The impulsive salesman clashed with the thoughtful executive. When others pointed to the need for more considered behavior, the cerebral side of Hanley won out.

Hanley was very careful not to take a show of hands. Technically, the CAC was not a decision-making body. Those who had the courage to take him on occasionally got great satisfaction. Every month there was a little more questioning and disagreement, and greater participation. Jack had moved them from easygoing management to discipline, from ambling along to direction. That was a wrenching experience. Now he was saying the time had come for him to pull back and let his team run the show. However, when he felt strongly about an issue he had a difficult time restraining himself from expressing his views. There were times when aggressive, probing questions at these meetings evoked Jack's ire, especially if they embarrassed someone or implied Jack might not have done his homework. When he erupted, it shook them. He would say, "I want you to ask a question, but to the extent that you cut off the conversation, that can be a problem. . . . Do we have to do it quite that way?" On the other hand, Jack would say, "That's a question that needed to be asked. We don't have the answer to it."

In 1978, with the appointment of H. Harold Bible as vice-chairman, Hanley was able to turn over the chairmanship of the CAC meetings so that he could attend to the external aspects of the CEO role. Jack knew that he was going to be spending more of his time fighting the battle for the chemical industry. Although he still attended about 80 percent of the meetings, Harold was always there. That shift also gave him a chance to back off from the chairman's seat and listen to how others reacted and become more a part of the discussion. In that position, he was less inclined to give his opinion until everyone else had and was relieved of the pressure a chairman feels when he must move the meeting along. The meetings were also more easygoing, which resulted in more discussion. When Jack chaired the CAC, it was difficult for him not to communicate which way he was interested in going, mostly by his enthusiastic support of whoever was presenting the issue that he favored.

Planning

Hanley quickly learned that various parts of the corporation had styles so different that a manager transferred from one to another would have to get to know the new setting as if he had come from the outside. Monsanto needed a coordinated planning system, and once that planning system was in place, ideally supported by an improved personnel development program, it would lead to a common management style. Then Monsanto would be in a position to move its broad portfolio of businesses into aggressive attack.

Hanley targeted earnings to double every ten years, substantially above Monsanto's historical pace, but he didn't immediately share his thinking. He played his hand close to his vest, exposing a card at a time. Only retrospectively could people see that he had been sequentially installing systems, concepts, and elements of new managerial environment piece by piece.

The Resource Allocation Program (RAP), a method for analyzing and weighing the needs of each component of the business, became a major component of Monsanto's planning process. Just implementing the rudiments of this process took Hanley into 1975. This delay to avoid straining adaptive capacities exacted a trade-off he later regretted.

> "I *know* I made a mistake here. I did not attempt to say to the corporation, 'Stop everything until you guys learn what I regard as a sensible analytical process!'
>
> "I knew very well in 1973 and 1974, even into 1975, that some of the investments we were making were going to turn out terribly. I didn't know which ones, obviously, or I wouldn't have made them. But I knew positively that some of them were cockeyed, because they were not the product of this careful analytical technique. . . . The reason I did [proceeded with the investments] that was . . . that we would have had a two-year [investment] hiatus which would have been absolutely tragic in terms of the perception

of their future on the part of the management group. So I said,
'Okay, let's keep going.' "

They not only kept going, they got going. Hanley expedited capital
investment from a level of $250 million to $600 million. The "cockeyed"
investments were in support of the then burgeoning nylon business in
Europe, which Monsanto subsequently wrote off. The implementation
of the analytic tools, especially RAP, also had to await a regrouping
effort. Hanley had to get competent executives in place who trusted his
intentions.

What were the signposts Hanley looked for to decide when to hold
back on the next phase of the planning system? "It's purely intuition.
I would kind of look at the glaze coming over the eyes of my associates.
. . . And once in a while [when] Harold Bible [then executive vice-
president] . . . would come in and close the door, I would know what
was coming. He'd say words to the effect, always couched in nice civili-
ties, 'Jack, you're doing a great job, but for Christ sake you're going to
drive us right up the wall if you don't ease up. You've got to slow it down
a little bit, Jack. . . .' I knew that it was not time."

A few others, like Bob Berra, vice-president of personnel, played the
same role. Berra had two themes: one was the "crack the whip" theme.
As Hanley heard it, "You know, Jack, you sit in your office and you make
a decision that's relatively high level, but by the time it gets down to
the foreman . . . it's world-shaking and they're not ready for that yet."
The second theme was the degree of understanding, acceptance, and
utilization of these programs at lower levels of management. "He could
say, 'Here's what's going on down there,' which in effect would say,
'We've got to take a little more time, we've got to make a little more
effort, we've got to be a little more sensitive to this. You've got to take
the pressure off here, take the pressure off there, put the pressure on
here.' "

Monsanto had been run loosely with considerable delegation. Managers typically understated targets, within the range of what they thought
their superiors would accept, in order to avoid the negative sanctions
they anticipated if they fell below a more realistic projection. There was
complaint that in the new management style Hanley was pulling power
back to himself. Hanley said it was his intention to delegate authority
to the lowest possible level, but given the fact that each of the business
units was doing more than a billion dollars, he could not delegate strategy to the business units.

In September, 1975, Sommer retired as chairman of the board, ending a forty-one-year career, but he elected to remain on the board for another three years. The board named Hanley to the additional role of chairman. Sommer was Hanley's next-door neighbor in the D Building until his retirement. "No one short of the good Lord Himself could have helped me more, especially during the first year of heavy homework," recalled Hanley.[9] But less charitable observers alleged that Hanley quickly sensed that Sommer abhorred confrontation and pushed him out of the picture from the outset. Deaths and retirements from the board in the early years allowed Hanley to replace all but one of the outside members, giving the organization a more pronounced Hanley stamp.

Technical Innovation

Jack Hanley took a hard look at Monsanto's technological health, and, like Reg Jones in a previous chapter and Tom Watson in the next, had some qualms. As part of the process of long-range profit forecasting, he calculated the percentage of future profits coming from products developed in the previous ten years and then extended this calculation back into the company's history. As in so many other companies, the profit trend from older products was declining, but far too precipitously for Monsanto's future health. Hanley initiated a fresh set of dialogues between senior executives and people at all levels in the technical community of the company. Visiting the twenty-six worldwide technical centers, he listened and talked. He found bits of evidence that suggested that "our technical community is having a hard time rallying around a leader."

Monsanto undertook to equip a research laboratory at the Harvard Medical School and to finance its basic research in molecular biology. The company agreed to spend up to $23 million between 1975 and 1986 and to work to commercialize discoveries made in the course of research. Roundup, an agricultural herbicide that promised to open up an entire new area of weed control, was approved by the Environmental Protection Agency in 1975.

The move into a program of product development based upon the life sciences did not arise solely from Hanley's fertile mind. Since he was not technically competent enough to suggest the technical direction of the corporation, that direction necessarily was a product of long and open debate with his senior associates (as it was for Reg Jones and Tom Watson). His functions, as he saw it, were to bring together a small group and to decide the level of support for the decisions. The debate was free. Each in turn, including Hanley, had been persuaded by the logic of the others.

Still, Hanley tried his own hand at innovation. For example, he thought that the carbon fibers that are used in golf clubs might have application in the automobile industry because of the fibers' lightweight strength. He had known the inventor of the material for years and went to San Francisco to talk with him. Hanley studied all the literature on the subject and became persuaded that this was something Monsanto ought to undertake. His reasons: (1) The precursor for carbon fibers is acrylonitrile, of which Monsanto is the largest manufacturer in the world. (2) Monsanto had the technology to form the fiber. (3) His perception of the marketplace was that the product would sell. He anticipated higher-mileage domestic auto requirements in the years ahead, requirements that would force automobile companies to use some carbon fibers to replace metal. "It's going to be one pound or ten pounds per car." If it were to be ten pounds per car, the company would profit handsomely; if one pound, there was little to gain. His associates persuaded him by their unanimity that it was going to be one pound, not ten. Hanley threw in the sponge—temporarily. "I've got it in my bottom drawer," he said, "and I'm going to keep probing at it."

Developing Management

The controlling, strong executive model Hanley exemplified to establish his position was followed by his effort to develop strong followers. Hanley had come to Monsanto with a commitment to himself and the company to transform its management and to build in succession. Hanley sized up senior managers during the first three months by calling each in for a review of his operation and by traveling extensively with them. The principle: "to identify some people who will grow with me, who will be sympathetic with the infusion of a new style of management and new management disciplines, get them out of present spots if inappropriate for growth and get them located, get them trained, get them coming our way." As was the case with each of the other chief executives described in this book, not all found wanting were discarded.

"A man who had run an autocratic but damned successful operation
. . . continued to do that until very recently. Now he's retired. There's
no sense in trying to make him miserable and me miserable by trying
to remake him. . . . And, God knows we didn't have enough forces to
replace everybody, so he just went on."

According to Monsanto's 1970 performance appraisal system, two-
thirds of Monsanto's top hundred managers had been rated outstanding. But there was no systematic correlation between performance
ratings and pay; money told the real story. To sort out the stars from
the satellites in the Monsanto universe, Hanley knew he would need
help. He had promised the Monsanto board they would not have to go
outside for another CEO. He had told Monsanto employees that it was
not his intention to start bringing in executives from elsewhere.

Hanley must have gone through several dozen operational reviews
in early 1973 before Earle Harbison's number came up. Harbison
made a two-hour presentation to Hanley on the Management Information Systems Department—an area with which Hanley was familiar from Procter & Gamble days. The productive meeting ended, and
Harbison accompanied Hanley to his car. "If something were to happen to you," Hanley asked, "which of those men I met today would
you recommend we put in the job?" "Well, with all due respect, I
think that's the wrong question," Harbison replied boldly. "What do
you mean by that?" "Well," Harbison explained, "that assumes that
one of those men is the proper guy to put in the job, and I think what
you ought to do is to assess the value of that job to Monsanto, because
I happen to believe that it's a very good training ground. It is a totally
intact business. The guy who runs that has his own world. He's got
worldwide responsibility. It's a high technology job. It's a sales job to
the people within the company to get them to utilize computers.
. . . You ought to decide what you want to do with that job, whether
you *do* want to use it as a training ground as well as one obviously to
preserve and enhance our position in the automation field. And on
the basis of that, you ought to make your decision as to who should
go into it, and not just say, 'Gee, which one of those three guys
who report to you.' " "Thank you very much," said Hanley and sped
away.

Several months later, Hanley called Harbison to his office. Management development, people development, was his concern. Was Harbison satisfied with Monsanto's management development programs?
"Certainly not. And the proof of it is you're sitting there." Hanley
reiterated his commitment to promote from within. At the end of the

discussion, Hanley said, "I'd like you to come over here and work with me on management development."

During the third quarter of 1973 Hanley and Harbison concluded that simply running more management training courses would not do. If Monsanto were to grow as rapidly as Hanley envisioned, it would need broad-gauged managers who could run with the new concepts and tools he planned to institute. Developing broad-gauged managers meant a reversal of the Monsanto norm of promoting people mostly within the narrow confines of a particular operating unit or a functional specialty. It also meant other executives had to do the same intensive coaching that Jack did, even two or three levels down.

To put his management development effort into high gear, Hanley called on Ed Schleh, a management consultant with whose work Hanley was familiar from P&G days. It was soon apparent to Harbison that plant-by-plant introduction of the Schleh system would be inordinately protracted. The program would have to begin at the top and cross the mass of Monsanto concurrently. It was top down despite its intention to stimulate initiative. Schleh feared that substantial benefits of the program would be lost in mass application. Hanley wrestled with that dilemma a couple of months and finally concluded despite the risk, "We'd go the whole way."

Earle Harbison adapted Schleh's management philosophy to Hanley's and worked the result into a format and language that could be understood, appreciated, and executed by Monsanto managers. Hanley called the new program Management by Results (MBR). Together they hammered out the details. Hanley stayed often until 8 P.M., humming to himself as he rewrote segments.

As he had urged at P&G, Hanley wanted to tie pay to performance, and to assure a manager who had met his goals that he would be rewarded on an objective basis. A new salary and incentive program was integrated with Schleh's system. If a superior didn't want to grant a bonus to a manager who had met his targets, then that superior had to bring that decision to Hanley's attention. Furthermore, he had to have a one-year plan for the substantial remedy of the man's problem or fire him, because such a decision meant the manager was in deep trouble.

Despite the intention to encourage coaching and provide more psychological incentive for people to be creative, the program ran into the common trap of using goals and objectives as a device for change. Predictably, managers played to the concrete and measurable. Schleh had warned that if compensation were linked to the MBR system, there would be severe administrative problems. Apparently he knew that to do so would nail managers to the concrete number targets that Hanley and Harbison wanted to avoid. The qualitative aspects of managerial practice they wanted to achieve would flounder as they had in all other corporations that tied compensation to specific goals alone.

Building a team for the future through all-out management development efforts aroused feelings of obsolesence in older executives, as it had in Citicorp. Hanley's moves of managers from role to role, intended to test them and to integrate line and staff functions, were interpreted by some as clever maneuvering to eliminate the old guard by assignments to jobs of lesser complexity or responsibility, thereby provoking early retirement. Also, as young stars were identified and moved up, their commitment to the new Monsanto management style and their attachment to the figure of Jack Hanley drew comments that they might become unable to act independently. This perception was accentuated by Hanley's personal mentoring. For all his time pressure, Hanley made time to teach those in whom he saw promise. He was not hesitant to criticize. The calls came out of the blue, triggered by something Hanley considered a significant piece of behavior. When a subordinate said, "You know, I don't think it was wrong. I think that's what I set out to say," Jack's rejoinder was, "I don't give a damn what you think was right. I'm telling you that didn't go over the way you intended it to go over, even though you think it did." While these protégés did not like to be told the errors of their ways, some, aware that such attention indicated their star status, were flattered that Jack would take the time to teach them. As would Tom Watson in the next chapter, Jack tempered his criticism. According to one protégé: "Once he's made the point, and it's all done, he'll say, 'But of course, if I told you it was a perfect job that you just did, that wouldn't be very productive, would it?' "

Hanley also corrected presentations at CAC meetings, demonstrating his mastery of subject matter. "Let me add a few words if I may. . . . Let me see if I can help clarify that or help explain another aspect of that," Jack would break in, rising to his feet. He then held forth for a few minutes with ad lib comments, perhaps feeling that the constructive criticism outweighed how it must feel to the presenter to be publicly second-guessed by a powerful boss.

Jack's style was to give only a bare minimum view of a problem at the outset and follow it with a maximum of exhortation. At an annual management conference, Hanley listened to a top subordinate paint a scenario of disaster if new products were not developed. The speaker traced the decline of new products as a percent of Monsanto's total sales, urging the assembled to get on with new product development and offering examples of success stories. Hanley called the subordinate into his office and said, "That was a good speech, not a great speech, a good speech." Jack began his critique: "I went through that speech and I found seventeen places where you scared me. You know, it reminded me of being at a tent revival. By the time I had sinned for the seventeenth time I was on the floor and by the time the preacher got to pick me up it was too late. I was wallowing in my sins." When the same man gave another presentation, within a half-hour of his talk, he got a personally delivered note. It read, "The tone this morning was just perfect. I loved the way you did it. Jack."

Jack used object lessons to dramatize a point in the mentoring process. A managing director wanted to transfer a subordinate to an important assignment in Europe. In order to avoid placing the man in the embarrassing position of having to turn down a formal offer for personal reasons, the managing director approached him obliquely to test whether he might be interested. His affirmative answer led to negotiations that proceeded to near confirmation of the move.

One Sunday morning the managing director got a call from Jack. "What are you doing? Come on down to the apartment." At the apartment Jack said to the director, "I've got a job for———. I've decided to make him———." "Jack, you can't do that," answered the anxious director. "We've got him on his way to Europe." Jack countered, "I don't know anything about a European assignment. I've decided I want to put him in this U.S. job." "Well, you really can't," the managing director protested. "That's precisely my point. You've taken away my freedom. You've got this guy on an airplane to Europe and he's in a group of top managers that are corporate property. They're just on loan to you. The top fifty guys are my troops, and I want to know about those fifty guys. I need to be part of the process of planning their careers!"

Hanley repeatedly asked managers what they were doing to teach people a couple of levels down. "Did you help him afterward to realize it was a lousy presentation and help him make it better?" was a typical Hanley query. Executives learned to respond immediately to their subordinates' performance.

Commenting on the MBR program, a skeptical insider remarked:

"As a matter of fact, there are many very fine features to this program. If you're my subordinate, we at least have three good sessions a year where we sit down and talk about your job. We have a period in September, called the JRA [Job Results Analysis] when we both agree as to the environment in which you're going to be doing your job next year or the environment in which we're going to be relating to one another . . . these are the key areas in which I think I ought to be held accountable for a goal. Then, we move from there to the establishment of certain goals—weighted goals— for the year . . . and that's another session [in January of the next year]. We always negotiate these because that is going to be the basis for some of your compensation. . . . Then there's a midyear review. . . . At the end of the year we have a Results Review session where, in effect, I kind of tell you how I think you did on your goals, and you have a right to battle me."

It became known that Hanley personally passed on everybody at the general manager and department head level. You didn't become a general manager if Jack Hanley didn't know you. It was not a matter of Hanley's running down into the ranks and yanking people into a general manager slot, but rather of a screening process in which he asked senior executives for their detailed oral evaluations of their top subordinates: "How is————doing? Do you think he can be a managing director in the company?" A negative reply elicited an "I don't understand why," from Jack, followed by elaboration from the boss. Over the years a general manager had to have the capacity to manage a $300 million business, a managing director a $1 billion to $1.5 billion company. Executives were reviewed yearly by their managing directors and every two years by Hanley.

In the early days of implementing the MBR-incentive system, Hanley used his numerous company appearances to inveigh against inflating performance ratings. "We've got to avoid forced ranking of people. We've got to realize that a good solid performance is what runs the corporation, and there's only this handful of superlatives, and I'm only satisfactory." Hanley himself didn't use many superlatives. One can only wonder whether his own very high standards for himself truly left him with no more than a "satisfactory" self-rating.

Hanley had placed himself out front when he made the MBR program his own, instead of something initiated by the personnel department, realizing that it would be more difficult to get the program across to the operating people if it were construed to be just another personnel innovation. The program was clearly identified with Jack, and he had to take the flack when it came time to appraise the damage in the aftermath of such a deluge of change. And there were complaints aplenty.

Hanley knew that although the various management systems that he had installed were intended to be constructive, they had been instituted quickly and across the company and therefore could not work equally well everywhere, even if the systems themselves were perfect—which, of course, they could not be. "In other words, he'd rather flood the situation and get it going, and then back off and let the water recede and find out what should be the next move," remarked an observer. At the beginning of 1979, it was time to make a course correction.

Hanley undertook a Yankelovich survey to take the pulse of the organization. Bob Berra did a telephone poll and conducted focused discussion groups. In the managerial ranks, there was concern, particularly among junior managers, about the gap between goals and results and the impact on their compensation. And Hanley was concerned about the degree to which the system encouraged the managers to play games with the numbers. It was time for fine-tuning on the basis of the data from below. These were summarized into major topics that became an agenda for an off-campus meeting of the CAC. Hanley intended it to be a transition as well.

He set the stage, asking for candor and pointing out that there were some errors in application of the systems, that it was time to correct them. Furthermore, he wasn't going to be there forever; he intended to begin transition of management responsibility for the corporation from himself to "them." He was carrying too large a share of the total responsibility, he said. The transfer of responsibility presumably would give the corporation better management. It would certainly train them and prepare them for the day when he was gone.

Hanley was satisfied that his top management had taken him at his word. During two tough days of frank discussion, they reviewed the survey results and established priorities. They avoided developing any formal remedial programs, both because they were too far from the immediate issues to know how best to do so and because it would be better for all concerned if those who had complained were part of the effort to solve the problems they had complained about. The meeting reinforced Hanley's view that the eyes of his top management group were no longer glazed and that group had just about caught up with his initiatives. No one wanted to abandon the systems.

Pursuing the Initiative

In his first four years of stewardship, Hanley was mastering science-based Monsanto's technology, analyzing its businesses, and "clocking" the stable of executives on parade. Man-on-the-run Hanley was characteristically a meticulous listener, planner, and, like all the previously described CEOs, always super-prepared. "He gets it across, I suppose, by looking you straight in the eye and stating what he wants done in language that you can understand," said one executive. "He just doesn't make any bones about the fact that he thinks that we've got to aspire to be the best company in the world [an aspiration echoed repeatedly in these chapters]. . . . He repeats it in a variety of different ways every time it's opportune . . . he says it with an intensity and a feeling, perhaps, that suggests that that spirit is one of his major driving forces. . . . He feels it in every bone in his body."

By early 1974, ideas were honed, placed into a final format, and sold to the CAC, the board, and finally to the key management group. Nineteen seventy-five was the year of implementation of a strategy for change that was led by Hanley's shock troops. Each of the shock troops was titled Director of Results Management (DRM) and devoted his full time to the project. They were widely recognized as eight of the best people in the company. The first wave and successive waves of DRMs spread out over Monsanto's managerial landscape, assuming leadership positions over the years and altering its topography.

The Hanley Style

Hanley's optimistic, upbeat, cheerleader style was expressed in his focus on a ten-year horizon of Monsanto success, despite short-term setbacks. It was also echoed in his sensitivity to the reactions of others, despite his sometimes apparent insensitivity to the feelings of his subordinates. When the executives of a foreign subsidiary (shut down years later) were presenting data to justify capital expenditures, they ignored ten years of poor results, focusing on the good earnings of the previous year and their profit projections. When one senior executive asked for this historical data, he was chastised the following morning with, "You can't deal with people like that. For Christ sake, you know, they've come here from. . . . That's what they believe and you're totally insensitive to their feelings."

His intolerance for that kind of insensitivity was reflected in a similar incident. In preparation for a Hanley-hosted breakfast reception for distinguished visitors from Israel, the coordinator of the event, a top executive, was asked by his own secretary what he wanted for breakfast. He was unaware that by answering he was setting the menu. At the end of a ham-and-eggs breakfast, which had been modified for the visitors, Hanley angrily refused to accept what he thought was a lame excuse by his subordinate for his evasion of his responsibility.

In social situations Hanley regales listeners from a wide repertoire of stories and memories. In his pre-Monsanto days, Hanley was known as a practical joker. He still jokes. Visiting the Soda Springs plant near Pocatello, Idaho, with an associate, he was met at the airport by the anxious plant manager who had boned up on every conceivable question he could anticipate that Jack might ask. As he alighted from the plane, Jack asked with a deadpan expression, "May I make a request: I want you to take me past the Princess Theater." The bewildered manager shook his head. "I remember Judy Garland singing that song in *A Star Is Born,* about being born in a trunk in the Princess Theater in Pocatello." Jack's hearty laugh confirmed his joke.

Hanley high jinks are also bestowed upon close associates. On a trip to Iran, Hanley and his associate found that they had a rare free half-day. While taking in the local sights, Jack spied a water pipe, which he requested his associate use as a prop for a candid photograph. Ten days later, the associate's wife received a letter from Jack: "Dear————, Your husband is totally out of control. Enclosed is an example of what he did on our last trip. By the way, ask him about the belly dancer. Love, Jack."

The Body Blows

Three body blows in 1976 knocked the wind out of the apparent Monsanto juggernaut. First, the U.S. Food and Drug Administration (FDA) prohibited the manufacture of Cycle-Safe plastic beverage containers, effectively killing that program despite Hanley's decision to challenge the decision in the federal court. This write-off reduced earnings by 55 cents per common share. Second, withdrawal from the expandable polystyrene business in the United States, reduction in the scope of nylon operations in Luxembourg, the closing of a fiber texturizing plant in West Germany, and withdrawal from several unprofitable segments of Monsanto's European plastics and fibers businesses—all part of Monsanto's continuing program to divest low-profit potential business—further reduced earnings by 39 cents per common share. Third, a higher tax rate and currency exchange and translation losses each reduced earnings by 90-plus cents. Yet Hanley increased development funds 16 percent, and capital investments were maintained in the $600-plus million range.

In 1974, Monsanto had invested heavily in the start-up of Cycle-Safe, a recyclable soft-drink container. Monsanto had great expectations for the product, which was already in use in two-thirds of the country. But in 1976, an industry-sponsored series of studies found acrylonitrile, a material fused into the plastic, to be associated with abnormalities in rats fed amounts at the upper end of the dosage. Extrapolating from the rat data, to duplicate the lowest level of acrylonitrile used in the test, an individual would have to consume 1,600 pounds of it daily, according to the 1976 Annual Report. The FDA announced it would suspend approval for the use of this product, an action Monsanto considered extreme in view of the inconclusiveness of the findings. Although no time schedule was set for this action, some bottlers and retailers understandably backed off from using the containers until there was definitive approval by the FDA. It was a hard and unexpected blow, for the company had made a determined effort to stay in touch with the Environmental Protection Agency and the FDA.

A colleague observed how Hanley handled the stress: "I didn't see him flinch on it. He just took the disappointment, didn't like it, very unhappy, but was able to move through that without conveying any kind of panic to the people. Saying, 'We'll fight it!' . . . I thought he handled that [well]. . . . He's not a guy that's going to . . . overreact to the big problems." "We had a thousand people who were out of work, just like that, over a weekend," he continued. "Three hundred of them were salaried people. And the ability of the organization to pull together, to close ranks and say, 'We're going to take care of those people first, before we do anything else' [was remarkable]. And the effort that was put forth to get them other jobs, I thought was real evidence of maturity on the part of the organization. . . . Jack . . . has done a great deal to bring that social consciousness here."

Meanwhile . . .

The downturn in earnings from the three major blows exposed Hanley to some internal criticism. Clarity of information and integrity of relationships weren't for everyone. An insider gave this perspective: "In 1973 and 1974 when this company's earnings turned around, there weren't very many critics. . . . Being in a big commodity chemical business, we were highly dependent on the cost of raw materials. Things haven't been as easy for the past five years. . . . Critics are more critical when things aren't going all that handsomely, but they're still burdened with all the extra system. And it's very easy to gripe and say, 'What are we getting for all this style?'"
One of the senior executives noted that the system of integrating each subordinate's goals with those of his boss looks perfect, but "it is not a system that can react fast enough when something happens."

"The system is so burdensome that it doesn't [change quickly enough]. . . . Companies run on a much more dynamic basis than a set of goals put in place at the beginning of the year and changed in the middle of the year.

"It comes unglued for certain disciplines. . . . Our R&D people would maintain that the whole system is lopsided toward the attainment of short-term objectives, and that you can't invent on that kind of a basis.

"It doesn't work in a staff operation. . . . If you're our antitrust lawyer, I'd have a very difficult time trying to get a set of goals from you, because you don't know what or where we're going to get challenged this year in the antitrust area."

In addition, there was the problem of raised expectations. According to the same senior executive:

"We began a technique with our employees of telling them everything, and we raised expectations to a point where we haven't been able to deliver. For example . . . one [manager] volunteered . . . that, 'It used to be fun to give a man a raise. You'd tell him he was getting an 8 1/2 percent raise, and he'd thank you. It was a happy occurrence. Now, when you . . . tell him he's getting an 8 1/2 percent raise . . . he knows that his performance is evaluated as 1 or 2, he knows the ranges for the salary grades for the various kinds of performance, he knows where he's supposed to be in the salary grade in four or five years, and he'll argue why he isn't getting an increase of 9.2 percent.' We've actually gotten to the point where the so-called open society has turned around to bite us."

Said another of Hanley:

"He's got warts like everybody else. . . . One of them is the fact that his rhetoric tends to outdistance our ability to produce, so that can result in increasing the expectations of our people beyond our ability to answer them in the short term. Because he gets so enthused, and he's so confident, the logistics can get away from him . . . you've got to be sure you've got in place the things that can make that happen. . . . What people tend to miss is that we've always done it on a sandwich-type basis . . . if we're going to move in a new general manager, we'll make sure that the managing director has been in place for a pretty good period of time, or that the team under him is a pretty solid team. . . . Those guys that really made the contributions had to think in terms of five, ten, fifteen years out . . . I think he's got that thing going . . . and the thing we want to be sure of there, as we move, is that those guys remain unawed by him. . . . I think we've got enough budding hair shirts so that we won't have too much trouble. But I think that could be a danger."

Jack Hanley's presence seemed to some to overshadow his associates. His one-on-one approach to his direct subordinates, the three executive vice-presidents and the vice-chairman, and his preference for using the cumbersome CAC to get things done were perceived as restricting the opportunities of his top group to get a picture of the top job. Might not this interfere with grooming a successor? That method was also seen as making them vulnerable to being pitted against each other, instead of working as a team. Some thought that Hanley really could not build a close team. One of the members of the board of directors is reported to have said, "It's like a chandelier over a dinner table with one 600-watt bulb surrounded by a series of dull 50-watters. Hanley is a pretty bright bulb, but the fact that his associates may appear to be dull 50-watters by contrast doesn't bother the 600-watt bulb at all."

One close observer reported, "As I watched the man every day . . . certain of his characteristics impressed me a great deal, but I also

realized that he had nowhere near the self-confidence that he appeared
to exude. . . . He doesn't let anybody bubble up to challenge him, but
in the process, he doesn't let anybody bubble up to help him either. To
me, that says that despite his handsome appearance and well-organized
life, there's a basic insecurity. . . . When Jack was down the line at P&G,
he was a guy that liked to relate to people, but being up in the top spot
he doesn't do it as well."

As hard-driving as Jack Hanley is perceived to be, associates say he
is too easy on people that "blow it," a characteristic shared by several
of the other CEOs. This is applied to the way he handled alleged ineffi-
ciencies in the technical community, where his knowledge is limited.
"The guy, in my view, tends to generate a great deal of respect," said
an intimate:

> "Almost, to some people, a feeling of awe. Now, you know from
> your own relationship with people that you respect a great deal
> that it doesn't take much from them to cut you right to the quick
> because your greatest wish is to look good in their eyes. Hanley
> understands this. Consequently, he's got a calibration that says,
> 'I've got some people who work for me who have already flogged
> themselves so badly before they've come here that my doing it any
> more isn't going to help the situation.'
>
> "So I have seen him, where people have made big mistakes, be
> more forgiving than I would have been. . . . He would put himself
> in the boat with them: 'Okay? That was a judgment we all made.
> We made a mistake. Now, how do we get out of it? Let's get in the
> boat and row together. Let's move it on.' The guy knowing full well
> that Jack has the ultimate responsibility, but that undoubtedly he
> was the one that said, 'Look, in effect I'm staking my reputation on
> this, and I recommend that you do it.'
>
> "I've very seldom seen Jack Hanley raise his voice, or say, 'You
> know, you really screwed this up.' He may once in a while say, 'It
> would have been better if we'd have thought about this ahead of
> time, wouldn't it?' Usually 'we.' [Much like Reg Jones.] But the
> severity comes in terms of the anxiety, or the desire on the part of
> the people to look good in his eyes . . . you can tell when they [top
> management] sense that they've let him down, and therefore
> they've let themselves down, in his eyes. That's the way I see him
> having his greatest impact on a lot of people. . . . Jack did not often
> show his anger. His tone was stern. People knew when he was
> disappointed, that he was not going to tolerate disappointment

repeatedly. The occasions when Hanley did express his anger were devoid of table-pounding or expletives. He just got a bit agitated.

"Jack's ability to communicate with people varies according to his own chemistry with them. If Jack doesn't feel as close to an individual, that individual won't feel quite comfortable. Consequently, there would be a cycle that feeds on itself . . . that's why it takes strong men to deal well with Jack Hanley."

This same observer continued:

"I've never seen him ever get upset for more than a tenth of a second . . . any guy that has that kind of a position doesn't necessarily want you coming in and saying, 'You screwed this up.' But you can do it. You can say it just that way, and he'll maybe sometimes . . . back off, and he'll say, 'Okay, that's what I'm paying you for. Tell me what I did wrong.' And then once you get into that, he'll shut up and just listen to you. He'll ask a few questions somewhere down the pike. . . . He can spot fairly soon where you're not fortified with the facts. Plus the fact that I think it's important to have a chemistry based upon a history of having built that credibility slowly."

Another staffer's view was:

"Things that he thinks he knows—like people planning—he comes on loud and strong. . . . Anything where he can do it himself, he's super. At anything where he's dependent on the input [of others], he's less good, because his style doesn't allow him to actually sit down and rap with a group of guys and allow them to participate in the conclusion. This company, for example, needs desperately to grow externally—from an acquisition. We've got to have about three or four guys go off a couple of weekends a year and just sit down without a lot of paper and talk that out. That's not our style. Our style is to have presentations before twenty-three people, a show of hands and—as a consequence—we'll never get anywhere on tough problems requiring joint input."

Still another observed:

"I see him beginning to move away and say, 'You know what I want, you know the main direction, now go do it. Let's see what happens.' One thing we don't want is surprises. And you learn that early in the game with Hanley. You'd better get it out, but you'd better have some idea where you're going, and have some kind of solution when you bring the problem to him.

"Occasionally, though, the people will say, 'Okay, this is where we are, but dammit, Jack, you've got a perspective I don't have, and I'd like to get your input.' In which case they will come and sit down and chat with him about that, and he'll give them his concept and his ideas, and then say, 'What else do you need?' 'I don't think I need anything.' Okay, back to the drawing board, and then they'll come in [the second time], and they'll make their pitch.

"I sense more and more of his saying, 'Do it on your own.' Now, you've got to remember that many of the managing directors . . . have not been in those jobs all that long. And so, it's gratifying . . . to see them grow in that way."

While some say that Jack is not reluctant to admit a mistake, others to say that he rarely will admit error during a one-to-one discussion.

"It's very, very difficult for him to ever state to you, 'Dammit, you were right. I wish I'd paid a little bit of attention to you.' It's just not in his makeup to do that. . . . When it turns out that you were dead right, most people would feel just a wee bit better if you were more honest with them. . . . I think he admits it to himself . . . but I think if you're building a team, you've got to do a certain amount of admitting it to the key guys on the team, too. . . . One of the things I find most frustrating about this style is when he calls you and asks if you have four or five minutes to talk over something. You don't have any more idea as to subject. He opens a folder, and he's been working on something you don't do right; he's got four or five pages of these little white pieces of paper. He's handwritten everything you do wrong—you don't tie your shoelaces right, to you don't do this right, et cetera. He's all organized. He comes on at you like gangbusters. Walking in, you didn't even know what the subject was. Now he's done that to just about everybody around here, and that is difficult."

Jack's overpreparation is said to discourage participation at board meetings. "You haven't got any men on the board who are gonna question anything Jack Hanley says," noted an observer. "He has the capability of overwhelming any one of them on a one-to-one basis, and he runs the meeting. . . . There's a little concern by some of those people, but they're forced underground with that grousing."

The Thespian and Communication

Hanley instituted the Annual Management Conference in December, 1973. He added the corporate people to the annual multiday meeting of the worldwide operating companies. It was 100 percent business in the early years at these 500-person swarms, topped by Hanley's after-dinner state-of-the-company speech. Intimates say Hanley's oratorical talents give these annual management meetings the ambiance of a revival sales meeting, with Hanley displaying his understanding and breadth of knowledge of Monsanto's business. All this was a far cry from his predecessors, who were considered poor public speakers.

His thespian talent sparkled at the April Annual Meeting of the shareowners. In one virtuoso performance, Hanley departed from his traditional formal presentation. He had the executive vice-presidents answer questions, and he himself devoted ninety minutes of "ad lib" responses to questions submitted with proxy statements. That performance became the talk of Monsanto. Tall, erect, impeccably dressed, and "endowed with reasonably good looks" (his phrase), Jack Hanley strode out in front of the shareowners, put on a microphone, fingered the cards he held, read a question from one in a strong baritone voice, and then threw the card on the table, got his glass of water, and punctuated his remarks with occasional sips. Those questions had been handpicked earlier and meticulously researched by Monsanto specialists.

Jack's public relations experts had briefed him on the seating location of a group of nuns and the name of their spokeswoman, expecting a question on an issue about which they had earlier expressed concern. The moment the sister raised her hand Hanley told the assembled, "This is Sister MaryAnn McGivern, chair of the investment committee of the Sisters of Loretto." Another shareowner asked Hanley about Monsanto's handling of the fundraising effort within the company for the United Way. Jack was national chairman for the United Way that year and had been written up in the local press for allegedly making a donation to this charity a condition of employment. He used the question as a platform to extol the activities of the United Way and Monsanto's social responsibility. Said an executive who watched the process, "He just made the guy look like a 'boob' in terms of who wouldn't support the United Way—this thing that does great things for mankind."

A bigger company also meant media attention. Jack, anticipating that his top executives would be taking on an increasing responsibility to speak for the company, took seven of them in 1977 to a training program for instruction on how to cope with the media. According to one of them:

"The first thing he did was to say, 'Look, you're going to get burned, okay?' Now that was the difference. We used to be so afraid that we would get burned that you wouldn't say anything. So Jack just plain opened it up and said, 'You're gonna get burned. You're going to be misquoted, or you're going to say something that's a proper quote, and you're going to be sorry you said it. Now let's start with the fact that you're gonna make some mistakes. But we gotta get out and speak up about what's right. Our side *has* to be heard.' He took us up to Chicago and gave us the Thompson course for a couple of days, where they really put you through the sweats. . . . That was the first indication that he meant business."

Another top associate describes the experience in similar tones:

"Well, as you watched those eight people respond to this very abrasive and unnerving exposure to a TV newsman, without doubt the guy who handled it best was Jack. . . . They started out by saying, 'Why the hell did you leave Procter and Gamble? And what do you do to earn $400,000 a year from Monsanto?' And about halfway through, the guy got rough.

"Sooner or later, everybody pretty much got rattled. It was designed to accomplish that. Clearly, Jack was able to handle that better than any of the rest of us . . . he came closer to not letting the guy get under his skin in his presence . . . sort of letting the man know that he hadn't rattled him, and making some light comment before he addressed the question."

It was not long before top executives were making the rounds, speaking at the Chemical Manufacturers' Association, before the financial analysts and other audiences.

Hanley exercised his mentoring bent in this arena as well. Young people made several presentations to Hanley and to other top executives before they had their maiden voyage before the CAC. Later, he left that training up to the subordinate's direct superior. If it was a presentation on a major issue before the CAC, Jack would be given an overview and all of the data. If a new person was being broken in for a presentation to the CAC, Jack would get the relevant data the night before, or if the presenters were in a hurry, they would give Jack a brief update so that he could approve the direction of the presentation. "I take my young guys in there all the time, because I *want* them to see how Hanley operates," said one of his senior executives.

"Rather than *me* go in and make the presentation, we'll have . . . one of my two lieutenants and two of his younger guys who are high potential people. We've been doing this now for several years with a succession of younger people. . . . Now, when we bring these guys up [from an operating unit to corporate], part of that is to get exposed. Hanley is beautiful with them. He just sits back and he listens to them with great respect, because he knows how hard they've prepared for this. . . . First of all he would try to put them at their ease, 'Okay,'I'll say, 'I don't know if you remember Bill.' 'Yeah, of course, Bill, Decatur, Alabama.' He'll know that . . . because he's privy to my long-range plan for people.

"They start with their presentation. He'll listen them through. He may ask a question here or there. He permits them to answer the question, and only if it gets to be a difficult one where it may look as though the man may not have the answer, he'll sort of look at me. . . . He will treat him in that office as though he were an equal to me . . . which I think is marvelous. He's tough . . . he's assuming that this person has as much knowledge, if not more, of what he's talking about as I do. . . . He only looks to us for the wisdom.

"You see [him] moving from the point of building the confidence at the beginning, then making sure that the guy doesn't fail to realize that he's got to have the facts, [and] he's got to present them correctly. It's a combination of what I would call a sympathetic discipline—firmness. . . . If he were going to be critical, he would be critical of me for permitting the guy to come in without preparation, but not there.

"after that the guy is now ready for his test . . . before the internal board, [the] CAC. . . .

"Jack says, 'When I lay down the hod,' his very words—the brick-layer laying down the hod. 'When I'm done, when I lay down the hod, one of the greatest satisfactions I'm going to get, (or speaking to me, you're going to get) is watching those younger people that we put in place succeed.' "

Hanley would not place himself in the position of being used by his subordinates. As he told one executive who was about to make a presentation: "Look, I hear what you're saying, I *think* I buy it, I'm not going to go in there [CAC] and necessarily support you until I hear what the other guys around that table have to say. They may come up with some thoughts that I haven't come up with. So I'll tell you again. Go, but don't go with the idea that I'm in there saying, 'Yeah, Jack Hanley supports it,' because I like the direction but I want discussion."

Hanley did not attempt to change the communication preferences of those already in his cabinet. If a senior executive felt more comfortable communicating with Hanley in writing, Jack would not object, realizing that some were uneasy discoursing with him. "The diffident person moves too slowly in his thought process," noted an intimate. "If you're going too slow . . . you can just see he's beginning to think about his next appointment."

Succession and Expansion

By 1979, 100 percent of the general managers and 96 percent of the corporate staff directors had been changed. On February 22, 1980, the board of directors approved Hanley's roster for management succession by electing Louis Fernandez vice-chairman and Richard J. Mahoney president. Hanley remained chairman and CEO. The decision was prompted not only by the board, but also by Hanley's increasing activity on the public scene, an activity that consumed nearly half of his time.

Hanley-watchers saw that he had paved the way for acceptance of his candidates. He walked the Executive Compensation and Development Committee of the board, all outside directors and his appointees, through the qualifications of his candidates long before a vote. Sensitive to the statesman role of the CEO, Jack showcased his protégés. Mahoney (and subsequently Fernandez) was Hanley's Florida house guest. Golf and dinner parties at the Lost Tree Club exposed Mahoney to corporate America. Hanley was instrumental in pushing Mahoney into the Arts and Education Fund in St. Louis. In the process of raising $2 million, Mahoney met all of the key people in town. Mahoney and Fernandez had major roles at the December, 1978, Worldwide Management Conference.

Despite a net income drop of 55 percent in 1980, capital expenditures zoomed 38 percent to $780.5 million; research and development costs rose 27 percent to $204 million. Hanley pointed to the strengths that were building: a plant expansion for Roundup herbicide completed in Belgium, the near completion of a third plant for this product in North Carolina, and a fourth unit on the drawing boards; expansion of the world's largest electronic-grade silicon plant, in South Carolina; expanded oil exploration to help ensure adequate feedstocks, with proven reserves of approximately 130 million barrels of oil and equivalent gas —an asset estimated at $1.774 billion; the completion of a new research building in St. Louis, with a 30 percent increase in research space at the site; the acquisition of approximately a 30 percent interest in Collagen Corporation, which had developed proprietary methods of processing and purifying collagen protein from animals to replace lost or defective tissue in humans; the purchase of a $20 million interest in Biogen, a genetic engineering company, which was added to the company's equity positions in two other leading genetic engineering firms—all giving Monsanto "windows on new technology and the flexibility to broaden our range."

In 1982, research and development spending rose to $260 million. Monsanto pooled resources with several British universities, including Oxford and Cambridge, to establish a $17.5 million venture capital fund in London that would invest in high technology start-up companies in Europe. Monsanto's action was the first major entry into Europe's venture capital community by a U.S. industrial company. Monsanto also awarded a $4 million five-year grant to support basic research in plant molecular biology at Rockefeller University, and a $23 million five-year contract with Washington University for research on peptides and proteins.

Achievement

If he had to do it over again, what would Hanley do differently? "If I had it to do over again, I should . . . do what I'm doing today, which is to follow my own instincts when they ring loud and clear. What the hell, I take the final responsibility so I might as well make the final decision!"

What about his managerial role as CEO would have given his parents the greatest pride? His answer emphasized his mentoring activities and his recognition by important world figures: "I think my father would take some comfort in my interest in skills, in dedication to developing young [managers]—the human relations part of my work, which is a genuine joy to me. My mother, being much more political than my father, would take considerable pride in her little boy—only child—being a noise on the national scene, even if not much of a voice. She would think that was pretty good, that a guy from Parkersburg [West Virginia] could be dealing constructively with the president of Brazil on some programs that are very important for Brazil and Monsanto. . . . She'd think that's pretty good stuff."

Notwithstanding Jack Hanley's frequent references to managing by reducing uncertainty to an irreducible minimum, obviously he leaned heavily on his own depth. He combines a wide store of knowledge and intellect with experience. He is therefore able to reach down into himself and, as it were, pull up a perspective or insight. And he has the optimism and the courage to be affirmative.

Hanley infused Monsanto with his own vigor and standards. He gave it new purpose and direction, and built into it a system for regenerating managerial personnel. He recognized research frontiers and bet big dollars on what they would yield for Monsanto. Like the elephant pictured in his office, he charged into his task. Sometimes that managerial style was neither smooth nor congenial. But no one could say any longer that Monsanto was moribund, nor that Monsanto's renewed vitality was tied solely to Jack Hanley. He gave the Monsanto management confidence in themselves and a future based on solid, diversified research.

Coda

In early January, 1983, Hanley reduced the number of operating companies from five to four. Additionally, he planned to skew capital spending toward research facilities. He was continuing to move from commodity chemicals toward the manufacture of proprietary, or patented, products.

Disaster threatened again. All herbicides must be registered with the Environmental Protection Agency (EPA) before they can be marketed. The EPA inadvertently disclosed the formula of Roundup in response to a Freedom of Information request by a Washington lawyer. That threatened to undermine Monsanto's hold on the herbicide market, which had accounted for $450 million in sales and nearly 40 percent of its profits in 1981. The EPA settled a Monsanto suit by agreeing that any applications it received to register similar products would be reviewed by a scientific advisory panel to determine if they had exploited Monsanto's patent. But that won't keep foreign competitors who learn from the leak from making an imitation.

Hanley became involved with another threat, as a project for his retirement years. A member of his family became chemically addicted and was saved by the program of the Hazelden Foundation in Minneapolis. Jack, Mary, and their three children undertook to sponsor a Hazelden Clinic in Palm Beach. "And there will be others," Jack promised.

In July, 1983, John W. Hanley, now sixty-one, announced his retirement. He was succeeded by Richard J. Mahoney as president and CEO, and Louis Fernandez as chairman. Hanley remained as chairman of the executive committee until his formal retirement in March, 1984. He said he had decided to step down because years of succession planning had been completed and his successors were clearly ready to assume increased responsibility.

Thomas J. Watson, Jr.

INTERNATIONAL BUSINESS MACHINES CORPORATION

IN 1956, the year Thomas J. Watson, Jr., became CEO, brokerage houses regarded IBM's stock as one of their selected issues. Said the confidential internal advisory memo of one, "Stock sells high in relation to earnings but earnings are in large part recurring, because derived from rentals. Considering that the company's machines are used by a wide cross-section of industry, and considering that it would in many cases increase a company's costs to cut back on the use of IBM machines, the stock bears strong attraction for long-term resistance to decline. Added to this is a powerful growth potential that derives from the company's demonstrated ability to create new markets through research . . . backlog of orders is at the highest level in the company's history."

It could easily be said of IBM that it became so successful because its long-time and dominant CEO was the founder's son. True, Tom Watson, Jr., did have certain advantages. But not as many as it might seem. Being the boss's son is great if your father owns the local department store, but it can't help you when running the business calls for imaginative plunges into frontier technology based on decisions that often have no precedents.

Though Watson, Jr., was without technical knowledge, he did not merely preside over IBM; he gave it decisive, creative leadership. That leadership was a product of meticulous attention to personal and organizational details, high standards, and the expectation that his followers would commit themselves to the organization. His demands were sometimes fractious, sometimes embarrassing, but always in the interest of the highest possible quality and service. Reputation was the first name and urgency was the middle name of his competitive game. Not all could meet those competitive demands. Even he himself had a coronary as a result of the pressure he put on himself. Yet the result was one of the world's most profitable and respected companies.

In 1979, we asked Watson: "Did you have something in mind that you thought you'd like to be able to achieve when you got to be CEO of IBM?" "I wish I could tell you that I did," he replied.

"What I really wanted to do, and I was always conscious of this, was to prove that I was a worthy and able son, and this was far above any other ambition that I had. . . . I told my wife that I thought maybe in order to prove my point I'd gotten in a little over my head. Maybe there were easier ways to prove that point. But that's what I was aiming at.

"I wish I could tell you that I saw the great future of the computer business, that I marched in to take advantage of that. One of the first things I did in 1946 was to go see Presper Eckert and John Mauchly, who had produced the ENIAC . . . at the University of Pennsylvania, for the Aberdeen Proving Ground. And I saw a large room . . . filled with vacuum tubes and shook my head, and Eckert told me how fast it was working, and I came home. It didn't move me at all. Probably like some of the people that saw the Wright Brothers' airplane."

Observers quote him as saying, "The company is in the family unconscious."[1] Some claim Watson, Sr., began grooming his first-born for succession from birth. In childhood, young Tom visited company factories, took company tours, and attended sales conventions with his father. Probably he was closer to his mother, Jeanette; often she was a refuge to her children.

Poor grades, erratic attendance, and a playboy life style that included nightclubbing as well as yachting, skiing, and other sports did not prevent Tom, Jr., from graduating from Brown University in 1937 at twenty-three. Whatever pain these breaches of his father's Calvinist ethic caused, all seemed forgiven when, shortly before graduating, young Tom asked, tongue-in-cheek, "How do you go about getting a job at IBM?" His armor pierced, the elated elder Watson is reported to have declared an alliance that mitigated his apparent loneliness: "The one thing that I am looking forward to now with so much pleasure is having you to counsel with and help me plan my future programs. I suddenly realized that now I have somebody in my life upon whom I can look with confidence."[2]

Nevertheless, Tom Watson, Jr., continued to fly his own course. Over his father's objections, he bought a small Fairchild airplane and continued his nightclub circuit, though, by his own admission, his interest in this after-hours activity reached its peak in 1939. He was elected president of his class at IBM's sales training school in Endicott, New York. His first sales stint was in Manhattan's financial district, easy pickings for IBM's products. Tom's associates, wishing to please his father, went out of their way to assure the junior Watson's success. Not surprisingly, young Watson qualified for the Hundred Percent Club (salesmen who met their quotas) in his first two years, making his monthly sales quotas in a breeze.

That "achievement" was not success, Tom recalls: "It was a very unpleasant time for me. My father was forty years older than I. He didn't see through the subterfuge of what was happening with my sales records, and I just thought it was hell on wheels. I was so glad to get out of there and get in the Air Corps. Boy, that was the biggest relief that ever hit me." Watson ferried airplanes across the Atlantic and flew generals and other dignitaries to Europe, including Moscow when it was under siege.

Crystalizing Identification

Watson attributes the final impetus for his decision to return to IBM after the war and pursue the top spot to a discussion he had near the end of World War II.

"It all went back to the odd automobile ride from the Pentagon to a small apartment my wife, Olive, and I occupied in the Park Fairfax during the war. I was driving a retired general, Major General Follett Bradley, home. . . . I had worked with him most intimately, and gone with him to the Soviet Union and flown him all around. He had had a heart attack and retired. Olive and I were simply having him for dinner. On the road, and I can even remember the point on the road, he said, 'Tom, what are you going to do when the war ends?' And I said, 'Oh, I think I'll try to be a pilot on an airline for a while and then get into the administrative side.' And he said, 'That's funny, I thought you'd go back and run the IBM Company.' And I said, 'General, my father doesn't own that company. He doesn't even own 5 percent of it.' And he said, "Oh, it wasn't for that reason. I just thought you'd go back and run it.' So I said, 'Well, do you think I could run it?' And he said, 'Of course.' So I said to Olive that night, 'Gee whiz, you know, General Bradley thinks I could run the IBM Company.' . . . Having made that decision to go there, I never had anything in my mind but to aim for the top seat. . . . From the word 'go' I wanted to be chief.

"It was odd, because as a youngster I don't think my father ever asked me to do anything much. But, by inference, I knew a lot of things that he wanted me to do. And at a very young age I thought that he wanted me to run the IBM Company. And I remember going home to my mother, and I couldn't have been over thirteen or fourteen, from school crying, and saying, 'I just can't do it, I just can't do it.' So, without his having ever mentioned it, it was a great pressure on me. I've always kind of wondered why I was so absolutely lousy in school. I was terrible in school and college. I suppose today a psychiatrist might say, 'Well, that was an unconscious effort to avoid doing what you didn't want to do.' "

In January, 1946, Tom Watson returned to IBM, a father since 1944, his full head of hair prematurely graying and, according to observers, presenting an athletic six-foot-two-inch frame and possessed of striking good looks. Watson was apprenticed to forty-three-year-old Charles Kirk. Eighteen months later, Kirk died of a heart attack. Tom inherited the title of vice-president. Kirk had been the senior Watson's potential successor. Tom was now just below his father.

Tom Watson's interest in electronic devices had come from contact with them during the war. In 1946, he accompanied his father into the recesses of the IBM building marked "Patent Development."

"I was wandering around the building with my father. He used to sort of go into the corners at 590 Madison in New York City, and we came upon a keypunch, and the keypunch was hooked to a box with black covers. I said, 'What's this?' and the man said, 'Well, we're using radio tubes to add, subtract, and multiply. And it does it very fast.' He said, 'It takes one-tenth of the card cycle to do this, and nine-tenths of the card cycle is waiting for the mechanical operation of the keypunch to punch the answer, to go to the next card.' They were doing a payroll—social security deductions, retirement, medical deductions, and so forth, and coming out to a net pay. That impressed me as though somebody had hit me on the head with a hammer, because it was a relatively simple device. And I said, 'Dad, let's put that thing on the market, and let's call it the first electronic multiplier.' I don't think people were using the word computer in those days. And he said, 'Why not?' and within a year we announced it. And, you know, we thought we might sell a couple or three to justify the ad, because we took full-page ads in the *New York Times*. But we sold . . . twenty or thirty, and everybody who bought them said, 'Well, if you could just make it do the following we would order a lot more.' And we did make it do the following rather rapidly, and then we sold literally hundreds."

It ultimately became IBM's first major electronic product, the 604 calculator. Though the young Watson hadn't yet seen "the great future of the computer business," he already had the ability to see the marketing possibilities for a new invention.

The Handwriting on the Wall

But the punchcard was doomed. Metropolitan Life had three floors filled with punchcards and couldn't afford to pay that kind of rent to store information that could be put on tapes. IBM had the whole addressing and promoting job of Time, Inc., but it required three punchcards for every name. Roy Larsen, Time's president, complained, "It's too slow. It isn't going to work, and I hear about this linear processing."

Tom formed a task force of the brightest salesmen to study the feasibility of tape machines. Like those who see a glass half empty rather than half full, they saw only the sluggish forward movement of reels of tape, not the whirl that could retrieve a tape segment in an instant. They turned thumbs down. He convened the best minds in the business in a running seminar over a three-month period in 1948/1949. They concluded nothing could be done, that IBM's punchcards were a better approach.

Coming into His Own

Tom, Jr., disagreed with his father on the commercial viability of computers and on the process through which new products find acceptance in the market place. When it came to developing new products, Watson, Sr., had a reactive approach: make products to meet the commercial customer's immediate and expressed needs. The salesmen then had the limited task of convincing the customer of the product's utility. The senior Watson's 1948 answer to the all-electronic ENIAC was the Selective Sequence Controlled Electronic Calculator (SSCEC), a faster electromechanical machine, the last of its kind.

Still, he allowed his son's experimental work on the Tape Processing Machine to proceed at the IBM Poughkeepsie, New York, laboratory before the Korean War. That was an electronic calculator to which programming and a memory unit were added. As it turned out, the Tape Processing Machine was the prototype for a line of computers. Tom had a calculator built using only electronics, just to show that it could be done. The 604 multiplier was a spectacular success that gave notice electronics were coming and that he, for one, was dedicated to them. Said an observer, "The thing just sat there and hummed and did A times B at several hundred per minute, instead of kerchunk, kerchunk, kerchunk, kerchunk—multiplying it out on punchcards."

Young Watson was not only impressed with the technology of electronic computers but also saw a major business market for them once businessmen were familiar with the technology. The father-son hassle continued. Watson, Sr., saw the market, at most, as being limited to scientists in large laboratories where the machines would have to meet the need for rapid, complex calculating based on the input of a few long numbers. As Reg Jones would do later, despite his lack of technological expertise, Tom, Jr., took an aggressive stance toward the marketplace, a style that would characterize his tenure. By 1949, Tom could envision automated factories and computers in banks and offices. He pushed his father into supporting the ongoing development of scientific computers for use in laboratories and factories.

The Turning Point

Developing computers was one thing, deciding to produce them was another. The prod to do so came from two quarters—the outbreak of the Korean War and a major competitive challenge.

Shortly after the outbreak of the Korean War on June 25, 1950, Watson, Sr., sent a telegram to President Harry S. Truman, volunteering IBM's resources in the service of the war effort. Tours of defense plants and government agencies, including the Pentagon, led to the production of a scientific computer twenty-five times faster than the SSCEC and only a quarter of its size, and then to the Defense Calculator 701.[3] The 701 was priced to rent for $10,000 a month. There were eighteen orders from government agencies, defense suppliers, and aircraft companies. To IBM's chagrin, the cost to customers worked out to $20,000 a month. No one canceled.

That was how IBM got into electronics. It was not, as Tom, Jr., had said, through any great foresight. Nor was it because of his technical proficiency. "It was all highly confusing," he reported, "because mainly I was an airplane pilot."

Meanwhile, Remington Rand had installed several of its machines commercially before IBM had any, including Rand's first computer, Univac I, which was sold to the Bureau of the Census on June 14, 1951. Tom's response was to meet every Monday morning in his office with his special management task force for moving IBM into electronics, until things were going in the direction he thought they should be. He had a consistent ability to keep attention focused intensely on a problem, and the marketing success of the 701 enabled him to convince his father to approve a total push. Driven by Tom, Jr., into developing a technical base, IBM overtook Remington Rand within about twenty-four months. IBM delivered its first two 701 computers to Douglas Aircraft Company in 1953.

The Task Force

Watson's thrust into commercial computers, including the 702, 704, and 705 models, was spearheaded by a special management task force. Overall responsibility for this foray fell to Louis "Red" LaMotte, a vice-president with a superlative sales record and thirty years of service. Red, almost like a father to Tom, was a powerful influence. He became head of the new Electronic Data Machine Division.

T. Vincent Learson, sales manager of the Electric Accounting Machine Division and later to be CEO, directed the sales attack and was the troubleshooter. Why Learson? Almost everyone in the company knew that if you needed somebody to get something done quickly, Vin Learson was the person to do it. Learson was so confident that he would solve the commercial computer problem in a year or so that he never moved from Bronxville, New York, to Poughkeepsie. It's still an IBM practice to take the best sales manager, district sales manager, or regional manager for some tough job that he or she may not know anything about.

Former salesman Albert Williams, a CPA and IBM's controller and a vice-president, was charged with developing leasing arrangements and a price structure. According to insiders, without Al Williams, the transition between the electrical accounting equipment and the computer would have been almost impossible. Observers say he was the senior Watson's surrogate son while Tom and the younger Dick were away in school and the military, and that he not only took part in orienting young Tom but also mediated father and son arguments. As viewed by colleagues, Tom brought out the best in Al. Their relationship was extremely close.

Tom and Al Williams were a management team. For a number of years just the two of them ran the business. They were quite different but complementary. Al was steady and methodical. He thought things through, slowed Tom down, got the detail work done. (The importance of a number-two person to manage the detail will be seen again in the next chapter.) Tom was creative, driving, and responsive, and he dragged Al forward. Predictably, they scrapped. Both Al and Red LaMotte could tell Tom he was wrong and Tom could hear them.

Response Time

While the 701 held off IBM's competitors, thanks to the company's "ground floor" placements of earlier products and its aggressive sales force, orders were being taken for the still nonexistent 702s in 1954. The first of fourteen placements was made in the spring of 1955. Edgar Monsanto Queeny, son of the founder and chairman of the Monsanto board and a longtime friend of the Watsons, achieved the goal of having Monsanto be the first corporation in the world to install IBM's new data processing technology.

The explosive marketplace growth and technological change in the data processing industry generated sharply overlapping phases—research and development, announcement, and delivery—in the birth of new products. Even as the 702 was nearing completion, a task force of salesmen and engineers—favorite management tool of Tom, Jr.—concluded its review with a judgment that the 702 was clearly inferior to the Univac, despite the 702's use of tape processing. Tom, Jr. ordered that another machine be designed and produced immediately.[4] IBM's response time was awesome. Even before the first 702 was shipped to Monsanto, Tom, Jr. announced that orders for two new models would be accepted; the 704 would replace the specialized 701 scientific computer, and the 705 would supersede the newly produced 702.[5]

"Regardless of any other people, any engineering studies, or whatever success-motivating factors were involved, Tom was the guy that caused that response time to happen," noted an intimate. "And that was simply by just turning the organization upside-down and saying, 'Look, we *are* going to do it, and we're going to announce, in this case, the 702 machine.' We knew we could do it and we did it. The motivation was fantastic . . . twenty-four hours a day, seven days a week . . . a whole organization that were jolly well going to make it happen because their careers were riding on it."

By this time, Tom Watson, Jr., had come into his own. In 1952, he was made president. From 1952 to 1956, Tom, Jr., was making most of the decisions. He had enough good people around him so that when it came to crossing the technological bridge from the electromechanical into the electronic world, his vision was guided and supported by a strong staff and solid technical and marketing-systems personnel. They were sufficient to point the direction IBM should go.

The numbers told the story of Tom's winning ways. From 1948 through 1950, IBM's long-term debt had been a flat $85 million, compared to gross revenues of $162, $183.5, and $214.9 million, respectively. Long-term debt jumped to $135 million in 1951, $175 million in 1952, $215 million in 1953, and $330 million in 1956. By then IBM's gross revenues had skyrocketed sixfold from $120 million a decade earlier to $734.3 million. In the same decade its net income had more than tripled, and its long-term debt soared elevenfold.[6] That capital infusion was needed to nourish ongoing production of products and to fuel an ambitious expansion into overseas markets. Watson, Sr., was reluctant to dilute the stock. Instead he continued to borrow from the Prudential Insurance Company. At one time IBM owed half a billion dollars to Prudential. Just before Watson, Sr., died, IBM sold a limited amount of stock.

On January 21, 1952, the U.S. Department of Justice instituted an antitrust suit against IBM, alleging that it was a monopoly. Four years later IBM agreed to a consent decree that did not admit wrongdoing but led the company to change parts of its operations. "Father was very resentful of the case," Tom reported. "I was trying to settle it." An executive reports that while Tom, Jr., was in court to sign the decree he received this note from his father:

> 100%
> Confidence
> Appreciation
> Admiration
> Love
> Dad

Tom Watson had proved that he "was a worthy and able son." In May, 1956, Watson, Sr., formally gave the helm to Tom and the World Trade subsidiary to the younger Dick. The founder had just celebrated his eighty-second birthday. He died of a coronary on June 19.

Tom Watson's ambivalence about his father surfaced often. "My father and I had terrible fights. He seemed like a blanket that covered everything. I wanted to best him but also to make him proud of me.

I really enjoyed the ten years with him. I used to tell Olive I wouldn't
go back another day. He'd call me in the middle of the night, and
Olive would pass me notes to keep my temper. The old gentleman
must have known before that he would die soon, and he made me
chief executive in 1956. That was better than having it fall to me after
his death."

Reorganization

The fundamental task that faced Tom Watson when he assumed
leadership of the company was to maintain balanced growth. The limits
had to do with how fast the company could finance itself, how fast it
could find engineers to put in its laboratories, how fast it had to go to
stay abreast of competition. A growth business can die from growing too
fast or it can be timid and let somebody else take the advantages. There
were many able competitors. Tom knew there would be considerable
risk and that he would have to take it. He could not be passive, nor could
his managers. Out of that urgency came his desire to develop managers
and test them. In the years before taking the helm, Tom, Jr., was talent
scouting. His mobility as a flyer got him out of the Ivy League North-
eastern corridor. For example, he would fly to the West Coast where
a group of IBMers were known as a renegade outfit. He admired the
way they were running the business so he started a managerial movement from west to east. Tom was not interested in where a manager
had gone to school or what his family did; nor was regionalism an issue.
For example, only two years after joining the company, Dean R. McKay
and his wife had dinner with Tom, Jr., in Butte, Montana. Watson asked
him to go to New York. McKay became a senior vice-president.

Tom had a variety of devices for soliciting ideas, including the standard IBM mechanism for spotting comers. A senior IBM official who is
to attend an official function for a branch will first go to the branch office
and sit around with ten star salesmen for a couple of hours. The ten
salesmen will have been picked by the local manager. The senior person will note three or four who stand out and either recommend that
they be put on a fast track or have one of them assigned to headquarters
for further observation. George B. Beitzel, a senior vice-president, is
where he is today because Tom was impressed with him on a Philadelphia trip.

In 1956, after becoming CEO, Tom Watson launched a major reorganization. He felt that, having grown at an 18 percent rate for the previous decade, the business was too big to be managed as one business. As did Walter Wriston, he wanted to put some competition into it. He set up divisions and corporate staff, and the beginnings of what became IBM's famous contention system. The contention system concept held that the vigor of a corporate entity is enhanced by the churning and competition within, out of which come better solutions. If one manager wanted to put a system in place that made demands of another, part of the second manager's job was to review what the first proposed. The first manager could not proceed if the second manager did not concur. If they differed, both took the issue to higher authority. If a manager agreed with a plan, and it failed, he was as responsible as its progenitor. The competition extended to the laboratories. One IBM executive reported, "We would frequently use the tactic of having one problem being worked on by two or three different groups." Ian MacGregor used a similar device.

The contention practice was illustrated by the case of an executive assigned to head a service function that was in conflict with a marketing group. He tried to be a statesman, expressing his understanding of the marketers' problem and assuming some of the blame. Tom objected vehemently, "Look, you can't do that. You are commander-in-chief of the service function and you've got to represent those people flat out and not try and understand the other guy's problems, because that's a marketing problem, not a service problem. . . . If you come in here and diminish the vigor of your argument because you're trying to understand the other guy's problem, that's not going to help the business at all. What you've got to do is pound the table and say, 'Here's what the business has to do to solve the problem from my functional standpoint.' . . . Don't try and help them out with their problems. I'll deal with that."

As for the quality of the product, after being burned a few times by products that didn't live up to what his managers promised (an experience that paralleled Jack Hanley's frustration), Tom brought product-testing into his office. He didn't delegate that. The rule was, "Don't put out a product unless it's ready to go." Tom put the best people he could find—future division presidents among others—in the product-testing assignment. Their careers would rise or fall on how well they told him a product would perform. That visibility indicated his seriousness and lifted the status of product-testing in the business. It had a material effect on giving the salesmen and customers confidence that, when a machine was announced and shipped, it was *ready* to be announced and shipped.

Tom was concerned with detailed and comprehensive staff work. Someone once remarked that he had never seen a staff like IBM's, short of the German army. In IBM, people are not promoted along a single track, line (which does the manufacturing and selling) or staff (which handles the control and support functions). Rather, the best marketer, manufacturing person, or engineer, might be on the staff at any given time. That makes for strong staff and minimizes doctrinaire line-staff conflicts. (Line functions often complain about staff ignorance of their work and of staff hindrance.) It also means that the staff members have had line experience, and so are in a better position to assume responsibility for their work. When something goes wrong—for example, if a product does not meet its forecast—it is expected that both the staff person and the division will admit responsibility. Two people should be holding up their hands.

The reorganization facilitated Tom's practice of constantly reshuffling the business, moving people around and testing them in new spots, in order to not allow anybody to "get fat, dumb, and happy." That mobility stimulated the growth of general managers. (It was a technique followed also in GE and Monsanto.) Each had to become capable in more than one discipline if he or she were to move up. Nobody could have a given managerial job for the rest of his or her life because IBM didn't have jobs like that. But all the managers in IBM knew they had a job, unless they stole from the company or violated its ethical standards. Tom had a strong conviction that IBM ought to promote from within. It should let managers go as far as their abilities would carry them, and support them liberally with education, motivation, and compensation. The only specialists he hired were lawyers and outstanding scientists.

The Primacy of Research

"When I came in here, we had only a few engineers with advanced degrees in the whole business," Watson said. "The rest of them were clever, the people who could think things up, and either commit them to metal and screws, or have them committed to metal and screws. . . . I knew that to compete in electronics, you couldn't do it that way. . . . Although I was not a technician, I suppose I put much more emphasis on that [research and development] than any other thing in my years of beginning my stewardship here." (We heard the same themes from Jones, Wriston, and Hanley.) With Wally McDowell in charge of the laboratories, the numbers of engineers with advanced degrees zoomed from near zero to 200 in two years. Those with bachelor's degrees numbered about 1,000. "The laboratories [at Poughkeepsie and Endicott] were always the places that I'd be in," Tom recalled.

"I called on colleges, I tried to get very eminent people to lead our scientific effort. I started a pure research laboratory . . . at Yorktown Heights, New York. I . . . am still needling them about why they don't have a Nobel laureate out there. (They have two Nobel laureates working there who earned them elsewhere, but every time Bell Labs runs an ad about its laureates, I clip that right out and send it to the chief scientist, and say, 'Why not us?') I started a computer research operation at M.I.T. I went on the Cal Tech board to try to draw myself closer to that scientific community. I knew Robert Oppenheimer, at the Institute for Advanced Study in Princeton, New Jersey, finally went on the board down there. I did everything I could to command the respect of scientists and get some of them to work here. I couldn't get scientists to come from the West Coast, so I went out there and bought a supermarket that had not yet been occupied. I put a very gifted inventor in that supermarket . . . and he had a way of attracting other fellows that were good. . . . They developed the disks and the magnetic materials for random access storage. We now have a complex there of 12,000 people, but it all started from this half dozen people in this chain store developing these memory devices."

Following Edgar Queeny's Monsanto example, Watson created IBM Fellows, scientists who had scored significant breakthroughs. As a result, they can do what research they want, with an impressive stipend. Contests among employees for suggestions on how to improve products or methods provided the winners with 25 percent of the money the company saved in the first year it adopted the suggestion. Some of them got as much as $75,000. Watson himself gave much of his time to these efforts.

One Down

Between November and December of 1970, nearing his fifty-seventh birthday, Tom Watson was stopped in his tracks. He explained it as a product of his intense, continuous effort. "I used to get so damned tired, and I thought of myself as indestructible. I was almost fifty-seven when I turned up with that heart attack and I couldn't believe it. I had pains in my chest—not very much. And they told me at the Greenwich hospital, 'You're having a heart attack.' Impossible. Father didn't have a heart attack. But, it was just that constant punch, punch, punch."

Image and Environment

For Tom Watson, design was a major principle of organization leadership. His interest was to make everything that the public sees—the product, the work environment, the buildings, the literature—exciting and modern. He described the awakening of that interest:

"I wish I could say that I was lying in bed one night and this great vision hit me. What hit me was a great envelope filled with stuff from the manager of the IBM company in Holland, who was very outspoken. And he said, 'Dear Tom, I have collected here the Olivetti total corporate image, and I put it against the IBM corporate image, and if you will unroll the two rolls of paper, you will see IBM brochures of their products, pictures of their products, pictures of their plants, and pictures of their news releases, and the same with Olivetti. Roll them out, and you can see the contrast.' Ours looked like directions on how to make bicarbonate of soda, and theirs were filled with color and excitement. At that point, I decided we were going to use the best architects, the best color people, the best contour designers we could find. We were going to try to fill our places with modern art."

During IBM's heyday of growth, Tom Watson selected the locations of facilities with an eye to attracting talent by offering the amenities of life style. He had the ability to put himself in the position of prospective employees and to decide whether something would appeal to them. He put a facility in Rochester, Minnesota, the location of the Mayo Clinic, and another in Boulder, Colorado, the site of the University of Colorado. There are others in Lexington, Kentucky, a horse-breeding area, Boca Raton, Florida, and Burlington, Vermont. All have universities nearby and pleasant surroundings. There is a research facility in Switzerland because Europeans didn't want to come to the United States. IBM used to provide recreational facilities at all of its plants, though the growth of the organization slowed those efforts.

Tom worked closely with Eliot Noyes, a great among architects and industrial designers, creating a corporate design program, which dealt with everything from product design to buildings, from interiors to the image of the company. Tom won an award from Tiffany for excellence in design.

The Penalty Box

One of Tom Watson's managerial techniques was what insiders called "the penalty box." The penalty box was directly or indirectly a career setback. It removed the penalized manager from the position he had achieved and from the direct competitive path. The penalty box might be a lateral assignment. It could even sound like a promotion: "So-and-so is returning to the Pacific Coast as regional manager after serving as Mr. Watson's assistant as the head of whatchamacallits for the last three years." Some believed that Learson's assignment to the commercial computer task force was a "penalty box" assignment, the result of a quarrel with Tom. Many close to Tom suffered one such stumble, and were put in the penalty box for some length of time. Those who saw that they were never going to get out of the penalty box or couldn't succeed in IBM left the business. Many became prominent in other companies.

Tom was straight with people. He articulated the rules clearly. He would tell people what went wrong and why they were being transferred or demoted. He would assure the person that transfer or demotion didn't mean he was out of things forever, only that he, Tom, had to send a signal throughout the company that the subordinate's action wasn't right. Even Tom's brother Dick, who headed the development and manufacturing side of the data processing business in 1965 and 1966, was taken out of his job. That division was overcommitted and missing shipments.

The penalty box was tougher for people at the top because Tom had less patience with them than with those lower in the hierarchy. Sometimes Tom jumped to incorrect conclusions because of his tendency to see people in black and white terms. He might have a totally inaccurate picture in mind of some situation, but no one could persuade him differently about the person involved. Tom's rigid point of view might play a role in that person's progress in the company.

Tom himself fired only three people in his career, all for breaches of integrity. Firing people required a special posture, Tom noted: "After I went through several of them, I got very arbitrary because I found that if you were really involved in the melee of the thing you could always find more reason to keep the man than to let him go. And that if you stood at a distance and asked, 'Was he honest or dishonest?' and forgot how competent he was, how important he was, and everything else, and just said, 'No, that's the way it's going to be,' then you could maintain a high moral tone. And I only did it a few times, but I was always told that I was going to wreck whatever I was doing. And wherever I did it, I always prospered."

When it came to mistakes, Tom Watson was at one with his father. "There is a book written about my dad called *The Lengthening Shadow*. [7] The writers say something in there quite profound. They say that Tom Watson was not unlike any other boy growing up in the last part of the nineteenth century except in one way: he made every mistake in the book but he never made the same mistake twice. And I always wanted to avoid making the same mistake twice. It didn't make any difference to me what mistakes we made, but it seemed to me highly unproductive to make the same mistake a second time. So I was always punching on that." Some of that attitude became ingrained in company practice. A manager was allowed to make a mistake, but if there were a second or third or fourth mistake of the same kind, the manager was demoted and his or her pay cut 10 percent. That was so the manager *knew* he or she was demoted. If the manager made a comeback, the former pay was restored, sometimes even with a raise, so that financially the manager might not be hurt over the long run. But the point had been made. An insider claims that there is not an executive at the top of the business today who hasn't been through those ups and downs.

Executive Assistants

Tom made use of executive assistants both for training and to size them up. If it appeared that one of his administrative assistants was not strong enough, his colleagues would get him or her back into the field organization quickly. The assistants were stars, which was why they were picked, so they were still highly competent. Besides, no one was ever clobbered if he had been through the chairman's office. Furthermore, higher management was not going to have Tom set up as a giant ogre who chewed people up.

Watson's administrative assistants were apprentices-in-leadership, high-potential managers auditioning for the fast track, not unlike a general's aide. The job varied from the exciting to the mundane. One minute an assistant would be talking to a person high in government and the next worrying about placecards for a luncheon. Tom gave each a two-page memorandum titled "Completed Staff Work," which had been circulated in the Pentagon during World War II and Watson had found particularly helpful. "Completed Staff Work," the memorandum said, "is the study of a problem, and presentation of a solution by a staff officer in such form that all that remains to be done on the part of the head of the staff division, or commander, is to indicate his approval or disapproval of the completed action."

Tom taught his assistants. He had a penchant for lecturing. "I think he's a very good teacher," was the appraisal of one former assistant. "Drill and exercise is part of learning. And some of this drill and exercise is hard for people to accept once they think they're intellectually across the barrier. . . . Watson was like that as a teacher. Drill and exercise. . . . And it was very effective. . . . The things that he wanted to perpetuate were things that he felt he learned from his dad. He thought of his dad as a teacher, he thought of himself as a teacher. And he insisted that everybody has a role as a teacher."

Assistants would work up responses to letters that came into the chairman's office and attach to the letter a brief explanatory memo on a three-inch-by-five-inch piece of paper. One of the tasks in being Tom's assistant was to become precise and crisp in communicating with him via the three-by-five route. If the messages didn't get through, or the letters weren't signed, or if larger issues were raised, the assistant found himself explaining the issue directly to Tom in the back seat of a limousine en route from the Armonk headquarters to New York City, to a dinner or play or speech. Tom conducted much of the day-to-day business of his office while traveling from one meeting to another. For those prone to car sickness, this was a particularly difficult ordeal. It was tough to be under the scrutiny and testing of the chairman, trying to convince him of some questionable logic, while traveling in the back of a limousine or flying in a corporate airplane.

Assistants quickly learned that they had to draft letters for him in "Watsonese." That meant first-person pronouns were rare. For example, he would never begin a paragraph with, "I want to thank you for your letter." If he were declining an invitation, he never would say why or use an excuse because that would imply that "you're not as important as a lot of other things." There was no self-importance in a Watson letter. His style is ingrained among many IBM managers. As was the case with Jones and MacGregor, ego trips were not acceptable to him, and he was not above telling people that. If there were to be an ego trip, it would be his.

If an assistant hadn't done his homework on a project, Tom would say, "Well, look, I understand this is based largely on your feelings, is that right?" The assistant, of course, said, "Yeah." So Tom would say, "Well this is a very important problem, isn't it?" The other would agree, "Yes, it sure is." Tom would say, "If we're going to run this business on viscera, it's going to be my viscera."

To miss something or forget it resulted in mortified embarrassment. One executive, a former administrative assistant, recalled "a recurring fantasy in which I would go in and put this gag on him and make him sit there, and before he could ask me something I didn't know I would tell him everything that I knew. Because I remember many occasions where Watson asked me some silly things (I thought it was silly) or something which I didn't know. At that point he would say, 'Well, obviously if you don't know that you don't know anything about this whole affair.' "

Seating arrangements for dinners or receptions were most troublesome for administrative assistants. Tom was exacting about seating the right person in the right place. He related that penchant to his father's sense of doing things properly and sensitively when you're the host. A local manager would spend weeks or months working on a dinner. There would be no empty chairs at the head table, and the microphone would work.

Travel arrangements had to be efficient and well organized and at the same time not give the impression at the other end that there were many special requirements. On his trips into the field he didn't want to be ferried in limousines, followed by entourages. He needed a single room, no special arrangements, no fruit in the room, no booze, no special menus, no special dinners. Finding the balance between avoiding ostentation and being well organized while working with Tom was difficult.

Feeling the Pulse

Like Jones, Wriston, and MacGregor, Watson felt the pulse of IBM through informal channels. Throughout the system, and many levels down, there were people he could call by first name. He always had sources of information other than the bureaucracy. And he always managed those relationships so that no one was promoted or demoted unfairly.

Another executive's perspective: "Tom carried a Think book [a small pocket book with perforated sheets] around. He thinks all the time and he jots things down [as did Hanley]. He used to keep a recorder next to his bed. He'd wake up in the middle of the night and record his thoughts. Or if he was away on a trip, visiting plants or what have you, he'd come back and tear these sheets out of this little book."

Of Anger and Impulse

Although he could evoke almost explosive tension on the sixteenth floor of 590 Madison Avenue, Tom didn't use profanity or dirty language in public. (He loved to tell dirty stories, but only to a few people, and he would never use dirty language.) Sometimes he swore, but not *at* anybody. Tom has an expressive mouth. When he got visibly angry his upper lip and his chin started to tremble. He would get red in the face and holler at an errant subordinate. Then he almost invariably found some way to smooth over the explosion.

Tom liked to use a card dealer's gesture, rhythmically rubbing thumb and index finger. His point was that your fingers have to be very sensitive when you're dealing cards so you can understand the cards, and it was the same with people. He would go to great lengths to avoid confrontations with those who he felt would be offended or defenseless, a characteristic of each of our CEOs. On the other hand, with his close associates with whom he felt comfortable saying almost anything that was on his mind, he had no compunction about attacking. In many respects, his demands on and criticism of others were similar to those his father had inflicted on him.

Tom looked for people with backbone, people who would be pushed so far and no farther, people who had integrity and would give him straight answers. Subordinates differ on whether he tested for integrity or for the boundary of what the subordinate would take. Some say he saw it instinctively. All say he respected it. One associate reported: "I heard one guy say, 'Listen, Watson, you've got all the ammunition, but one thing I do have is my dignity and I'm not going to listen to any more of that.' And turn around and walk out. The next day Tom would call and apologize to him, but in the meantime it was really awful." How did one maintain one's self-esteem in the face of Watson's penchant for finding the one hole in a write-up when there was no opportunity to balance his criticism against one's accomplishments? "Well, don't misunderstand me. You didn't lose them all. Very often he'd say, 'Terrific job!' He was not without his compliments. Nor was he without the desire to be balanced about it. Sometimes to the point of being unbalanced in the other way, of overdoing it, saying, 'You did such a great job, and I know I made a fool of myself by being too aggressive and impatient with you and all that sort of thing, and so take your wife and go out to dinner.' . . . He has done so many things for *all* of us that worked for him. He had a sense of humor about it. So, you don't lose your self-respect."

Despite the fact that Tom could react emotionally and sometimes very harshly with assistants, he realized the position they were in. One recalled:

"I remember working with him very late one night in Armonk [IBM headquarters]. . . . It was a very heated discussion. As we left the building late together, he said, 'I'm sorry that I kept you away from home this long.' I made a comment that it was my wife's birthday. By the time I got home . . . Tom had arranged to have flowers delivered to our house with an apology to her for keeping me away that night. He was always interested in the people who worked in his office, their families, and what their children were doing and their home life. [Another characteristic shared by all of the CEOs in this book.] He would from time to time invite people from his office, secretaries, assistants, and his office manager, to spend time skiing in Aspen or go sailing, or to share a dinner. He could be very angry and unforgiving one minute and then immediately turn around with an expression of gratitude."

"Being so good about apologizing, now a good guy, a white hat, and personally picking the victim off the floor, that's how he got so many worshippers," said a colleague:

"For him to stroll down to the fourteenth floor and walk into some guy's office and lean against the door and say, 'How are you doing, Charlie?' and Charlie would say, 'F-f-fine, sir,' and he'd say, 'Gee, that was quite an argument yesterday, wasn't it?' And Charlie would say, 'Yes, sir, it was.' And, you know, the guy's life is flashing before his eyes, and Tom would just lean against the door and say, 'You know, I think it's a hell of a good program. I got a little carried away with that one part of it that I didn't agree with, but on balance, it's a good program. And by the way, everybody tells me you're doing a super job. See you later.' In fifteen seconds the guy's on cloud nine. He calls his wife, says, 'Jesus, I'm born again.' Very dramatic. And Tom knows it. He has a fine, intuitive sense of what he's done with great personal charm."

Before the contemporary structured compensation systems, if an employee did something dramatic, he or she might get a $10,000 raise retroactive to eighteen months before. Tom would give such raises to secretaries of whom he might have been extra critical.

The aura of power, together with a temper and an instinctive management style, tended to create a high level of anxiety. People, therefore, were apt to jump faster, to be more responsive to directions, and to argue or deliberate about them less. Such a relationship is not comfortable, yet a reasonable level of anxiety keeps people on their toes. They are more likely to anticipate problems, to be more responsive to ideas. They more readily push themselves to the limit of their capacities. The organization seemingly gets the best out of them, unless the tension precipitates physiological symptoms or emotional breakdown. If the managerial process is too democratic, the tension may be too low, or conversely, may be high because of lack of structure and direction. If it is too authoritarian and driven, people burn out. Sometimes the chemistry between Tom and some others resulted in too much tension. An executive observed, "It's worrisome to see a sixty-year-old vice-president literally running down the hall because the chairman is calling. It's undignified. He's too old to run down the hall."

Tom patched up bruised relationships with those he respected, but others attended to the casualties. If an executive was unequivocally a dud, it probably would not be Tom who would say, "Maybe we ought to think about another assignment for you." IBM had grown so fast that many managers had been promoted to jobs beyond their abilities. Many had moved too fast from one job to another without ever proving themselves. Those who rose too high for their capabilities usually sifted their way back down in what the computer people call a graceful degradation mode.

Developing Managers

How fast can you develop management? No one knows. Setting ambitious objectives is one way to test the limits. Tom could have done it at a more leisurely pace. But if he went about it intensely, he would attract people who were willing to endure the strain and tolerate the unsettled nature of rapid growth. People knew that if they reached their limit or overreached it, they weren't going to be dealt with too harshly. As at GE, they would have a chance to go back to where they had been successful. When someone failed, the people who put them there also would bear some responsibility.

People accepted ambitious targets and expected to be measured against them. The IBM culture is highly success-oriented. There is a sense of trying to beat your best. Though there is much rivalry at IBM, there is also much peer support. People can discuss the reasonableness of their plans before they commit to them. They can compete with each other and still compete with themselves in the sense of maturing. And they can help the business advance by exchanging information with the people they are competing against. As a matter of fact, that practice has helped successful competitors in IBM, people who have moved ahead,

to be balanced and cooperative with their peers. Tom didn't tolerate
a lot of backbiting or game playing. He had a good enough smell for that
kind of behavior that most of the managers at IBM would know it would
not get them very far.

At first IBM had only factory schools. Watson, Sr., wanted to upgrade women during World War II, so he had night schools in Endicott. Then came the widely known customer schools. These are now
only the tip of an educational iceberg at IBM, noted for its mammoth
human resource development program. Every new first-line manager
at IBM is given a week's training in Armonk in basic management
responsibilities. Every first-line manager and new employees are told
about IBM's famous open-door policy. The middle management and
upper management schools were developed following the model set
by GE.

The Guggenheim estate at Sands Point, New York, was purchased as
a site to prepare young candidates for later top management. When
Tom discovered nothing was being taught about IBM, Tom Clemmons,
who was in charge of the program, argued that he just wanted to
educate them to be good managers. "To hell with that. We're going to
educate them in IBM management. That's the idea of the individual,
going the last mile, spending a lot of time to make those customers
happy. You don't read that in anybody else's manual. That's what we
want to teach out here."

Starting in the mid-1950s, a comprehensive system of training IBM
managers was developed. The management principles were to be the
same in all divisions or locations. Like Reg Jones, Walt Wriston, and Jack
Hanley, Tom was always very closely involved with the management
development process. He spoke to most of the executive classes. Even
today, one or another of IBM's top executives appears at every one of
the executive schools. They personally review the curriculum and
course content. Each IBM manager is required to attend forty hours of
management development training unrelated to his or her specific job
function.

What didn't Watson do in executive development? "Only the Watson
brothers were known outside the company much because that's really
the way they wanted it," was the judgment of an insider. "Tom didn't
prepare enough senior people to assume roles of leadership as early as
he should have in their community and in Washington. Also, everyone
was so caught up with being terrific at what he was doing inside the
company that, with a few exceptions, most of IBM people didn't get that
outside experience. The best, most successful people were too busy

being successful. They didn't get that exposure then that now every businessman has to have."

"I am not a scientific manager," said Tom. "There are plenty of places for scientific managers in business, but I am not sure that the emotional, dramatic kind of manager can't hold his own with a scientific manager." A colleague supports this view: "He is a person. He's not an automaton. . . . Watson was not without his interest in the abstract part of a problem, but he damn well wanted to go see what the building looked like. What the guy who ran it looked like. How did he treat his secretary? Was he a decent guy? Did he keep his fingernails clean? That's the personal management as opposed to 'bottom line.' And he prides himself in that."

Another IBMer characterized the Watson style: "Some chief executives tend to be orchestrators; that is, their talent is in understanding in considerable detail all the pieces of the enterprise, engineering them, putting them together in a way that they run very smoothly. That master plan may or may not be explicitly stated, and it may or may not be terribly visible to the worker bees who are cogs in that wheel. Another type is really a forceful personality type. Tom, I think, is clearly in the latter category. He was always a very strong, up-front leader, never any question when he was around as to who was boss."

Meanwhile Back on the Farm . . .

Another technological storm was gathering toward the end of the 1950s, and Tom Watson sailed into its eye. The intermediate-size magnetic drum machine, the 650, had become the most popular computer in the world by the mid-1950s; 470 were in operation in 1956 and 803 in 1957.[8] But it was downhill thereafter, with the introduction by Remington Rand of the first of the Model 80s in August, 1958. That computer was the first of the second-generation computers, replacing the cumbersome, heat-generating vacuum tubes with transistors and diodes. Transistors, invented at the Bell Laboratories in 1948 and licensed to other companies shortly thereafter, came cheaply within the reach of corporations in 1956 when the government ordered Bell to provide its patents on a royalty-free basis. Compared to tubes, transistors were smaller, cooler, more dependable, more efficient, and much cheaper to manufacture. Tom Watson had a major decision before him in the face of this competitive threat.

"With Al Williams's help, I made one of the bigger engineering decisions ever made in IBM, with no engineering knowledge or background at all. Japan had just started to turn out these transistor radios in great quantity, and we were putting our computers together with acres of electronic tubes. When you sold a computer, the customer had to install a great deal of expensive air-conditioning to take care of all the heat that was being thrown off. Here were these little transistor radios, working fine. The transistor was doing the same thing as the tube was doing and was throwing off practically no heat. Our people had barely learned to understand how to handle electrons in a tube, and this invention shocked them. It was something they pulled back from. [Shades of Reg Jones and electronics at GE!] I used to go up to the lab and say, 'Why not transistors?' Finally, Al and I wrote a memorandum that said, 'After June 1, 1958, we will build no more machines with electronic tubes. Signed, Tom Watson, Jr.' They were awful mad, and said, 'What the hell does he know about it?' But I kept giving them transistor radios. Every time they'd complain, I'd pass them a transistor radio."

Tom's recognition of the need for broad technical development led to his finding Dr. Emanuel Piore, a prominent Navy Department scientist, who led the development of the second-generation fully transistorized computers, and later in the 1960s, IBM's revolutionary third-generation 360 series. Said Tom, "About the time the 360 was coming out in quantity, my initiation of these decisions was almost zero. I follow the New York papers closely . . . and the magazines, and if I saw something in there about something being able to be done, I'd rip it right out and say, 'Are we on this?' or 'Can we do this?' and so forth. Some of these seem to be coming back haunting us, antitrust-wise now. I seem to be so aggressive. It's hard to think why we can't do everything. . . . I suspect that the person who is functioning now as I did then would be the individual division manager, prodded by the group executive."

Dealing with Crisis

Fortune called the decision to make the 360 IBM's $5 billion gamble, "The most crucial and portentous—as well as perhaps the riskiest business judgment of recent times." There were tremendous start-up problems in 1964 and 1965. The major problem was that the small ceramic plates on which the subassemblies were placed began to crack stripes. The stripe is essentially the wire between two components. No one could tell why they were cracking, or when they would crack more. They had to be taken out of all of the computers on the line. Engineers worked night and day with hot environments to try to make stripes crack, understand how they did, and then remedy the problem.

Meantime production schedules were aborted. Promised deliveries went unfulfilled. IBM's reputation was on the line. It wasn't at all clear that IBM was going to be able to pull it off. Many employees themselves were experiencing tremendous strain. Tom drove himself to get to see as many of them as he could. In crises like the 360 he was right there, in the forefront. "Here are the problems," he told them. "What do you want to do about it? . . . We're going to make it and here's why." Customarily on his visits he would walk through a laboratory or a plant, have a management meeting, then get on the loudspeaker and tell the entire facility what was going on in the business. He never would sneak in and sneak out of locations. To Tom, IBM is nothing more than the total of the individual contributions of the people within it. He would tell them that when things were tough. His message was, "Look, you can take away almost anything from IBM. You can take away our technology. You can take away our plants. You can take away our labs. You can take away any facility. You can take away our headquarters, but leave our people and this business will recreate itself overnight." He believed it. His people believed it. Out of that came a tremendous unleashing of human effort that brought the 360 program through at a time when IBM lacked today's sophisticated machine tools and advanced semiconductor facilities. Individual diligence and effort had to do the job. Tom understood that.

He would go to a Hundred Percent Club and say, "I can appreciate what effect this is having on your customers because we can't make our shipments as fast as we want. Here's how it happened. Here's what we're doing about it, and I want you to know we can make it. I've called on customers myself, and we're going to maintain customer satisfaction. We're going to take care of them and you can tell them that." And, in fact, IBM did. The salesmen went to the customers and said, "Here's the story. Here's what we can do to help you during the interim, and you have your choice. Here are the full facts. You make your decision now as to how you want to proceed." The customers were so disarmed by the frank discussion of IBM's problems, and by its confidence in breaking new ground with computers whose price performance promised to be so tremendous that the company was risking its whole business to bring it off, that they went along. It wasn't that they didn't have alternate sources. They believed that IBM was telling them the truth, which, in fact, it was. The first of the 360s was installed in April, 1965. Within two years the line accounted for nearly half of the company's domestic installations, while overseas it swept all before it.

Setting the Tone

Watson's methods of setting the ethical and managerial tone are legend in IBM. "Excellence ran through everything he did and in an extremely strong way," an intimate says. His view was that if he didn't act strongly, the last ripple at the end of the pond wouldn't be very strong. He often said, "I don't really give a damn about a white shirt but, if I wear a nice looking blue shirt, the next fellow down is going to wear a purple shirt, and then . . . we're going to have an aloha shirt down at the salesman level."

Tom used an expression, "to galvanize into action." If an issue involved two or three other people, or if he needed functional expertise or something of that nature, he would call a meeting on the spot. Everybody that was pertinent to that discussion would come. The meeting could be fifteen minutes or five days. It didn't matter. Everybody understood that that was the highest priority, and they'd stay with the problem until it was solved.

The organization earned a reputation for instant response. There are myriad folklore stories about somebody's computer going down, so the payroll for 5,000 workers would not be met the next noon. A machine would be flown in from someplace, people would work all night. At 11 A.M., that machine would start to grind out the payroll, and by 12:01 the checks would be spewing out the pay window. Then, of course, those IBM people would be written up in the company publication. Tom would say such effort was not wholly altruistic. Customers thought long and hard about ever buying anybody else's computer.

Soon after Watson took over as president in 1952, he called managers to task if their lavatories were not spotless. One of them reported, "If it were not clean he would have raised holy hell. . . . if we had a meeting of district managers . . . he'd say, 'Look gentlemen, I really don't want to be known as Dan the Latrine Man, and I was just in the john here this morning and I've been giving [the manager] hell about it, but I am so jealous of the IBM company, I am so jealous of its reputation, I want it to be such a shining jewel, that I just don't think you should have dirty johns.' " Why make such a big fuss about such a little thing? It was an approach to life that said, "There's nothing that is wrong that is too trivial for me to act on." He imbued that sense of responsibility and responsiveness in the business.

There is a hoary, oft-repeated story at IBM: A major public figure— the name varies with who is telling the story—was to speak at an out-door affair at Poughkeepsie. Clouds began to gather. Out came 5,000 umbrellas. The clouds drifted away and the sun came out. Out came 5,000 pairs of sunglasses. No manager was going to get fired because he was unprepared for the vagaries of the weather.

Much of what Tom had to say dealt with the way people were treated. A story about John Opel, now IBM chairman, is illustrative. Keith Funston, former head of the New York Stock Exchange, and George Harrar, of the Rockefeller Foundation, and a couple of others were going with Tom to Washington. Opel, then an administrative assistant, had taken the party to LaGuardia Airport and had then gone home. The weather became increasingly bad. As he usually did, Tom worked at 590 Madison until the last minute. The chief pilot called to say they could not fly. An assistant passed the word on. When Tom heard that several of the party were still at LaGuardia, he said, "Just have Opel drive them back to their homes." Not bring them back, but deliver them back in the IBM car to their homes. "John's gone home," his informant reported. "What do you mean, John's gone home?" "Well, John took them to the airport and went on home." "Get John back," Tom snapped. "I'll go get them," the informant offered. "John lives in Chappaqua, and. . . ." Tom, now angry, said, "You apparently misunderstood me. I said get John back." The informant called. "It's Halloween," Opel lamented, "I was going out trick-or-treating with my kids." "Yeah, too bad. Come on back." So John came in on the train. Tom gave him what reportedly was "the worst dressing-down in the world." "Look, any time you're going to take people like that, people that *I* associate with. . . ." The moral of the story was that you lock the door of the airplane and you watch it take off down the runway, *then* you go home.

Although Tom never said it, he acted as if IBM were a family-owned company. It wasn't, but up to that time only he and his father had been the chief executive officers. If an article appeared in the press implying that IBM's motives were wrong or that its integrity was in question, he would respond. He wanted the reporter to know that his information was not correct. Once *Life* magazine described the San Jose plant as "opulent." Tom was in Europe at the time. When he got back and saw the article, he immediately wanted to know if anyone had responded to it. That plant was a well-designed and cost-effective plant, but it was not opulent.

High standards of performance and meticulous attention to detail also meant high moral and ethical standards. For conduct that was unacceptable to him, like being involved with members of the opposite sex at a sales meeting, instant and violent action would follow—usually firing. A manager who got mixed up with his secretary would be fired instantly.

IBM and alcohol mix only on the side. In Watson, Sr.'s time, if you worked at Endicott, they used to say that you ought to pull the blinds in your kitchen before you had a drink. No liquor or wine was served at an IBM function. Tom rarely drinks and does not smoke. Some think it's because he would not be as fully in control of himself if he did. Others think he acceded to his father's wishes. At sales meetings many problem drinking situations were covered up by the "cold-shower crowds," the senior managers who would patrol the local bars and take anyone who had drunk too much back to the hotel. There was a great deal of protection and camaraderie. The usual scatological horseplay, suggestive slides to stimulate interest in sales presentations, and similar breaches of decorum were simply not tolerated at IBM sales meetings. If a customer from Oshkosh reported real skulduggery, Tom sent an assistant who was to report within twenty-four hours.

Watson once discovered two years after the fact that IBM's tax calculations were not accurate. Though the sum was minor, Tom personally called on the head of the IRS in New York to report the mistake. Sometimes Tom thought business ought to pay more taxes and said so (a thesis Reg Jones also advocated).

Early on, some vendors became too dependent on IBM. When IBM had to pull back work, they were in danger of going broke. Some smaller vendors in local communities suffered from competitive bidding. So Tom instigated a rule that no vendor could depend on IBM for more than 30 percent of his business, and another that IBM's procurement practices should not squeeze the little guy. To protect IBM's host communities, Tom established a policy that IBM would never exceed a certain percent of the work force or of the population. IBM plants are generally limited to about 6,000 people. IBM won't force itself into a community.

Tom used to get sore at a big company's elbowing IBM when it was small. He decided if IBM ever got big, he would be careful not to do that. Even before antitrust became an issue, before the government's interest in IBM, Tom tried to be a tough but fair competitor. How should competitors be treated? "Suppose that you were a competitor —small, precariously financed, without a large support organization, and without a big reputation in the field—but with a good product. How would you feel if the big IBM company took the action which you proposed to take?" Disparaging the competition is against IBM's ground rules.

Tom is a religious man, although he does not go to any given church on a Sunday. On big occasions in his life, when headquarters was at 590, he used to walk over to St. Patrick's Cathedral. Several very influential people in his life were priests. He has a sense of not being here forever and, observed one colleague, "I think he has a very strong relationship with his Maker."

With Watsonian morality goes frugality. IBM's first corporate airplane was a small twin-engine Aero Commander. Tom explained: "I always wanted to have a good many less airplanes per million of net profits than any other company. And I wanted to have less plush. I never thought that because you were the head of a business you were some kind of a damned king [an attitude verbalized also by MacGregor]. I've been in a lot of people's airplanes that were fixed up like palaces inside, and for what? What right does anybody have to do that? An airplane is a tool, and I was very much for that airplane business because I was going all over this country and hardly ever getting home, and the airplane simply got me home more often." Watson was wary about anything that might smack of haughtiness:

> "I think the most unattractive thing that I see corporation leaders get, and I must say not more than one in five gets it, is a haughtiness which makes one conclude that because they are the head of a corporation, they think they're a very big shot indeed, and that they should be fawned on by secretaries and employees, and so on. . . . I think a sense of humility is vital to running one of these jobs well. And the more humility, the better [echoes of earlier expressions by Jones and MacGregor]. You've got to have self-confidence —my God, you've got to believe in yourself, but . . . when you're out there on the line talking to the whole management, you've got to be humble. And you can't say, 'Do it because I said it,' you know. It's 'Do it because I think it's the right thing to do for the following logical reasons or at least they seem logical to me.' "

Executives from other companies would comment that IBMers did not treat themselves very well. Their desks were ordinary. There was a certain spareness to their offices. Managers didn't entertain with large, expensive French restaurant-type lunches except under very special circumstances. High expense accounts were looked upon askance. IBM had only seven cars for the headquarters of a whole multibillion domestic corporation. The reason was not the money greater luxury would cost, but the tone Tom wanted to set and keep. There would be a uniqueness about IBM.

An IBM benefit program or perquisite is for everybody. There are no names on parking places outside the Armonk headquarters building. (Although any employee can park in those close-in spots, they don't.) No regular meals are served in private dining rooms for the officers of the company. They get trays and then sit in the cafeteria like everybody else. That's also true at the plants.

Setting People in Motion

Tom didn't care where he got his ideas. He could get them from the barber or the elevator operator or the janitor, and could act equally on them. "Tom loved to have you pick up your own phone," an executive reported:

"I picked up the phone once and said, 'You know, Tom, our advertising is awful. It's really awful. . . . Why don't we have a B-52 soaring up into the air and 'An IBM computer made this possible' underneath it? I even had an artist draw a picture and I sent it to him. And I said, 'Do something like this.' I was at a convention about a month later and I was called to his room and Learson was there, and Tom said . . . 'Are you interested in advertising?' And I said, 'No, not really.' And he said, 'Well, you sent me this thing and it's a good idea. We're going to do it.' And I said, 'It's just that I thought the ads are dull, and they're not exciting.' And he said, 'Well, would you like to come back East and be the advertising manager?' Now that's the way he did things. He put people in totally unrelated fields. . . . But the environment was such that, if you had convictions and enthusiasm and aggressiveness, you could do it. Another fellow said, 'Tom, we're making a terrible mistake

to not use air freight.' And Tom said, 'My God, why didn't I think
of that before? How about you coming East and setting it up?' And
the fellow said, 'Fine,' and did. And that was his key to the
kingdom."

At the same time, Tom required people to stand behind their ideas.
Salesmen frequently feel that modification of a product requiring mini-
mal effort would dramatically increase the market for the product.
Every now and then Tom would do something dramatic. Once a man
was giving him this argument. Tom asked, "Do you really believe that?"
"Yes I do." Tom said, "All right. I'm going to have you work for me for
six months on that project and we're going to see what happens when
you and I together attack it." He gave the man a virtual carte blanche
to find out what those little gadgets could do on those great big machines. Tom gave him a budget to get engineers, and a financial man
to get the break-even prices. Six months later nothing had come of it.
Tom felt that in management you deal with myths and the way you deal
with myths is either to convert them into facts or else to smash and
discard them.

Though Tom demanded facts and logic from others, one of his greatest assets, as reflected in the transistor issue, was his own intuition. As
one of his intimates reported:

"Instinctively he knows the right answers to questions and he belit-
tles that instinct at times himself. He'll say, 'Well, I'm not really a
scientific fella. I don't really understand, but in my stomach, my
viscera, I think this.' And sometimes he wouldn't feel comfortable
putting that forth as the reason why he felt the way he felt. And
then, in lieu of saying it was really his instinct, he would buffer his
conclusion with some fairly faulty logic, and in the process, get into
an argument. Then you'd be obliged to argue, 'Your logic is faulty.
You're really doing this on instinct.' And then he would fight like
hell, and finally grin and say, 'Yeah, that's right.' Which was kind
of funny."

It's very difficult to reduce human factors to some set of rules, which,
if followed, will produce a machine that has great appeal. Some people
have great sensitivity for others' reactions to products. Watson was one
of them. He had a sense about design and utility and about the way
people would react to a machine's appearance as well as to the way it
operates. It wasn't all gut. The facts were important, too.

What he admired least were people who weren't willing to speak up and take positions when there were tough problems to solve. He was perfectly willing to listen to some very tough answers. The building at 590 Madison Avenue was old, and it had a rather narrow entrance and then a bank of elevators and a very small entryway. He saw the new Pan American Building at Kennedy Airport had an air curtain entrance instead of a door. He wanted to put an air curtain at the entrance to 590. He sent an emissary to the building engineer. After investigation, the building engineer reported that the Pan American Building was of a totally different construction. The air curtain wouldn't work at 590. It would be a violent funnel that would suck people through, the emissary reported. There was a surprised look on Tom's face. "I guess you misunderstood me," he told the emissary. "Tell the engineer I want an air door down there." In about two weeks, the engineer told the emissary, "Look, goddammit it, it will not work. It's going to cost an inordinate amount of money, $100,000 or thereabouts, and it simply will not work." Now the assistant delegated to get the air curtain constructed was in a dilemma. Should he tell the engineer to do it? Or should he go back to Tom? After he understood the engineering problem involved and became convinced himself, he went back. He stalled nervously, "Tom, look—about the door. If, if, if you want to do it, we'll do it but let me tell you you're wrong. Now if you've got ten minutes, I'll tell you why you're wrong." Tom looked at him and said, "What are you talking about?" "I'm talking about the air door downstairs, the Pan Am air door." "Oh yeah," he said, "Well, that's all right. Forget it." If the assistant had proceeded and the door hadn't worked, probably he would have been fired or transferred. Tom would say, "You know, I really can't use you in that capacity, if you're not willing to go the last mile and personally embarrass yourself to help me and keep me from doing something I shouldn't. . . . "

When problems recurred, Watson expected executives to bring new solutions to them. "It had to do with not letting people develop a grooved swing as far as your reactions are concerned, and to react differently to the same situation on different occasions, and not to be taken for granted," an executive reported:

> "We were discussing something with Tom that we were doing because we thought it had been successful the way it had been done the last time, and he had agreed to it. So we took his agreement for granted, as it were, and we went in and said, 'Now here's what we're doing about this particular sales program.' And he said,

'Well, I don't think that's the way to do it.' And we were startled, and we sort of implied that we had his tacit agreement. And he said, 'Well, you don't at all. I may have agreed to it a year ago, but that certainly doesn't mean I agree to it now. You're just following your nose. That's the same old yesterday's mashed potatoes. Nothing new. Nothing creative. Nothing innovative.' . . . we were still a little puzzled as to how we'd gotten trapped in assuming that he would agree with it. And he said, kind of halfway kidding us, 'You fellas should know by this time I will never run *with* you.' So you know he'd like to always be out in front and be the leader."

Just as Tom Watson gave himself a long tether to be spontaneous, depending upon intimates to restrain him appropriately, so he also gave others wide latitude in exercising discretion in meeting objectives. It would be up to the subordinate to let Tom know when further direction was needed, but not to return with intermediate reports for self-assurance. He didn't want to know any more than he needed to know to assign the task or make a decision. That latitude might leave the subordinate wondering. As one reported, "What does he really think I'm to do now with his million dollars for the next five months or five years? Now you would think he must know more about it than you do. Right away you think, he has a tremendous understanding of your field. So . . . you'd work like hell to put together the prospectus and think, 'I wonder if this is what he meant?' You'd work your ass off. It's a management technique that really puts the burden on you, along with great opportunity. . . . And you are going to work harder at coming up with what you think he wants as opposed to having it outlined."

Speaking and Listening

Tom began learning communication skills from his father. Many of IBM's major communications devices stem from Watson, Sr. These include personal contact, speeches, and the famous IBM open-door policy.

"I was born into an environment where I followed my father to a reception—an IBM convention—a thousand people. He'd spend thirty minutes walking through that room. When he was done, everybody would know him. They probably wouldn't have shaken his hand, but he had a magnetic presence, and everybody would know him. The only other person I saw who could do that was Soviet Premier Khrushchev. I had him to lunch once out in San Jose in 1959. He was a little fellow but everybody would know he was around. I couldn't do that very well. My brother Dick would do it, but it was hard on me. So I felt inadequate in large crowds, in IBM crowds and outside crowds. I think I was a reasonably good speaker, in retrospect, but I always felt inadequate when I had to make speeches, either IBM or outside speeches. I could make a fine speech if we had a cracked stripe, a defect in a computer component, and I had 400 guys in there and we had to fix that cracked stripe. If I had to tell them what was going to happen to the company, that was easy. But just to exhort them in a general way that was hard."

Yet a Watson colleague insists he is a good speaker: "He can be extremely warm and charming in the kind of semisocial situations you get into with government officials, heads of other companies, academic institutions. And the fact that he had done, in my view, such a good job in those kinds of things for the company over those years . . . without really liking to do it, was an indication of a dedication to his job. It was a new insight for me, even after having known him for all the years."

When his father died, Tom went to every one of the plants and held meetings with all of the people. He talked about what he thought, what he planned to do, what he hoped for the business. The point was to establish strongly and quickly that he was the new leader and that he needed their help. He wanted the people in the company to understand that, first of all, its reputation was very important—very, very important; that the integrity of the company, its reputation for honesty, for being the kind of straightforward company that people would like to do business with, was fundamental; and that every detail counted.

Tom maintained an open-door policy. Any employee could go all the way up to the CEO to appeal a management decision or complain about being treated unfairly. Some went directly to Watson. The open door was intended to be the equivalent of an ombudsman, a spokesman. The employee has to have someone he or she can talk to who will, in fact, take his viewpoint. That's what the open-door policy tries to stimulate. At IBM it has been tremendously helpful for people to know that if they think they're getting a lousy deal, they can go right to the top. Tom would try to find out at the end of the year how many people had written, how many decisions had upheld management, how many cases had not been correctly managed. He knew that a lot of the letters he got were self-serving, that the people writing them were using him to blackmail their management through the open-door process. He also knew he had to support management sufficiently, and yet when management had screwed up, rather than protect it he would let the mistakes, as he would say, "see the light of day."

"Yeah, I spent 25 percent of my time on the open-door policy," Tom said:

"Some people said I was crazy. I don't think so. I learned an awful lot about the problems of the little guy. And I learned a lot about the problems of what I called the Poughkeepsie Protective Association, or the Endicott Protective Association, or the Greencastle Protective Association, where management gets together in sort of a solid phalanx, and goes out after a little guy who sometimes is completely blameless. There was a fellow who got fired up in Poughkeepsie. I forget his name. And he came to see me, and he said, 'Mr. Watson, your people aren't treating me fair up there. I make more pieces than anyone in that shop per hour, and I get the lowest pay.' And I said, 'I can't believe it.' He said, 'That's right.' So I called up there, and said, 'Is that right, does he make the most pieces and get the lowest pay?' 'Well,' they said, 'he's a very uncooperative employee, doesn't belong to the IBM Club, he doesn't do any outside activities, he wears a blue shirt to work.' I said, 'That's not the question. Does he make more pieces and get less pay?' And then I got another, 'He has a very sloppy yard and a couple of old automobile wrecks lying on the front lawn, doesn't take care of his children.' 'That's not the question. Does he make more pieces and get less pay?' 'Yes, he does.' That caused us to go through every plant in America, and relate pay to pieces. I say we didn't have piece work, we didn't. But, we certainly wanted to compensate the top producer with the best remuneration. We weren't counting them, but my God, he knew he was making a lot more than anybody else. But, that was a revolution. Yeah, I think the open-door thing was well worthwhile. When they come in on family problems, it's very tough. You really can't get into family problems."

The open door is complemented by "Speak-Up." People could write, anonymously if they wished, a question or comment or criticism to the editor of the local IBM newspaper or a person he designated as coordinator. Sometimes the toughest speak-up questions were reprinted in other IBM newspapers. Tom often tried to answer the most critical ones himself. Policy letters and management briefings served to establish operational cornerstones and to make certain no manager could plead ignorance. Watson's other vehicles for communication included the company's *Think Magazine,* use of the loudspeaker box in the plants and labs, sometimes via telephone hookup, the Hundred Percent Clubs, and an organization (founded in 1961) called the Golden Circle. The Golden Circle included the top 5 to 10 percent of the marketing team. They and their spouses were given formal recognition at a meeting at a major resort hotel. The Golden Circle resulted from Tom's concern in the early 1960s that he was losing contact, and therefore the sense of family in the business, because he no longer knew most of the salesmen by name.

IBM managers are taught to deal with the individual rather than with groups. If a group of welders came to see a foreman two weeks after he became a manager, he would know enough to say, "Now gentlemen, I'll talk to you individually about your problems, but not as a group, because it's not a group situation." The company is not unionized, though avoiding unionization was not a goal in itself. Watson, Sr., said, "You can do a lot of talking to employees, and you can buy turkeys at Christmas if that's your hobby, but it isn't going to help you one bit to keep the employee happy. What's going to make the employee happy is what's in that pay envelope at the end of every week when he shakes it. And then the benefit plans." IBM instituted one of the first major medical plans, and the contemporary medical benefits plan is one of the best in the country.

Watson, Sr., had wanted to pay workers better and relieve the managerial pressure produced by piecework, so he eliminated piecework in 1934. In 1958, Tom, following the suggestion of Jack Bricker, vice-president of personnel, put factory workers, like white-collar employees, on a weekly salary instead of an hourly wage. No longer was anyone docked for an hour's pay if he or she were late. Tom felt that if you trusted employees and managed them well, they would act properly. His confidence turned out to be well placed. Despite the warnings to the contrary, product costs went down when IBM went on salary. Already assured of a lifetime career and the company objective of full employment, employees knew that if they worked hard, they wouldn't have to worry. That confidence allowed the company to change produc-

tion and automate, to train and retrain people. Many IBM people have
been retrained several times over.

Of Hobbies and Family

Tom Watson tried to climb the Matterhorn three times from 1977 to
1979. He flew his own airplane to Geneva on two of those trips. This
despite the fact that he was in his sixties and had had a serious heart
attack at fifty-seven. Why? "I am at the age where people tell me I can't
or I shouldn't do things. I'm just going to go out and do them." He has
a wide range of interests, from sailing to hot air ballooning to canoe trips
to river running. He has been known to fly a Piper Cub at fifty feet over
the waves into and out of various Maine inlets. He enjoyed driving a
bulldozer to clear his Maine land, where his son raised pheasant and
grouse, because it gave him a feeling of power different from that he
experienced in his corporate role.

Tom has a library full of books, many in his office. He is interested in
history and photography. All of his activities are individual. His wide
range of interests brought balance to the complex technology that he
was spearheading. On his trips he finds time to work the kids into things.
He has always been concerned about what his children were doing
despite his preoccupation with the business. Once he left a colleague
to pilot a twin-engine Beech H-18 while he sat in back and wrote a letter
to his son. (Although the colleague was also a pilot, he didn't know how
to fly a twin-engine plane or even how to switch from the nearly empty
fuel tank to the full one.) His was a close family. No doubt, in his role
as a father, he frequently remembered that it was not easy being a son
of a very successful person.

Tom sounded a warning note about becoming wrapped up in one's
work:

"I had a glorious fifteen years. I loved every minute of it. I couldn't
wait to get here in the morning. I think, if you're talking and
teaching and discussing executive relationships, however, that I
would have one word of caution to executives, young executives in
particular. I think that you can ruin your whole life by letting your
business become too much a part of you. I came close to ruining my

own. I've been married to the same woman for more than forty years and we're very, very happy. She describes me when I was really running this place. At night, she'd have shined up all the six little children. She'd been working all day with them, and I'd say, 'That child's sock isn't up, and that child's hair isn't combed.' I was carrying that total critical IBM attitude back to my house. I think people have to have a long look at that.... If I die tonight, I'll have had a marvelous life. I've had a lot of fun and a lot of business success, but you've got to have both. If [an executive says] . . . unhappily, 'I've never had the opportunity to do things with my children because my business took so much out of me'—I think the guy's a lousy executive. I just broke out of here and I took my kids to Jerusalem once, and I broke out of here and I took them for six weeks around Sweden on a sailboat. I broke out of here and took them all to Greece. I broke out of here and took them to Zermatt for Christmas once. I would always, you know, recognize that you had to have a family side."

On June 29, 1971, Tom Watson relinquished his post as chairman of the board. How did another Watson intimate see the differences between him and successor Frank Cary?

"The issues have gotten more complicated. . . . So I don't think you can operate today as well with the almost . . . towering personality approach to management. I think you would need something more systematic, so that at the top of the business I think there would have to be more bats—more turns at the plate. . . . I think Cary is a much more detailed, modern manager. Frank is more a process person, more deliberate, and Tom is more of an intuitive person. . . . If you look at the problems of the company today, just in the mode of operating internationally, it's changed so much, because of economic nationalism, and a whole host of currency problems. That's the kind of stuff that Frank just thrives on. . . . I think of Watson as a peppermint. Frank is a chocolate or vanilla, but he's not peppermint. . . . I never knew anyone in IBM who had the sort of quiet fortitude and the quiet confidence to follow the Watsons, as Frank had. . . . And I think that one of the other great insights Tom had, was knowing that the company was going to go through a very complicated intellectual period—product, legal, and all these other areas, and that you needed somebody like Frank."

Tom Watson made IBM the world's most respected business organization. His demanding standards, his continuous pressure for premier performance, his grasp of the implications of the simple transistor when those more technically proficient than he rejected it, and his capacity for taking risks combined to create a configuration that gave IBM character, aspiration, and reputation. The letters IBM are recognized all over the world. IBM's standards of product design and product performance are the yardsticks that competitors strive to exceed. A worthy and able son, indeed.

Coda

In the late 1970s there was some talk that IBM was slipping. Competitors were springing up all over the place with smaller computers, while IBM lagged. But then, the old IBM snapped into place. In August, 1981, it jumped into the mass market and established its personal computer as the standard for the industry. It quickly captured 21 percent of the market. It already had 40 percent of the world market for computers. At the end of 1982, its sales were $34.4 billion with profits of $4.4 billion, the most profitable U.S. company. Executives and managers who were "graduates" of IBM were sought by other major corporations.

IBM attained a big advantage in the personal computer market partly by inviting all comers to create software rather than developing its own and by putting its computer together with components manufactured by others and taken off the shelf. It acquired 15 percent of Rolm to gain the advantages of its electronic switchboard and thereby to compete more efficiently with American Bell, GTE, and GE, and 12 percent of Intel to gain access to its chip technology. IBM was prepared to compete intensely for office automation and communications business. It established retail distribution channels, created independent entrepreneurial business units that could bypass corporate bureaucracy, and special business units for innovative projects. It separated policy from operations by integrating the corporate office and corporate management committee into a sixteen-member corporate management board.

Frank Cary stepped down as chairman in February, 1983, to be succeeded by John Opel, described as "good plain vanilla," but a powerful leader, nonetheless. Opel moved to decentralize the company into seven independent business units, which are companies within the company. Opel, vice-chairman Paul Rizzo, and John Akers, the new president, became a three-member policy committee. Nine executives from operating groups became a business operations committee.

The government had sought to curb IBM's growing power by filing an antitrust suit in January, 1969. It took six years to bring the case to trial, and the trial itself lasted another six years at a cost of one-half million dollars a year. Then it was dropped in January, 1982. The Justice Department said that the case was "without merit." IBM suddenly began to blossom competitively again, almost as if it had held itself back during the trial. No longer did it introduce new products gradually. Its $10 billion investment in plant since 1977, financed by shifting emphasis from leasing computers to selling them, enabled it to become a lowest-cost producer. Said Tom Watson, Jr., "From the point of view of manu-facturing, IBM is a new company." Its new, more flexible production techniques enabled it to build several different models on the same production line and thereby launch new models rapidly, before com-petitors. Return on shareholders' equity was 22.1 percent.

In 1984 *Time* magazine called IBM the most profitable company on the face of the earth, leapfrogging General Motors and Exxon to be-come the most important and most powerful business in the U.S. *Time* contended that IBM was the lengthened shadow of Thomas J. Watson, Sr.[9] It was, more accurately, the lengthened shadow of his son.

Arthur O. Sulzberger

NEW YORK TIMES COMPANY

IN 1963, when Arthur Ochs Sulzberger became chief executive of the New York Times Company and publisher of the *New York Times,* the company was still privately held. The outside world knew only of the prestigious newspaper it published and of the typographer strikes it endured. "Good, gray" were the adjectives people used to characterize it—a trustworthy daily font of knowledge from all over the world. "All the news that's fit to print" was its motto. As at GE and Monsanto, inside it was another story. The strike settlements were draining its financial lifeblood. New suburban competition threatened its circulation. Management was a word, not a skilled practice.

Each of the CEOs we have discussed so far brought well-developed management skills to his task. Arthur Ochs Sulzberger, managerially unprepared, suddenly found himself following in his brother-in-law's footsteps. His task was to sustain the international reputation of what is probably the world's most widely respected newspaper—and to rescue it from a dangerous financial bind as well as from the chronic labor conflict that threatened its survival.

Sulzberger brought to his new responsibilities a long-standing family relationship with the company, modest reportorial experience, and an equally modest personality. He had an unusual capacity to wander among his people and to listen. Contrary to the expectations of many, he could take charge as well. Moving in slow but surefooted steps, he earned the regard of skeptical followers as he transformed the one-product company into a highly profitable business venture, a diversification that gave added strength to its journalistic mission.

All in the Family

Sulzberger, commenting on the *Times,* stressed the importance of the paper's high standards: "If there's any one word that we try to keep up to as to what it's all about, it is quality. . . . I sometimes get the feeling if we all went away, that the paper would just come out by itself, because there's so much pride in it and so many ingrained things. . . ." Such sentiments were all in the family for Punch Sulzberger. That nickname, bestowed by his father, comes from the traditional puppet show, Punch and Judy. (His sister's name is Judy.)

Punch's grandfather, Adolph S. Ochs, bought the *Times* in 1896, having gotten his start in the newspaper business by rescuing the *Chattanooga Times.* Through astute borrowing and deal-making, he had turned a losing property around. "His primary interest was the quality of the paper and not increasing profits," noted a *Times* veteran. Adolph had no stockholders he had to accommodate, so he poured the cash flow of the paper back into the product rather than into the profits. His was a great business achievement. From him the *Times* got its reputation, its traditions, and its place in journalism.

Ochs is reported to have been in direct control, managing in a one-on-one fashion, and knowledgeable about printing, printers, and printing machinery. Editors were given their heads, but all editorials expressed his viewpoint.[1] In an early draft of his proposal to take over the *New York Times,* Mr. Ochs had said, "I am certain I could not succeed as manager with any abridgement of almost autocratic power."[2]

Punch's father, Arthur Hays Sulzberger, started out in his family's textile business, married Ochs's daughter, and was publisher of the *Times* from 1935 to 1961. "When his [Punch's] father was publisher this was a floor [the fourteenth floor of the New York Times Building] on which only two people sat, really, General Adler [Julius Ochs Adler, nephew of Mr. Ochs and first cousin of Punch's mother, Iphigene Ochs Sulzberger] and Arthur Hays Sulzberger," reported an observer:

"He was at one end and General Adler was at the other. It was their floor and it was a very private floor—there was very little access to it unless you were summoned to it . . . the word came down from on high. And there was very little arguing with the word. The publishers of this newspaper have traditionally left the News Department alone. . . . There have been exceptions. If you read the Harrison Salisbury book [*Without Fear or Favor*], you'll find an example of Punch's father intervening when the CIA got to him [in 1961] and said to keep [Sydney Gruson] out of Guatemala. . . . His father was a relatively remote man sitting up here on the fourteenth floor, meeting with selected members of the staff, mostly at luncheons, but confining his camaraderie to a very small group, knowing people like [James] Reston and [Turner] Catledge, perhaps, but very removed."

In 1961, Mr. Sulzberger handed the reins to his son-in-law, Orvil E. Dryfoos, the husband of his eldest daughter, Marian. Dryfoos had a Wall Street background. He brought in other outsiders, such as Amory Bradford, Andrew Fisher, and Harding Bancroft, the first cadre of management types to enter the *Times*.[3] By 1960, Bradford, Dryfoos's closest friend, had progressed to the position of general manager.[4] "Amory had a very broad mandate from Orvil and had imposed his own cold, austere, difficult personality on many aspects of the place," said a *Times* executive.

On December 8, 1962, the International Typographers Union called the longest strike (114 days) in New York newspaper history over the issue of automating the printing processes. Bradford was the chief negotiator for the *Times* and the publishers of the other New York newspapers, who had to follow the *Time*'s lead. It was to prove a watershed in Bradford's career and the *Time*'s history. Dryfoos became ill during the strike and died on May 25, 1963.

As Punch reported it, "Orvil and my father had worked everything out perfectly. He thought my brother-in-law would serve as the president and publisher of the *New York Times*. . . . And then he would move on into retirement and yours truly would come along. And dad's scenario was beautiful. There was only one trouble. He hadn't consulted the doctor. Orvil died almost immediately after the strike, and that's when I came in."

When Orvil died, the trustees of the Ochs estate, who were his father (then ill from several strokes and in a wheelchair), his mother, and George D. Woods, the chairman of First Boston Corporation, named Punch publisher. He was prepared in spirit and in his understanding of the most important part of the paper, the News Department, but he knew virtually nothing about anything else. "I had to teach myself. I had no business background at all. I was a young reporter type, banged around in the Marines a couple of times, and at the *Milwaukee Journal*." An intimate says, "When he was to finally come here, the original plan was to put him in the promotion and sales department because it had contact with the whole paper. His father thought that would be a good training area for him, but he changed his mind and made him assistant treasurer . . . without any real duties. His father, too, had once been vice-president in charge of nothing and spent years trying to make a job."

Amory Bradford ignored Punch in those days, but the late Turner Catledge, managing editor of the *Times*, befriended him. Catledge brought Punch into a little cabal of executives that met night after night in Catledge's back office to drink and tell stories. When Punch became the publisher, Turner became not only an adviser but also one of his closest friends, mentor, and almost a father figure.

In a sense Punch had made himself an invisible man. He was modest to the point of being self-deprecating. His academic record through several private schools was hardly illustrious. After he was discharged from the Marines he took his degree at Columbia University. Because he had not shown a great deal of academic achievement, even the Sulzberger family didn't contemplate that he would be the head of the business. But Punch had had another kind of education during his formative years. The Ochs and the Sulzberger families had been accustomed to meeting with the great and the near great, with politicians, businessmen, royalty, and near royalty. They had learned to be at ease with important people. In addition, as had been the case with his father, Punch had acquired a sense of what the *New York Times* should be. "The important thing is not how much money the *New York Times* makes, but how good the *New York Times* is." The quality of the product must not be eroded.

The First Days of Power

When it was necessary in 1963 to appoint a new publisher, there were two possibilities, Punch and Amory Bradford. After discussing it with Punch's mother and three sisters, Punch's father proposed that Punch become publisher and Bradford president. But Bradford had not treated Punch particularly well when Punch was floating around in his never-never land, nor was Punch comfortable with Bradford's hard-nosed style of management. Punch rejected the proposal. Bradford left the day after Punch became publisher. At thirty-six, Punch suddenly became the boss of men who were much older and much more ex-perienced than he, but it wasn't difficult for him to establish a relation-ship with the senior people who became his subordinates. A participant in that adaptive process reports, "He didn't assume a competitive pos-ture. He didn't try to tell them how to run their departments. He would make a decision when a decision was necessary, but except for casual suggestions that we all make to each other here, he never told them how to do their jobs. However, he never hesitated to indicate if some-thing in his opinion was done badly."

Punch quickly recognized the need to concentrate on the business side:

"My brother-in-law devoted himself primarily to news and edito-rial and had let the business side drift to Bradford. . . . The business side was really in disastrous shape by the time I got in. . . . Every-body reported directly to Amory and he was the guy who decided whether this department should know what that department was doing and so on. As a result there was an enormous amount of suspicion and a lot of conflict. Believe it or not, we never had a budget. If you were head of the Circulation Department you were not to be concerned with little details like finances or what Adver-tising was doing. You were just supposed to go out and sell the paper."

The *Times* had prospered while the *New York Herald Tribune* and other New York newspapers had expired. The *Times*'s formula was based on the advertising director's philosophy of keeping very low retail rates. But that philosophy had its own problems. No one at the *Times* knew, until their computer told them in 1979, whether any given line of advertising added to the revenues or cost them money. Punch soon discovered how advertising rates were raised. "One day the advertising director came upstairs and he closed the door and said, 'Now we're going to raise the rates.' I thought, 'Gee, I didn't know.' We had about 250 different categories of advertising. And he said, 'We're going to do this, and we can't do that,' and I said, 'Fine.' There was no way to discuss it with him. It had been pretty much a fly-by-the-seat-of-the-pants way of doing it."

Punch focused his energies easily and knew on whom or what to depend: "The paper as a paper was really doing quite well," he recalled. "The content of the paper was good. I had some problems with the editorial policy, but nothing so frustrating that there was any cause for me to act immediately. The list of priorities was so obviously pushing me toward the business side. . . . Throughout this whole transition, Turner Catledge, the managing editor and one of my oldest and dearest friends, was a great aid and comfort to me. When I didn't know what to do, I would ask him." Punch leaned on other executives for support as well. He moved Ivan Veit, now retired, from directing promotion to taking over much of the business side of the *Times* and to integrating circulation and advertising. Veit became his constant business adviser. "Bit by bit, just by working at it, by hammering at it repeatedly, we got people to understand that if it was going to work, that they'd have to work together," Punch recounted. "When I first came here, if you saw an advertising person on the News Department floor, you knew that something was wrong. He definitely was not welcome. Advertising was perceived as something a little tainted. The only people who were pure were the reporters. I think the News Department has learned. Today the young advertising salesman is as proud of being an employee of the *New York Times* as the reporters. And they get along well. It was just a slow, slow process."

Having been a reporter, Punch could confidently express an opinion about the news operations fairly quickly. It took him longer to become immersed in the technicalities of sales, advertising, circulation, and promotion. As did Jack Hanley, for a long time he had to take the word of the people who were directly in charge of those operations. He never pretended to have knowledge that he had not yet fully acquired. "He didn't put up an executive facade simply to demonstrate his authority," one insider recalled.

With Bradford gone, Punch was suddenly faced with a number of executives who had been with the company for many years, each of whom had built a dynasty and felt that he was superior because of his knowledge of his operations and so was almost immune from authority. It was very difficult. Punch bided his time. Luck was in his corner. Not only had Bradford left, but his managerial troops were nearing retirement. The circulation and promotion managers each had forty years of service; and the advertising manager, thirty-five. In a very short period Punch would have four or five major openings simultaneously. Besides, "Most of the young ones that I knew had lived through the same strike and felt as I did that it had been unnecessarily protracted because . . . the relationship [with the unions] had gotten so very bad. When you sit around for three months with nothing to do you chew the fat about where you're going and what you'd like to do."

Punch Sulzberger's succession to the top of the masthead was reminiscent of President Harry Truman's taking over after Roosevelt's sudden death: both were greatly underrated. But Punch could tap a reservoir of good will, of loyalty to the institution that is the *New York Times*. "We found he was someone we could deal with and who could deal with us," recalls an executive. "He was bright enough to grasp problems. He didn't cover up his lack of experience by aggressiveness, and it didn't take long to see that he was learning fast. . . . It is easy to develop affection for him, you want to help him. That was our feeling then, we wanted to do what we could for him. . . . When he established with us that he wanted to do the best job he could, that he wasn't going to go beyond his depth until he learned to swim, naturally we wanted to help him. I must say there is a high degree of institutional loyalty here, and the Ochs/Sulzberger family represents the core of that allegiance."

In the early days, Punch had plenty to do to get an overall grasp of the structure of the personal relationships, which were very important because the *Times* had no real organization chart. Everything was done by personal relationships. He learned fast. He knew the major personalities. The most influential people on the staff were Lester Markel, Turner Catledge, Andrew Fisher, Monroe Green, Harding Bancroft, Ivan Veit, and James "Scotty" Reston. His whole demeanor invited their help. They went out of their way to help him.

One observer described Punch's method, his style:

"I've seen him absorbing advice almost the way a sponge sucks up water. What I don't see and which nobody else sees is where does the squeezing process begin and what is the factor that starts to force some of the water that's been absorbed out. I know this process he has of going to all sorts of people, listening to all sorts of different opinions, before making up his own mind. . . . He has a great habit of putting up a possible solution . . . just to see how it would be batted down. [A characteristic shared with the others in this book.] And you see after he's put it up for a while that he didn't really put it up except to be batted down. . . . I don't ever see what that final [decision] factor is. And he has developed over the years an inordinate ability to keep certain things to himself. . . . Yet Punch is terribly stubborn about certain things, some which others might regard as minute. He likes his own way a good deal."

An intimate commented on the Punch Sulzberger personality:

"He's given people a considerable sense of well-being. That emerges by a relationship developing and a personality spreading itself through the building. . . . And that is not something you can write about and nobody from the outside can see it firsthand. . . . His imprint is all over the place. . . . How does he put his imprint? Listen. The people are very human. He wanders around the place, the nicest guy in the world to everybody, secretaries, printers, cleaning people. . . . In all that process, people know what it is he wants. To the extent you're able to give the guy who owns the candy shop what he wants, people want to give him what he wants. . . . Pleasantness is probably the best word to describe the character that is on display to most of the people all of the time. . . . People are very protective of the paper and therefore the family. They're very protective of him because he is very protective of them. And people around here go to such extremes you'd be astonished. They work eighteen hours a day and they go to any length necessary. Some people will say what they think that he wants to hear to please him. . . . And in one way or another he makes it clear that you don't have to do that. . . . Very engaging, very open man."

Reported another colleague:

"He is very conservative from the shirts he wears to the striped tie. There are only white and blue shirts. There are mainly only striped ties. He wears a certain Paul Stuart suit. He's conservative in action. He doesn't leap over the parapet and say, 'Gung ho. Let's kill the enemy.' You go very, very carefully, a step at a time. You fortify as many positions as you possibly can, and you only proceed from one fortified position to the next when the next one's ready, and the one you've been in is so safe that you know you can get back to it quickly. And that governs an awful lot of his actions. And its been good for this company because he's had a number of people pushing very hard out of personal ambition . . . to try to do things that seem good from one's own personal point of view but which somebody has to take a look at from a much bigger point of view. He's very fortunate in that he's not only the chief executive officer, the publisher of this paper, he's also in a sense the man of the family; he represents the family that owns it.

"He has that marvelous security of knowing that, in effect, though we're a public company and we behave like a public company, to an extreme we are not only Caesar's wife but we are Caesar's wife multiplied many times. He has an almost incredible evenhandedness of approach, and dealing with people he can only be as evenhanded as the man who has no problems about his own position in the place. It's very apparent in the ease he has with dealing with what are often enormously intricate financial, economic questions."

When Punch became president in 1963, the company was a literal mess. There were four major problems: (1) vulnerability to the unions and the consequent draining of assets; (2) distant, money-losing editions; (3) internal fiefdoms; (4) the need to develop a management team. We will take each in turn.

Vulnerability to the Unions

Times Company executives experienced the 1962/1963 114-day strike as akin to being raped. There was a 47 percent wage settlement, with no right to automate. The *Times* faced a situation in which, technologically, its overmanned composing room was still literally in the nineteenth century: 1,100 typographers were setting type as contrasted with the 250 persons required today for an even larger paper. Later, in 1967, the paper agreed to a contract that guaranteed everyone a job for life with the understanding that it could automate. It took another five years to reach a stable level of relationships with the unions.

Meanwhile the unions were running rampant. Even after the strike they would shut down production impulsively. Neither reader nor advertiser would know if the *Times* was going to appear. During the 114-day strike, much of it the result of a conflict between unions themselves, the Times Company had no income and simultaneously was losing $5 million a year from its western and international editions. The Times Company shared ownership with Kimberly-Clark of the Spruce Falls Power and Paper Company in Canada, but took most of its paper production for the *Times*. It, too, therefore, contributed nothing to profit. The strike left the Times Company with only nine months of revenue, and twelve months of expenses. It became clear to Punch that if the company were to survive as an institution, it had to diversify, that it had to have a base that was somehow not totally the *New York Times* newspaper.

"We've changed a lot in the newspaper. A tremendous amount now," said Punch:

"It really is a much different newspaper. But we couldn't have done that until we got over that terrible problem of automation. . . . It took us ten years to get out of that 1963 mess. But we were just one of eight newspapers. I remember that night that they imposed the bar to automation. The publishers wrote language on automation, sent it up to Bert Powers [the union president] and went out to dinner. Some of them got drunk. Powers approved the language, sent it back downstairs, and they had a hell of a fight, and we rejected our own language. Powers imposed a ten-year ban on bringing new equipment into the newspaper scene in New York. We have very much speeded . . . that process. We had to get determination, and strength of character and willingness to take the son-of-a-gun on and that just took some years in getting our act together."

Diversifying so as to build a financial bulwark against union strike threats was no easy proposition, especially with Punch's father looking over his shoulder from the chairman's perch. There was a tradition dating from the pioneering Adolph S. Ochs that the Times Company could not invest in any other corporations to avoid the criticism of editorial prejudice. The *New York Times* as an institution had to be pure. Punch's father, for example, had no idea where his business managers placed treasury cash. He didn't want to know that because other people might think a decision he made on an editorial was somehow distorted as a consequence of that knowledge. Also, the Times Company could not own another paper because how could there be another newspaper that was up to the quality of the *New York Times?* How could another Times paper have an editorial position different from that of the *New York Times?* He didn't want to own a television station because he didn't want to be in the entertainment business. His was a philosophy of staying out, but Punch's was one of getting in. The long philosophical debates that preceded diversification were carried on in the figurative shadows of Ochs and Adler. The debates were not without guilt for the heirs. There were macabre jokes about Ochs and Adler turning over in their graves as the discussions went on.

Some preliminary actions preceded diversification. In 1963, the Times Company bought a 49 percent interest in Gaspesia Pulp and Paper Company, Ltd., agreeing to an annual purchase of 60,000 tons of newsprint from the 90,000-ton capacity facility. The Times Book division, established in September, 1963, to develop a variety of *New York Times* books by members of the staff, had published sixteen books by the end of 1964. Three had been selected as Book-of-the-Month Club alternates or dividends.

"The company didn't go public until about three or four years after I became publisher," said Punch. "We were a little late to get into the acquisition field. It took a while to convince my father that we should change. There are a bunch of steps that I would have wished that we hadn't made. We went off in some wrong directions. We started some products that didn't work. We bought some companies that weren't terribly successful."

Meanwhile, if the *Times* could not automate (according to union fiat), it could modernize in other ways to increase productivity. In 1964, new and more efficient stereotype equipment, specialized mail room machinery, and automated passenger elevators were installed. A new ten-unit press with two folders to replace an uneconomical thirty-year-old, six-unit press at Forty-third Street and two additional press units at the West Side Plant had been ordered. More than $6.5 million was earmarked for improving operating efficiency by replacing old machines with new ones in 1965.

On December 13, 1966, the Times Company acquired for $500,000 a 51 percent interest in Teaching Systems Corporation. In addition to publishing instructional materials both for general educational purposes and for training in industry and government, the acquisition developed specialized teaching materials, particularly for handicapped children at the elementary school level. Said a colleague who was close to Punch: "It was at that time a meaningless acquisition for us. And yet something about it attracted him. He went ahead and bought it, and it has now become a fine, profit-making, wonderfully managed, little gem of a company in the crown of companies around the newspaper itself. . . . I don't know why he fell in love with it . . . what attracted him to it. I think it may have been the man who ran it, Clement Daley . . . who was out of the Navy, had . . . I guess you'd call it a military bearing. That, from his own Marine days, he finds attractive. It's a manner he's comfortable with, which always catches his eye."

Certainly Punch was proud of his Marine experience. Salisbury says Punch "sent his Marine exam scores to his father and they showed him in the highest percentiles in interpretation of social studies, natural studies, literary materials and mathematical ability."[5] Salisbury's footnote suggests another hypothesis for Punch's interest in this little company. "Punch's mother and sisters believed he suffered from dyslexia, a childhood learning disability in which words and letters seem to be transposed. Punch's grandfather was said to have had the same malfunction, which may be hereditary and more prevalent among males. Iphigene Sulzberger and her daughter, Ruth, both insisted they were plagued by the difficulty."[6] Punch questions the dyslexia "diagnosis." Punch is left-handed. "At St. Bernard's school," he reports, "every time I wrote with my left hand I went to the front of the class and was banged with a ruler until eventually I wrote right-handed. And since then I have had trouble with reversibles." Punch also still has trouble spelling.

In 1967, the Times Company got a three-year labor contract in late March. It was the first time since 1960 that contract negotiations were completed without a strike. In 1969, the momentum of acquisitions picked up. The first real move into what was, for the Times, the big leagues was the Cowles enterprise in 1970. According to Ivan Veit, the Cowles acquisition came about in the following way:

"Ben Handelman [later a Times senior vice-president] who was working in the subsidiary-affiliated area, came to my office one morning early with that day's paper, pointing to a financial report of Cowles Communications. Ben said to me, 'You know there are good properties here. If we could acquire them without *Look Magazine* [which was floundering and later died] it would be very good.' So we went over the figures and I agreed. I went in to see Punch and briefly said, 'We think this would be a good major acquisition and the board is ready for it. Will you talk to Mike Cowles and see if he's interested?' He said, 'Sure.' And he did it that very day. It happened that we were very timely and he [Mike] saved us a problem by saying, 'Yes, but not *Look*. You don't want *Look Magazine.'* And of course we didn't."

The New York Times Company exchanged 2.6 million shares or 24.6 percent of the Class A common stock of the company, and a subsidiary of the company in which the acquired businesses were placed assumed $15 million of debt. Punch did not have to worry about control of the Times Company; after the acquisition the Class A common stock had the right to vote for the election of only 36.5 percent of the board of directors. The Cowles properties included television station WREC in Memphis, Tennessee; four Florida newspapers; *Family Circle* magazine; Cambridge Book Company, Inc.; and the Modern Medicine group of professional magazines.

When it came to presenting acquisitions to the board for approval, Punch was careful to review things beforehand to ensure the right emphasis. According to one participant:

"His method of operation would be to give people working for him plenty of leeway, plenty of authority. When he concluded that they were going in the wrong direction, that is, not doing things as he wanted them done, then he would step in and make personnel changes to get his management in place, then through consultation and discussion he would make sure that new plans evolved.

"This was not done in a formal way where he would call for people to sit around a table and brainstorm or develop a plan, instead it was done in a much more informal way. Discussions were held about problems or what might be done. He encouraged people to come up with solutions, or to propose solutions. The way that he works it is almost impossible to decide where the contributions came from (that doesn't really become all that important). What's important is the plan has been evolved (and to make sure that it's properly implemented) and that it succeeds."

The acquisitions continued: two newspapers in Florida, *The Leesburg Daily Commercial* and *The Palatka Daily News,* to add to the former Cowles properties, *The Gainesville Sun, The Lakeland Ledger, The Sebring News,* and *The Avon Park Sun.* The Times Company was following the population shift to the Sun Belt. By 1972, subsidiary activities had more than doubled their earnings. By 1973, revenues from all business categories other than the *New York Times* newspaper accounted for nearly 30 percent of total revenues. This was the kind of financial clout Punch Sulzberger needed in negotiating with the unions.

The labor scenario would be different when 1973 rolled around. Negotiations throughout 1973 resulted in two-year agreements with all but three unions, the Typographers, Electricians, and Operating Engineers. It was not until July 28, 1974, that a unique eleven-year labor agreement, retroactive to March 31, 1973, was ratified with New York Typographical Union No. 6, which gave the *Times* the unrestricted right to automate its typesetting processes in return for lifetime job guarantees for full-time regular printers and designated substitutes.

Capital expenditures in 1975 and 1976 totaled $37 million. An additional $24 million was planned for 1977. This three-year sum of $61 million contrasted with the $20 million in capital expenditures during the previous three years. Virtually all in-house classified and display advertising was already being photocomposed. It was time now to computerize the editing and setting of news copy. In October, 1976, the new automated satellite printing plant in Carlstadt, New Jersey, became operational.

Nineteen seventy-eight saw the return of an old nemesis, the strike. At one point, seeing no end to the strike, Walter Mattson, then in charge of production operations, warned Punch of the risk of waiting until they were financially weakened and then giving in to the union demands. Punch said he was going to stand firm and that was all there was to it. The eighty-eight-day strike of the pressmen, from August 9 through November 5, 1978, won for the *Times* the right to reduce pressroom manning through attrition and retirement incentives to levels competitive with the manning of the principal unionized suburban newspapers in the New York area.

The strike reduced earnings to $1.32 a share, giving a net income of $15.55 million on revenues of $491.56 million. However, by that time the affiliated companies had produced record earnings. Punch Sulzberger had achieved the financial clout needed to protect against threats to the Times Company's survival. That clout also positioned it to gain concessions from the union that could only increase that clout. This was all the more significant in view of the fact that the *New York Times* had sustained an operating loss of $12.6 million in 1978.

Punch moved vigorously in 1980 and 1982 with the acquisition of more newspapers, *The Sarasota* (Florida) *Herald-Tribune,* followed by eight daily and three weekly newspapers. The dailies were in Kentucky, Alabama, Louisiana, North Carolina, Mississippi, and Tennessee; the three weeklies in Mississippi, Maine, and Tennessee. This brought to thirty the number of regional newspapers the Times had acquired.

Punch had ensured the viability of the business.

Distant Editions

The *New York Times* Western Edition had begun publication in October, 1962, just before the strike. It was in hot water from the outset. It became abundantly clear that the *Times* decision makers hadn't done their homework. The edition's circulation of 85,000 spread out over thirteen states resulted in high distribution costs. It could not attract sufficient advertising because of the widely scattered readership. It was engaged in a battle on the West Coast with the *Los Angeles Times*. It was losing $3 million dollars a year, and it would not be profitable by the end of a five-year projection. The new publisher shut it down. That decision was a complete reversal of Orvil Dryfoos's dream to expand the *New York Times* to a national newspaper.

In Europe, the *Times* was engaged in a head-on battle with the *Herald Tribune*, as it was in New York. Unlike the New York battle, which was won by the *Times*, the battle in Europe was going in favor of the *Herald Tribune*, and the *Times* was losing $2 million a year there. The senior Sulzberger had started the International Edition during World War II for American troops. It was first a weekly, published in Amsterdam, then a daily published in Paris. It was viewed in New York as a pale imitation of the *New York Times*.

An analysis by Sydney Gruson (now vice-chairman of the company) showed clearly there was no room for two publications of that kind in Paris. Within two weeks, Gruson and Punch worked out a merger with Walter Thayer, of Whitney Communications, and a representative of the Washington Post Company. A coin was flipped to see whether the line under the new title, the *International Herald Tribune*, would say published "with the *New York Times* and *Washington Post*" or published "with the *Washington Post* and *New York Times*." Punch won the flip, so the *New York Times* came first.

Intimations of a clash between business considerations and news considerations had surfaced with respect to the merger with the *Herald Tribune*. The news side was more opposed than the business side because of their concern for the *New York Times* as an international newspaper. How would its editorial voice be heard throughout Europe? The agreement provided that the partners would select the editor jointly, and that the *New York Times* news service would be available. Punch felt its importance among world leaders would not be diminished because the *New York Times* would reach all of the capitals in the world.

A *Times* executive commented on the decisions that determined the fate of the two editions: "Why shut down the Western Edition and not the International Edition? When we started the International Edition it was clothed in the altruistic cloak of a contribution to international understanding. Arthur Hays Sulzberger said that this is something we are committed to. He had never said we were committed to the Western Edition."

According to another executive, the merger produced "what is by a lot of people's standards the best paper in Europe, and a profitable newspaper. . . . Once the idea had been accepted, there was no hesitation; he [Punch] took hold of negotiations himself . . . there was no pettiness. The idea having been accepted, he doesn't permit the underbrush to stop him at all."

Internal Fiefdoms

Despite the success of the *Times* as a newspaper, it suffered from the conflict of fiefdoms. Punch saw that "there was a great deal of the feeling, 'You stay out of my turf and I'll stay out of yours.' And that meant that when they couldn't resolve a difference, it came up to my desk. I was prepared to resolve it, but they could have resolved most differences themselves. We were running two separate newspapers here, a daily on the third floor and a Sunday on the eighth. They did not talk to one another. We had a Sunday editor, a great guy, Lester Markel, tough as nails."

Punch realized that Markel would never accept Catledge as executive editor, and therefore had to be removed before that appointment could be made. Punch had to set aside consensus and ordered the merger of the News and Sunday departments in 1976. "If you sought the consensus on that," recalled an intimate, "you would have had the

Sunday people holding out for separation and the daily people, knowing they would get the power, wanting to take the power. So you couldn't reach consensus."

Punch doesn't relish confrontations. He would prefer shaking hands to chopping heads. But when he knows something needs to be done he does it. Despite the fact that he had been brought up to respect senior editors, Punch went down to Markel's office and said that he wanted to put everything together, that there would be an executive editor. He brought Markel up to the fourteenth floor. That was a signal that there was strength in the publisher's office.

Punch's plan to merge the News and Sunday Departments and to reorganize the News Department went awry. Turner Catledge fell in love with the Sunday Department and never brought the two departments together. James "Scotty" Reston, one of the nation's finest newspapermen, up from Washington to run the News Department, admitted that editing was not his forte. And after about fifteen months, he fled back to Washington.

It took until April, 1976, before Punch managed to merge the two departments under one head, Abe Rosenthal. As Punch recalled it:

"I said to Abe Rosenthal, now look, that's it. No more. And we merged the two together and there is no more Sunday Department. It's just one big News Department doing its thing. Some do it on Sunday and some do it on Monday. But, you know, looking back I probably would have done it differently. I would have probably asked Turner to do it differently. I don't know if I could have. We even tried to do some merging in our sales area, but they weren't ready to do it. And it didn't work. In fact we haven't even merged those departments now. If anything, we've even separated them further. It looked like a good idea at the time and it turned out to be a lousy idea."

The tradition at the *Times* is that the publisher does not tell the News Department what to do. He may comment on performance or even make suggestions, but the News Department runs about as independently as a News Department can in any newspaper. Every day at four o'clock, there was a managing editor's meeting with the News Department heads. Typically, the publisher would attend that. Proofs of editorials were sent routinely to the publisher. Sulzberger, Sr., and

Dryfoos read every editorial every night before they went to press. Unless it was a very sensitive issue, or unless it was a recommendation of a candidate for office, the publisher would not necessarily be consulted about an editorial.

Over the years Punch had seen editorials he took issue with. He decided it was time for a change. As he described it:

> "There are little things that make big changes. The change of editor of the editorial page to Max Frankel, I think, made a big change. It's not that we violently changed our editorial position. I think we just became a little more thoughtful, a little less preachy, a little more considerate of the fact that there is usually more than one side to an issue and that everybody on the other side isn't a liar or a thief or something like that. . . . We were perceived as being antibusiness and I thought we were. I always argued that we were a business. To be antibusiness would be against ourselves. I think that we are considered far less antibusiness today. . . . If we're going to outrage the businessman, we're not going to get his advertising or his readership, both of which are important to us. . . . They called it a bloodbath because we got rid of some editors." [He laughed.] So, I don't know how subtle it was."

To accomplish this change in January, 1977, Punch had to ask his own cousin, John Oakes, to retire before reaching the mandatory date. John's mother died when he and his brother were tots, and Punch's mother, Iphigene Sulzberger, was practically a surrogate mother to John Oakes. "How do you confront a situation like that?" asked an intimate. "It wasn't that John was incompetent. He was an able editor but he wasn't performing exactly as Punch would have liked. I dare say he would have made a change sooner if John were someone else's cousin. . . . Punch didn't want Max Frankel reporting to Abe; that wouldn't work too well . . . they're both senior people. He wanted to name Max editor of the editorial page, reporting directly to the publisher. Many people thought he would wait until John was sixty-five. But no, it wasn't right. He couldn't allow a point of view to continue that didn't feel right to him."

One of the major managerial practices that Punch learned from his grandfather was: "Don't look over somebody's shoulder all the time. Pick the man who you want to do the job, and then let him alone to do it. And if he doesn't do it, change him." According to Punch's subordinates, he has an unusual ability to cut his losses and to be absolutely ruthless in facing situations that he believes he has to resolve for the good of the newspaper. Said one: "It's not easy to say to people you've worked with for ten, twelve, thirteen years, 'That's all. For the sake of this newspaper you've got to stop. You've got to, in effect go away.' He takes a lot of time working out the mechanics of the changes he wants and who he wants in the new places. Then, with less emotion and less reaction than almost anybody I know, he can do it."

Some people are still bitter about the way Punch brought Frankel in as editor. To do so, he had to clean out the old editorial board as well. But apparently Punch has the capacity to heal as well. John Oakes remains in the *Times* building and now seems a reasonably happy man, despite his regret.

What did Punch do for those deposed? According to one associate: "To the extent that arrangements can be made to look after them, they're looked after. Where they have to be retired, they're retired. To the extent that he can be generous, where company policy permits generosity, he's generous. Where it doesn't permit generosity, sometimes he insists on generosity anyway."

Developing Management

After the Times Company went public in 1969, management methods gradually changed to maintain quality and profitability simultaneously. It was a case of either teaching old dogs new tricks or waiting for new dogs to come in. Punch began to change the roster of executives on both sides of the business. Over a period of years, budgets were developed. Promotion and sales became more important and more aggressive. Internal controls improved. There was more planning, and, of course, the acquisition program.

Punch Sulzberger tried to initiate an atmosphere that would pave the way for the management systems to come:

"So I took the gang away . . . loaded them up in a bus and drove to Atlantic City in February in a snowstorm for the first meeting of all the top executives. And I remember telling them that we had a whole bunch of pine trees, all growing straight up, and it never came together at the top excepting through me, and I wasn't going to spend my life doing that, that was crazy. . . . Since then we've

refined that process and been away repeatedly, of course, changed
the composition of the group enormously. But that was the beginning and then we moved on slowly, in baby steps, into the budgeting process, which I thought was essential if we were going to
manage our business. I remember I got Turner Catledge, who was
the managing editor, convinced that we ought to have a budget.
And I thought if I can convince Turner Catledge that we should
have a budget, that would work. So I said, 'Do me a favor. You
explain how it's going to work to everybody who is highly suspi-
cious, of course, of what a budget is going to do.' So Turner made
an eloquent speech, in his southern drawl, at one of his meetings
about, not to worry, it's just planning. And we started on a budget.
About four months later something came up that he didn't like, so
he withdrew the News Department from the budgeting process.
But it was too late, he couldn't do it, he was stuck."

One of the abilities that Punch has is the recognition of people with
talent, such as Walter Mattson, who subsequently became president of
the company and, some say, probably the most respected newspaper
executive in North America. When Walter was a very young man,
Punch marked him as someone who had a future with the company. He
managed to keep Mattson with the *New York Times* when Mattson had
many offers to go elsewhere, and rescued him from the Dunkirk that
was the Western Edition.

Punch's eye for talent is further exemplified by Bill Safire. As part of
the effort to undo the antibusiness slant and to get rid of the *Times*'s
alleged left-wing image, he wanted to bring a conservative on board.
He met Safire at a party and said, "This is the guy." His colleagues
protested that Safire was not a newspaperman but a public relations
flack, tainted by his association with Nixon. But Punch in his stubborn
way was absolutely unmovable. Safire later won a Pulitzer prize.

At first there were three committees called NOG, COG, and SOG
(newspaper operating group, corporate operating group, and subsidiary
operating group). Punch was the head of the newspaper operating
group; the chairman, Harding Bancroft, was head of the corporate
group; and Veit supervised the subsidiaries. They met as an executive
committee every morning. The next step was to name four senior
vice-presidents to clarify the overlapping activities in the executive
committee: Walter Mattson, who was in charge of production operations; John McCabe, the advertising, circulation, and marketing activities; James Goodale, legal and corporate; and Sydney Gruson, who had

the subsidiaries. Then the executive committee met once a week with those four senior vice-presidents, and every other week the whole group would meet with the labor relations people because that was a constant preoccupation.

By the end of 1972, there had been a marked increase in the number of officers and corporate executives of the New York Times Company, as distinguished from the *New York Times* newspaper. This executive group had grown from fifteen to nineteen, with most holding the title of vice-president. The subsidiaries had been structured into the magazine group, the broadcasting group, the Florida newspaper group, and other subsidiary activities.

But Punch knew these steps were still part of the period of transition. This was not the structure that he wanted ultimately. When Veit's retirement neared, scheduled for 1973, Punch postponed it for almost a year to think through the next step. That was to appoint three executive vice-presidents: Mattson, for newspaper operations, except news and editorial; Gruson, for the subsidiaries; and Goodale, for corporate, legal, and financial. They, with Punch, became the executive committee. Veit retired on April 1, 1974, and became a board member. Punch added other directors in 1973 and 1974, most executives of major corporations to bring a business perspective to a growing business.

Goodale had come to the Times Company originally as a member of the legal department. His area was corporate affairs and financial administration. He moved in very strongly on both the budget and acquisition processes. He and Walter Mattson were clearly the competitors for the presidency, because Gruson was twenty years older.

In September, 1974, Punch and Mattson sat in the publisher's little den in the back of his office and chatted about some needed personnel changes. The circulation director had to go. The advertising director had to go. The controller was dying of cancer and would have to be replaced. A new team would have to be built. Punch had anticipated Mattson's analysis, and agreed completely. Mattson gave himself until September, 1975, to get his team in place. Punch met with the candidates Mattson brought to him for approval. Punch was a major salesman, persuading attractive candidates that things were different at the *Times,* that this was the place to work, and that he, Punch, was the kind of fellow they would want to work for.

But Mattson was the engine of reorganizational change. "The fact that you could . . . move him through the organization, then have Mattson turn around and recreate in his image the empires that we're giving him, was a change in organizational culture," said an observer.

"Punch never said much about the reorganization until it was all clean and tidy and done. He moved Mattson right through the organization, past one staunch guardian of the status quo after another, in the most startling fast manner. Mattson reorganized each area that he headed. In the process, he created quite a different substructure of the newspaper. Punch knew exactly that that was going to happen. He had this troika, Mattson and Goodale as the forty-year-old base of the isosceles triangle, and the older Gruson at the top. He operated advantageously with that setup for about four years."

Then it stopped working. It began to be difficult to get decisions out of the executive committee because the struggle for power was so intense. Mattson in his own quiet immovable way was digging in. Goodale was trying to establish himself as president without the title. Neither Mattson nor Gruson were going to permit him to do so, and they prevented it by jockeying and blocking. Punch knew someone would have to get hurt, and he took a long time to do it. He brought McKinsey and Company in, ostensibly for the purpose of studying the company and recommending a reorganization that would best meet its needs for the future, but really to validate what he had already decided.

The marketplace demanded a change. The company had to be better led, better managed. Mattson was the man to do it, and Punch understood that. Mattson had straightened many things out—the union situation, the production process, the selection of new people. The company was a new entity with many subsidiaries that required a different corporate structure. Said one observer, "He couldn't do without Mattson; he could do without Goodale." Goodale resigned in January, 1980. Mattson was named president and chief operating officer of the company. Sydney Gruson became vice-chairman. Both were named to the board, and, with Punch, comprised the executive committee.

Mattson is viewed as a strong character, a very competent workaholic, with good judgment. He can be ruthless. He has fired people rather abruptly. He plays his cards close to the vest. He keeps his finger on everything. He delegates less than had been characteristic before. He knows what's going on.

Punch stressed the attention to placing people in the right roles, using Mattson as an example:

"People in the News Department are not usually very good business managers. They are much more concerned with news. . . . They needed help and they weren't getting the kind of help that they needed. There was a constant backing and forthing and each

one blaming the other for all kinds of things. And you remember
how sloppy the old editions were, with the typographical errors.
When Walter came along this thing started to resolve itself. He
quickly won the confidence of the News Department, [so] that
when Walter said, 'We'll print it for you on Thursday night, a
special section,' by God it was printed on Thursday night. And
when he said, 'I'm sorry, but I can't . . . ,' there really wasn't any
point in arguing with him because he was telling you the truth. And
I think that we've bubbled up a lot of people like that now. And
when they say they can, they can. And we've taken a lot of baloney
out of the thing. And they're a lot more professional managers.
We've gone outside and we still bring an awful lot of them."

The Times Company base for decision making is still too narrow. The
company hasn't developed the middle management it requires because
it hasn't yet developed a structured developmental program. The
Times personnel staff has been working on that program.

The Sulzberger Style

Punch described himself as "Reasonably easygoing, I would guess.
Reasonably trustworthy, reasonably trusting. I like my associates. My
best friends are my colleagues, with a rare exception. So when I'm done
at the end of the day, I'm perfectly happy to go out with them at night.
And, you know, that's a kind of an organization I like. I like to like my
associates, and . . . a cold, calculating, professional manager and I don't
get along very well."
One close associate described the Sulzberger style:

"You usually find his conversation has humor; when staffers reach
notable anniversaries, they come up here for a drink with the
publisher. They may be messengers or clerks but it doesn't take
more than two minutes before they feel there is a warmth between
them. There is no sense that the big boss is condescending to stand
with the person. At those anniversary social gatherings he would
approach with a smile, say, 'Can I pour you a drink?' He would say,
'Great record and I know you're proud of it, and we are, and I'm
glad we got to meet.' There are usually three or four other principal

executives there, whoever can be swept into the office to give it more prestige, more aura. But he is the one who sets the tone. And the same thing is true in meetings. There are no meetings, except on the gravest problems, in which he isn't relaxed and he usually has a joke to break tension. It is a great asset. It has eased many situations. . . . There was no board meeting I can remember that he didn't have some spontaneous joke or pun or humorous reference to put things in that kind of tone. And I don't know anyone here who is mad at him."

He has a keen sensitivity to the traumas of his associates. When one suffered the breakup of a long marriage, Punch sat with him in a hotel room for two hours. "We're not going to play tennis and I don't like golf," he said. "We're not going to go for a walk. We're just going to sit here and talk about it, talk about what's really going to be a tough time for you and how I as a person, not chairman or boss, can be helpful to you."

An insider gives another perspective:

"He has a very high sense of the right thing to do. Where it affects people and things and ideas and in this case, the newspaper that he loves . . . there's practically no limit to his willingness to put himself out in any way at all. There is a certain lack of concern or unwillingness to involve himself where people or things or ideas that he doesn't care about or doesn't know about are involved. There is no all-embracing humanity, if you want to put it that way, for the stranger on the street, for the mere acquaintance. He has enough people he cares about who are close to him, I think, to use up all the compassion and feeling and love and so on, and on them he lavishes that very willingly and very easily and very givingly. . . . He will look after friends, in top and lowly positions . . . he will go to great, great lengths to protect them . . . he would see that they don't get hurt. He will make certain that the arrangements made are to 'take care of that person' and that person will be comfortable and will not be trod on or destroyed. . . . But there's a limit."

Punch doesn't really enjoy strangers. He doesn't like to be seated at a dinner between people he's never seen before. He'd rather be in his own house puttering around than visiting the great and the mighty and powerful. He has no pretensions to uphold. He is a very secure man and likes the familiarity of people and places.

The only exception to this preference for the familiar is his desire to see exotic faraway places. Punch has an enormous curiosity to see things, to go into the bazaars and just talk with and watch a lot of people. He has great curiosity about what is being sold in the shops. He's not as interested in visiting museums. Nor is he particularly interested in listening to an opera or a symphony or looking at paintings to figure out what an artist is trying to say. He spends so much time examining and asking and investigating and looking, that he would just as soon not do that for relaxation.

Like all of the other leaders described in this book, Punch is described by associates as having a neat, tidy, visual mind. Reported one, "His sister once said if you want your car washed just leave it for a couple of hours in Punch's driveway." Another story has it that Punch visited a friend for a weekend and began fixing the pipes, doing the gardening and other odd jobs around that house. This behavior was so predictable that the friend said to his wife, "Let's wait for Punch, he'll fix it all." A colleague leaves some pictures against a wall waiting for Punch to see the disarray on one of his visits. "If I just leave them like that, eventually he'll come in one day, go back and get his own hammer, and he'll hang them for me. He wanders because the nature of the man is not to stay still very long. When he sits down to get rid of the junk on his desk, he gets rid of it as fast as he can because he wants to go around and see people and talk to people."

"He likes things to be tidy," confirmed one of his associates. "He likes things to be neat and clear. He like things to be compact. He doesn't like to spend more time and/or words than are necessary. When managers came to present proposals of their operations to the board, he was very quick to praise those who got to the point and made everything clear and got it over with. I can't remember him cutting people off, but he would be restless with discursive presentations . . . fidget. But he wouldn't say anything critical while the man was there. He might say to us afterward, 'Jesus, can't you get him to come to the point faster?' " That, too, is a penchant he shares with the other CEOs.

"Punch is an easy man to read," said another associate. "You know his degree of enthusiasm by the manner in which he speaks, by the tone in which he converses, by the nature of the questioning, and so on. For example, you hear, 'Look, I don't want any of that. Goddamnit, ———, you know how I feel about that. Why do you do this?' or, 'Jesus, do you have to?' Or you get a series of questions such as, 'What do you think this would do for the place?' or, 'What do you think the effect will be on X and Y and Z?' and so on. There are grades between those two reactions, but he is not a hard man to read; he keeps a lot of things to himself, but I know when he's keeping things to himself."

Punch's associates can read his state of mind by attending to the body English he demonstrates. Some think tense situations at the Times Company may be correlated with flareups of his back problem. One says:

> "When we're talking and there's not total concentration, I can almost see his mind floating away from me. Then I know there are other things on his mind and I've only got a certain percentage of his attention. I stop because I know, unless I've got his mind, that there are so many things going on that I'll have to come back to it anyway. We're not going to go where I want with the issue at hand or the question. I knew it almost from his body movement, really. . . . There's a tightening of his shoulders. His eyes are very telltale. When he's uncomfortable with something, he expresses it in a motion of the top of his body. The top of the torso and the shoulders roll a bit. . . . When he's worried the focus is 50 percent or 60 percent, and the mind is dealing with you but it's also dealing with the problems, whatever they may be, coming from other directions. . . . I've heard him say, 'I'm just not going to have that. Now goddammit it, they might as well know I'm not going to have that.' That's about as much getting up his back as he does. But when he says, 'I'm not going to have that,' and the issue is a strong enough one, that is it. He's open to discussion, argument, persuasion, possibly to a greater extent than almost any man I've known who has that much power. . . . When he's angry, he's angry. He comes straight out at you."

Another associate noticed that Punch "bites a little harder on his pipe" when he is tense. You also know when he is angry. Said one errant executive, "He sat in that big conference room and he never said one angry thing to me. What he did was to say nothing. Absolutely nothing. . . . By not saying anything he let me know let's not let this kind of thing happen."

In an officers' meeting, Punch lashed out because equal opportunity employment goals were not being met. One who was there reported, "He wadded up a piece of paper, and he stood up and threw the piece of paper on the floor, and he said, 'Goddamit, how many times have we talked about it? How many times have I tried to impress you that it's not enough just to make the effort. We've got to get the results.' There was just a flash fire. . . . It was apparent that he felt passionately about the issue."

Making Things Happen

Punch maintained a very delicate balance between the business operations of the newspaper and the News Department. Said one informant:

"If we were going to develop a new section, it required a commitment from the Business Department to generate the revenues to support the editorial costs. Punch would allow that to develop between the Business Department and the News Department. He would encourage business management and news management to work together to develop a plan to bring to him.

"He wouldn't call the two together and say, 'I want you guys to do so and so,' but rather he would encourage each side to work with the other. He would say, 'If you run into a real problem come on up and I will break the tie, but I want you to develop the plan. I want to know what the plan is, then we'll discuss it and go over it.' So he's involved through encouraging, on a one-on-one basis, everyone's best energies and talents. He's involved in trying to put together the people who will not only develop but also implement the program without his being the person on top who is forcing the issue. In the selection of the personalities, in his way of encouraging things to happen, Punch accomplished what had never been accomplished in the history of the newspaper. . . . The conflicts between the business and the news operation are practically nonexistent at this point. In my experience . . . only once did we ever bring an issue to Punch for Punch to resolve.

"He has in his office a little sitting room in the back and the habit of calling executives back to his inner office where they would chat on a one-on-one basis . . . relaxed, jacket off, just sit there and have a friendly conversation . . . smoking his pipe. The perception of the publisher is that he is a very relaxed individual in the sense that he puts you at ease. I think that is one of his most significant attributes. . . . Only on one or two occasions have I seen him operate by giving an absolute command. In most cases there's persuasion involved, and discussions and listening, and going back again and a pat on the back, sitting down talking about what we are trying to do. . . . Physical [pat on back] very, very important."

Punch believes that there is less politics at the *Times* than elsewhere because he tries to identify the right person to do a given job, grant him the authority to do that job, then let him alone but be available when that person wants him. Punch abhors large meetings "to pour holy water on something that's already been decided."

"If the people down below can figure it out without me, great. They usually know a lot more about the particular situation anyway. And, as long as we all go along in the same path, steering in the same direction, that suits me to a T. . . . We have made some . . . silly mistakes because . . . of my philosophy of letting people grow and develop and do their own things. [Walter Wriston could say the same.] And sometimes, if you let it cook too long, it develops a life of its own, and by the time it gets to you, even if your instincts tell you that it's wrong, there's very little that you can do about it without causing an enormous lot of damage."

A good example was Punch's decision to go along with a major new consumer biweekly, titled *Us.* Intensive testing and a research program were under way in 1976, and the new publication started in April, 1977. It would be sold at newsstands and supermarkets, employing the supermarket and chainstore sales force that had made *Family Circle*'s average monthly circulation soar to more than 8.5 million copies. *Us* was aimed at young adults and their interest in personalities in the news and the world of entertainment. Bill Davis, the new head of the Magazine Division, and Sydney Gruson were behind it. Said Punch, "I guess by the time it got up here—the magazine group had developed it—it really did have almost a life of its own. I should have said no. I just didn't like it. . . . It didn't feel good, it didn't feel like something that the Times should be doing. And, you know, great hindsight, it didn't work out. If it had worked out, of course, I don't know how I would have felt about it. And I remember talking with some of my colleagues who didn't like it who said to me, 'You can't stop it now. You've got to let them try because it's gone so far.' There's something wrong with that.

"I learned a lesson," he laughed.

"Next time I get that gut reaction, I'm just going to stop, and if they don't like it, that's just too bad. At least I'm going to stop it until I have the chance to think and not get swept along by the emotion of the time. . . . it became very rapidly apparent that we were incapable of producing that kind of an editorial product. . . . The magazine division is separate from the newspaper, and we haven't traditionally borrowed from one for the other. They had no expertise in the magazine division to edit that kind of publication, no experience. . . . If you're going to have that magazine, you've got to first have an editorial concept and the ability to carry out the concept. And we started it ass-backwards. We started out with the fact that we have a delivery system. Now let's go find a magazine that fits the delivery system."

Us was sold in 1980 to Macfadden Publications. Punch didn't spend any time wringing his hands and weeping.

Another insider said of Punch: "When he approves of a deal he will support it, but he is not necessarily an innovator. We went through the staff process each time we had a major decision to make. Then we would always go to Punch, discuss it, and he could say no or yes. It wasn't often that he would say, 'Let's do this big thing.' Usually, those things are staff generated." The Sulzberger style from another perspective:

"Punch, in his own patient, conservative, yet quiet daring way, saw an opportunity here and set a group of people to work. . . . This is the way he works, this is the essential working quality of him that has never changed in all the years I've known him—he starts with the idea and people run, having given the instructions to go ahead, take a look at it, lets people run very hard. But in himself is terribly, terribly slow-moving about it, very deliberately deliberate, so that whatever enthusiasms are worked up by the people doing the work that he has sent them, they are always countered by this deliberateness, this decision of his, which is always unspoken, to go slowly. . . . Yes, he's willing to be the first publisher or owner or member of the owning family to change it drastically, but he's going to do it with such care, such deliberateness that the chance for error is going to be as minimized as a human can make it. It doesn't mean you're not going to make mistakes . . . there have to be mistakes in order to have the successes. We've had our share of mistakes

. . . that he's played a part in and wouldn't attempt to run away from. And I think where he went against his natural instincts he got into trouble."

Although Punch doesn't like detail, he has infinite patience with those details that relate to the design and content of the newspaper. For example, when the paper changed from eight to six columns he was concerned with what would remain as part of the regular format. But the detail of the figures and the analysis behind the figures, all the back-breaking stuff that are part of daily corporate life, are just not for him.

"I do not have an MBA background, or a business school background. I am *constantly* frustrated by computer printouts of economic matters," he laughed.

"Which may be all right, because I insist that they put it in English so that I can understand it. . . . It's a highly frustrating thing. . . . I walk down the hall to our controller and say, 'Tell me in English what this means.' And you know, I guess one of the grave troubles of computers is that they grind out so bloody much. And I get very, very confused when I get into that. Someone comes in and hands me stuff like that, I don't even know where to *begin.* I can work my way through the stuff I send our directors with no trouble. And I think it's probably pretty good, because I've insisted that they put it in English. But don't bring in a big, complicated thingamajigger and say, "Now, based on this, were do you think we ought to go?'

In his office, Punch is at home with the new technology as well as relics from the past. He uses an old Underwood manual typewriter to help him think; a habit leftover from his days as a reporter. "I had it sent up about . . . twenty some odd years ago, I guess. I just hung onto it. I still use it. When I really want to think of something, I drag out my old piece of paper and type it in. . . . The old reporter in me," he laughed. "The computer terminal keeps me in touch with the world now. . . . It's the only way I can really find out what our editorials are going to be. There are no more galleys as they used to have, so I have to call them up on the terminal. And if I see something I don't like, I can put into it what I think ought to be said or done or something like that and communicate back and forth. I can call up the Associated Press and United Press wires, some of our national and some of our Washington stuff and foreign stuff, and I hope soon to be able to get the entire circus, all of our five data systems."

Punch doesn't like sitting for hours at a meeting. His limit is usually two hours. Then he'll find some reason to leave. Sometimes people think his tolerance is less than it ought to be for certain problems. But his style is very deliberate and says to people, in effect: "I will listen for a certain amount of time."

Punch's preference for one-on-one consultations with senior executives occurs in the context of his peripatetic style. As described by one:

"He would wander around these halls and pop in on Dave Gorham, the senior vice-president for finance, to chat about a problem, and Gorham will give his opinion. Then he'll wander next door to Mike Ryan and he'll chat with Ryan. Then he may wander into Mattson, and then there's this ebbing and flowing of ideas around him. . . . He's a great wanderer. . . . You may notice there are no closed doors up here [on the fourteenth floor]. He likes to wander around, and if a door is closed that's a sign to everybody that there is something going on that shouldn't be disturbed. And even Punch, 99 times out of 100, respects that. He may not, if it's particularly somebody he feels very easy and comfortable with, and he will pop his head in just to say I want to see you for a minute. But he wanders. He goes to the tenth floor and sees Frankel [editorial page editor], he goes to the third floor, talks to people in the News Department."

"We've created a newspaper that has given away, in my opinion, none of its seriousness and has put into it a major amount of service and lightheartedness that had to be unless the paper was to atrophy," said a participant in the creation.

"Sulzberger, Sr., had a few friends within the paper. Dryfoos had more. Almost all of Punch's friendships are with those on the paper. Therefore he knows more about the people and more about what is going on with the development of the paper. He's with new ideas from the beginning of the development of the idea. For example, at the end of most days he has a drink with Abe Rosenthal [executive editor] in Rosenthal's office. Punch has involved himself with the actual newspaper and the people who edit and report the news.

The News Department responds to him more as a co-worker than just their boss. It would never have entered his father's mind to have sat with the newspaper and designed a section of the newspaper the way Punch does."

To sustain the imaginative and independent spirit of a paper, the publisher must be willing to accept a give-and-take discussion of ideas and to recognize that the expertise of others may be greater than his and that their ideas may be different from his but grounded in a professionalism that he can't ignore. Punch deliberately set out to create this atmosphere. "He was faced with a marketplace in which the paper's future was threatened unless change was created. That was the big challenge and it was in the meeting of that challenge that is a major mark of his success," explained one colleague.

Another intimate discussed Punch's relationship with the news side of the *Times.* "A William Randolph Hearst or the publisher of the *Post,* Rupert Murdoch, would dictate news play and display to the editors. Punch does not do that, but he does criticize and suggest. There are constant discussions of ways to improve the paper, new formats, developing news areas and how we will cover them. The publisher doesn't usurp the role of the managing editor, but he is certainly involved in the larger questions of maintaining and improving the quality of the *Times.*"

Punch himself takes a personal interest in developing people close to him. For example, Punch insisted that Mike Ryan attend college as a condition of his staying at the *Times.* While Ryan was attending law school at night concurrent with his job in the financial department of the *Times,* Jim Goodale offered him a job in the new legal department. When Punch learned of it, he typed a personal note to Mike saying how delighted he was that Mike had decided to join the legal department and that it was important to the future of the company as well as to Mike. The couple of typos in the note and Punch's signature indicated Punch had used his old manual typewriter. Another *Times* staffer was faced with a problem with the military draft, wanting to meet his obligation in a way that would permit him to continue his education. One day Punch buzzed the staffer to come to his office. There, chatting with Punch was the commanding general of the Marine Corps. Punch suggested that a six-month tour in the then active reserve program would fill the bill.

Although a deliberate person who takes no impulsive risks, Punch nevertheless will take risks once the requirements of the situation, the advantages, the options, and the dangers have been presented to him and he has been able to weigh them. He has to be convinced in his own mind pretty firmly, before he takes a drastic step.

The case of the Pentagon Papers is an example. Louis Loeb, who was the outside counsel, and Herbert Brownell, the senior partner of Lord, Day and Lord and a former attorney general, both said the *Times* could not print the Pentagon Papers. A couple of editors agreed. Punch heard all the warnings. He also heard other editors say it was the *Times*'s duty to print. Scotty Reston said he would even be willing to go to jail for doing so. Before deciding whether to print the papers and, if so, whether to do it all at once or in a series, the *Times* set up a secret editorial office in the Hilton Hotel, and a secret, locked and guarded composing room on another floor in the *Times* building. While the editing was going on, Punch and Ivan Veit were scheduled to go to London. Punch told the editors he would not decide on whether to publish until he saw the final copy before he left. The editors finished, and he made the decision to publish both the papers and the interpretive story that went with them. It was a very delicate legal situation. He decided with the editors that doing it as a series and with the documents was a better public service.

Remodeling the *Times*

Nineteen seventy-six was a year of thunderous change. The *Times* changed its format from its traditional eight-column page to a "six on nine"—six-column format for news, nine-column for advertising. This maintained news content, improved readability, and saved 4 percent on expensive newsprint. More importantly, the *Times* became a four-section paper with the introduction of the new Friday section, *Weekend,* a guide to entertainment and the arts, and the introduction of the *Living Section,* a Wednesday "magazine inside a newspaper" devoted to food, culture, and other amenities of living. March, 1977, would see the start of the *Home Section.* The *Times* increased its coverage of business and financial news with the largest team of business reporters in its history. Their reports and analyses were in a separate section *(Business/Finance)* of the newspaper four times a week. Early in 1976, two new Sunday sections, the *New Jersey Weekly* and the *Long Island Weekly,* were launched for readers in those areas. The *New York Times*

Magazine was spruced up, now printed on a premium-grade paper, providing advertisers with superior color reproduction and readers with a more attractive product.

Punch assessed the change in newspaper format:

"It's not only a newspaper of good hard news everyday, but it's basically a magazine also, with those C sections, which have been very good for us. Our circulation has grown while other circulations across the country have declined. . . . I think much of the magazine concept came out of our Business Department. . . . The News Department likes to claim some of that credit, but I think that the fact of the matter is that it was a response to a business need. The News Department grabbed that opportunity and has done, I think, extraordinarily well. The business need was one that . . . was fairly imperative . . . the circulation problem was the major one. The suburban newspapers had grown. Instead of being little dinky things, they had been acquired by big powerful companies. They were producing a product that satisfied too many people. And we were being squeezed from all sides. Every time we had a labor dispute, they'd move in one notch more on us. We had to do something that would excite our readers, something new, something fresh, something they really wanted. And we also had to put to use a section that would be interesting to advertisers. We had never, for instance, been able to crack the food advertising business. Grocery chains apparently thought the *Times* readers never ate. So we decided that we had to do something about it and we started off with the most obvious section. We also had seen the enormous growth of service magazines, such as *New York Magazine, Cue,* and the *New Yorker,* in some respects. And here they were, putting out in a magazine all of this information about the theaters and restaurants. We had all that stuff in the house and we were throwing it away. So we started with that Friday section on *Weekend* and took an enormous jump in street sales. We had 35,000, 40,000 overnight. And it fits. Then we went with the food one, a little bit slower, but the same response by the reader. And since then we have moved across the board for five days a week. We have generated new advertising and new reading interests. . . . It was a business response to a business situation, magnificently supported by the news department.

"This pretty much came out of Walter Mattson's concept. We were also having enormous printing troubles. The four-section paper is actually easier to manufacture physically. I don't think I got two letters from people who noticed the difference when we changed from an eight-column format to a six-column format. We've always tried not to shock the reader. . . . I think, as a result, we've had a slow and rather steady firm growth, which is a lot better than going up and down on the roller coaster."

Nineteen seventy-eight ushered in the rounding out of the four-section format of the newspaper. The *Business/Finance* section was made a separate, fourth section of the paper and renamed *Business Day*, appearing Monday through Friday. Formerly part of the second section on Saturday, *Sports Monday* appeared in January, 1978, and *Science Times* was introduced in November.

Another *Times* executive claims that the change to a four-section paper was one of the most important decisions in the history of the *New York Times* and one of the most adventurous. The *New York Times* dealt with hard news—foreign, national, cultural, financial. It was a two-section paper that had had the same formula and the same format for decades, and it was losing its momentum. Punch, the executive said, was fully prepared to take the criticism that might flow from introducing these soft news sections, because he believed that it was the right thing to do. It has unquestionably proved to be correct. According to the executive, Punch held firmly to his decision: "Even though he had a period when the profits of the newspaper were dwindling down to almost nothing, he never once wavered in his commitment to excellence in the guts of the paper. Even when things got a little dicey he was convinced over the long run that the formula of the newspaper was going to succeed. There was no harping about what happened, how we had gotten to where we were, on his part. There was only interest, a drive and encouragement to change the situation that we found ourselves in and to improve it."

The idea for the four-section newspaper evolved from Punch's one-to-one methods. Punch became persuaded that it was the correct course of action, and he gave his approval. Through formal and informal communication networks, Punch knew what was being developed so that when the four-section concept came to him through Walter Mattson, it was not a great surprise. However, it was a novel event for a major business figure on the paper, Mattson, to play a major role in the development of the newspaper itself. There were feelings on the part of some managers at the *Times* that this innovation was the breaking of a great tradition. The hardliners were in the news organization, but the top management people in the News Department were behind the changes. Punch not only told the old guard but, by his actions, demonstrated that he wasn't going to waver. He assured people that there would be no wavering from the commitment to excellence of the product, and he made funds available even during the most difficult periods for the *Times*'s continued excellence.

Punch gave the same attention to the subsidiary papers. One editor reported his early contact with Punch: "The first thing he did was to impress upon me and my closest colleagues that the way we grow our companies would be different than . . . anyone else in the newspaper industry. . . . And that was that we start with a deep and abiding commitment to product. . . . I really wondered whether that could be done because I'd never really been offered that luxury in the small town newspaper business. . . . He said, 'Let's spend some money on these products, let's hire more and better reporters, let's put more emphasis on writing.' Now we have put together a news team that goes out on location and reviews products."

The Future

News reports speak of the wonders of automated communications and their implications. Yet many efforts to combine newspapers with computer-based video transmission have failed. What does Punch see as the dominant problems his successors will face?

"Pretty much the same kinds of problems we're facing today, which is where is our business going in terms of the communications business? I just can't visualize people getting up in the morning and looking at computers. . . . I don't see how you take it into the john, or subway, or, when you're all finished, put it in the garbage can and throw it away. . . . The cost of business is going up so much that I don't know whether fifteen years from now *what* we're going to be. But cable is something that is going to happen . . . with TV. We're in the software end of the computer business with microfilm companies also. And all of these things, I think, are going to weave their way together in some way. At this point it's a very cloudy picture. I think the next person in this chair will have to have a better idea of where we're going than I do. So I'll spread the base and they can then narrow it later on if they want to."

But the combination of print communication and video transmission is on its way:

"The technology isn't terribly far away that you'll be printing a magazine, not in a whole series of pages which are then folded and twisted and cut, but literally page by page. And if you know when you print that magazine that it is going to go to John Jones, 1300 Broadway, Stamford, Connecticut, there is nothing to say that you can't address all the advertising to John Jones at the same time. . . . Because if you find out that I'm interested in race cars, and I'm not interested in baseball, you could really start to tailor that publication. . . . Our problem with the *New York Times* is that we don't know who it's going to. . . . But down in Gainesville, Georgia, we know 99 percent of the people who are going to get it because it's all . . . home delivered. . . . Of course the idea of having every ad in the place addressed to you personally, I think, is revolting.

"Fifteen years from now . . . we're going to be hooked into everything in some way, shape, or form. . . . The [cathode ray] tube is not going to be some thingamajigger that people fiddle with, but probably in almost everybody's home."

Yet, as Punch found out, it's not that easy to use the same journalist in different media; each medium requires its own staff. Punch continued:

"We've tried, on occasion, to jiggle our great news organization just a little bit. For example, we have a wonderful radio station downstairs [WQXR]. Someone had the bright idea to let correspondents phone in their stories also for broadcast. . . . It doesn't work. You can't give a guy out in the field too many jobs to do. He loses track. . . . We ran into that when we were running our West Coast Edition and our International Edition. There were three deadlines and it just was a hell of a mess. . . . Of course, the moment you see that one of them isn't doing very well, you concentrate your efforts on that. So Big Mama was suffering for the sake of some tiddly little West Coast Edition, and our priorities got *all* mixed up. *All* mixed up . . . if you tell the guy that he's got four masters, he's not going to do well for any of them. I think *Time* discovered this with the *Washington Star.* They tried to use people for both. It's very difficult to work for a weekly magazine and for a daily newspaper at the same time."

Establishing an adequate data base for decision making and personnel selection is as difficult for the *Times* executives as it was for the other CEOs. None of them was satisfied with his degree of success in resolving these problems. Nor was Punch:

"The perpetual business problem for us is that of decent information to make a rational decision. . . . Like every other company, we screwed up on our introduction of computers. We had to go back and start it all over again. That is one that you just keep constantly working on and constantly getting frustrated, starting all over again. Another is people, I mean every time you think you've got just the perfect team in place [knocks on wood]—that's what I think right now. But, so far, it hasn't been the perfect team. . . . We tend to make the same mistakes over and over again. I think . . . we get people who we think will be perfect, and that we've misjudged. . . . It's getting better. We look more now for the specialist than we do for the generalist, across the board. Even with the newspaper. When we have an opening, if we're looking for a restaurant critic, we're not looking for a general assignment reporter. . . . Everything's getting more narrow. We use a fair number of headhunters. We've had *fair* success with them. . . . And we do a fair amount of it ourselves."

Quality Achieved

Punch's mother's greatest pride is the way the company has moved from being a single-product, union-bound company with marginal earnings to the kind of company it is today. His own, he said, pointing to a copy of the *New York Times,* is: "That. The way it's changed, the way it's looked upon, perceived, growing. The things we're going to be doing that are going to make it better. . . . We don't run it to maximize the profits of the paper. If we did, I could double the profits tomorrow. Shut some bureaus down and start using Associated Press, and muck around, use stringers who really don't work for us, and look as though we have somebody there, cut down on the news. Doesn't take any genius to do that. . . . You wouldn't even notice it for a while. . . . And we'd be just like everybody else." In short, the quality.

As did each of the other CEOs in this book, Punch Sulzberger turned out to be a builder who nurtured a heritage. Although he was unprepared managerially, he was prepared in personality to mature as he led his company to new maturity. He was uniquely able to capture the leading edge of the growth of key subordinates with a managerial method that allowed them and the *New York Times* to flourish; indeed to blossom into a new and different form while still remaining its enduring self. His quiet, consistent authority in the context of his pursuit of quality provided a rock of stability upon which to defeat union exploitation and to build expansion and innovation. He sustained tradition yet reversed it. He invited help, and from well-selected staff and directors alike, got it. He had only to be himself.

Coda

It was not until March, 1980, that the issue of a national edition would be raised again. The *New York Times* announced that it would print an edition of the newspaper in Chicago starting in late summer. Its competitors saw this initiative as tantamount to a national edition. Observers saw it as a willingness to go head-to-head with the *Wall Street Journal*, whose then 1.9 million subscribers gave it the largest readership in the country.[7] The new edition was made up of a front section of national and international news and selected features, and a back business section. It would reach readers in key cities throughout the Midwest and be flown to Texas and the West Coast. The revolution in newspaper technology, satellite transmission, could transform a layout in New York to an exposed negative in a remote location in a matter of minutes, from which a press plate could then be made. The paper could be on doorsteps the next morning. There was no need for the large typesetting and printing operation that had hobbled the Western Edition. Moreover, there had been a vast growth of well-educated and well-heeled people across the nation since the earlier ill-fated Western Edition. And the *Wall Street Journal* had been successful with its four editions for twenty years and had used satellite technology since 1975.

In April, 1982, Punch Sulzberger announced the August printing of the *New York Times* National Edition in California. It would provide same-day distribution to major cities in thirteen western states. The National Edition was already being printed in Chicago and in Lakeland, Florida. This two-section paper now included selections from the *Sports Monday, Science Times, Living, Home,* and *Weekend* sections in its weekday issues. Punch anticipated that the California operation would raise the edition's combined press run to more than 100,000 copies on weekdays and 200,000 on Sundays. Still, in his deliberate way, Punch is pondering whether the National Edition should become a truly national newspaper, not like *U.S.A. Today* but in the *Times*'s own image. To make such a paper available to large numbers of subscribers nationally will require a major investment. If history is a guide, Punch will roll it out step by careful step.

In its 1984 survey of American leaders, *U.S. News and World Report* found Punch Sulzberger to be regarded as the most influential person in the communications field, and outside of government, the fourth most influential leader in national life.

8

In Sum...

THERE ARE many ways to analyze, summarize, and integrate the data of these chapters. All will necessarily be arbitrary and based on the predilections of the analyst. What we learned from our data on these leaders can be summarized in the following definition of leadership. The leader: (1) is able to take charge; (2) has a strong self-image and a powerful ego ideal; (3) interacts with customers, employees, and other constituencies supportively; (4) provides permission to take risks; (5) is a thinker as well as a doer.

Taking Charge

Although the issue is little discussed by contemporary theorists of leadership, clearly the leader has to be able to take charge. Participative efforts will flounder without careful and guided direction from the leader in the form of specific actions. Even in the examples of temporary organizations which Warren Bennis and Philip Slater use, somebody is in charge.[1] Somebody has the right to hire and fire. Somebody has the right to make final artistic, conceptual, financial, or other decisions. A major fault of contemporary theorizing on leadership and organizations is precisely that it does not discuss this issue. It is as if writers were unable to differentiate between being authoritative and being authoritarian, and, therefore, the appropriate exercise of authority is viewed as being not good managerial behavior.

None of the CEOs we interviewed spoke of a specific charge from a board of directors about what he was to do when he took over. Nor did any of them start out with a vision, as MacGregor, Watson, and Sulzberger specifically indicated. Each had to define his own problems and map out his methods for resolving them. That meant that each had to fall back on his internal road map, based on his organization's history and his previous experience. Each had to be an expert diagnostician. Jones laid out the six problems he faced at GE, Hanley the three major issues he faced at Monsanto, and Sulzberger the four most prominent concerns at the *Times*. Each set out on a path of resuscitation and recovery. Wriston saw the world as one economic unit and the need to prepare to compete in those terms. MacGregor saw a world of declining natural resources and rising inflation, and therefore advocated acquiring more mines. Watson discovered that Univac had taken the computer lead and threatened IBM's customer base; at his insistence, IBM engineers overtook Univac in two years. Sulzberger saw no adequate management and the looming impoverishment that would follow the continuous union drain on the resources of a single business unit. All were clear about what they were going to do and how they were going to do it.

But diagnosis is never enough, nor is ad hoc action a satisfactory basis for continuity. Certainly, it does not give meaning to the organization or form a coherent focus for the needs of the people in it, nor does it provide a structure to translate that meaning into continuity of organizational behavior. The point to note, therefore, is that each of our CEOs took charge of his organization and took it in a new direction. In the mode of adapting animals who lose some functions in evolution only to develop others that enable them to survive, they deliberately altered their organizations. Survival meant to be different but quintessentially the same.

Thus, although their organizations, by and large, did what they knew how to do best, each of our leaders shifted the focus and direction of his organization into unfamiliar areas. Jones and Watson pushed into electronics, Wriston into consumer financing, MacGregor into aluminum manufacturing, Hanley downstream into proprietary products, and Sulzberger into acquisitions. Yet for all of the transformations they initiated, their companies did not lose their identities. They were, like children grown to maturity, recognizable but unrecognizable. They were outgrowths of what they had always been.

In order to make these changes, each of our leaders attacked entrenched perceptions and practices that had become set in organizational concrete—product, technology, structure. Each insisted on a new definition of reality in keeping with his own diagnostic perceptions. These leaders were like trout swimming against swift currents. They couldn't stop. They stayed alive in a metaphorical sense by encountering and enduring in the cold, harsh, forceful environment in which they lived. Indeed they sought the advancing currents; they sought change. Theirs was an upstream orientation.

Throughout the process of transformation each of our leaders was clearly in control, both formally and psychologically. None had difficulty taking charge and maintaining that control, either by managing the purse strings, like Jones, MacGregor, and Hanley, or by sitting atop the vast information heap. When edict was necessary, it came. Watson set a deadline, after which there would be no more computers with tubes, and delivered edicts regarding personal behavior. Sulzberger said there would be one paper, daily and Sunday, and not two. Wriston himself took charge during the New York City financial crisis. Each grew further into his role, whether through internal maturation in the organization, as did Jones, Watson, Wriston, and MacGregor, or by having to confront crisis, as did Hanley and Sulzberger.

Despite self-doubt, each of these leaders was strong and took a position when that was necessary. MacGregor opposed the Hochschild faction to make a deal with Pechiney and fought that group repeatedly. He faced down his putative rival, Donahue. He could be stubborn about the nickel business. Each of the others stood against the entrenched wisdom of his organization and even against those who knew technology better than they. They did not vacillate, at least publicly, in the face of decisions that often required spending hundreds of millions of dollars. They were able to stick with their convictions until they brought their followers around. What they achieved, therefore, was not, as Hanley would have it, just dumb luck. Each could have failed despite the enormous resources behind him.

The thespian talents of our leaders, another form of taking charge, bloomed late but well. Each developed a platform presence that added to his stature as a public figure. That same presence allowed subordinates to take pride in the public figure whose handling of the public aspect of his role redounded to the advantage of the company. Each had his share of Potomac fever and enjoyed the association with governmental power and famous figures. Though Sulzberger does not have thespian talents, his warm, self-effacing style quickly wins over groups and audiences.

All of our leaders except Hanley had been involved with their organizations early on. Hanley, who came late in his career to Monsanto, had been at Procter and Gamble for all of his prior executive history, stayed at Monsanto for the rest, and invested himself in his new organization beyond the specific behavior required by his role. Each of the others did the same. Jones, Watson, Wriston, and Sulzberger appeared to be more highly influenced by the organizations they led. MacGregor was not satisfied with being able to get along with his board. He clashed with them because of his vision of what AMAX could be and did become. He was committed to achieving that vision for that company, although, as history confirms, he easily could have gone elsewhere. Each appears to have made his company more important than himself.

Yet none was blinded by this commitment to the organization. Commitment can easily turn into a personal cause, which can turn into narrow and rigid pursuit of an impossible ideal. Their commitment was not to exploit the organization for a personal cause, whatever that might be, but to integrate their personal causes with the organizations' needs. Of course, they may well have rationalized the gratification of many of their personal needs by justifying their actions as organizationally necessary. All executives, being human, do that to some degree. But here the organization came first. They knew their organizational histories and took them into account. "Working with the grain," Jones called it.

Each had to do what his own personality enabled him to do. Each established a comfortable degree of fit, although it was harder for a new man like Hanley to do so. Indeed, when their successors took over at GE, Citicorp, IBM, Monsanto and AMAX, they were different men who now had to confront different technical, financial, and competitive worlds, requiring a different kind of fit.

Self-Image and Ego Ideal

The leader must have a strong self-image and some ideal toward which he or she is striving. The self-image, how one sees oneself at any given time (which is often only partly conscious), operates in conjunction with the ego ideal. The ego ideal is that view, mostly implicit, of that ideal self toward which one is always striving; it is an internal psychological road map of which one is only partially aware. There is always a gap between the self-image and the ego ideal. The greater the gap, the angrier one is with oneself, and the harder one pushes to narrow the gap.

A high ego ideal contributes to a strong conscience. In turn, a strong conscience is necessary for powerful motivation to achieve at any level. A person has to have a sense of obligation to himself, his trade or profession, and to his employer to develop a conscientious work role. Similarly, one must have a sense of obligation if one is to assume the responsibilities of a family, or to maintain the complementary activities of a friendship, or to discharge one's share of the duties of citizenship. One must have an even more powerful conscience, coupled with intellectual capacity, good judgment, perspicacity, and certain qualities of personality to become the successful builder of a major business organization.

All of the leaders in this book worked hard. They were concerned with controlling their organizations, but they were able to allow many others to do things in their own ways. They were able to lay the groundwork for succession and to yield to it in five of the six instances. What factors contributed to that leadership behavior as contrasted with the extreme behavior of executives who cannot or do not do so?

To develop both the self-image and the ego ideal, the leader has necessarily made use of models and, therefore, comfortably holds himself or herself out as a model. By doing so, he or she offers clarity of direction for himself or herself and for his or her followers, particularly if that direction is built on realistic competences rather than some magical unconscious strivings for omnipotence (a factor that has led to much irrational expansion of conglomerates). This is what Abraham Zaleznik and Manfred Kets de Vries refer to as powerful ego strength.[2] The leader must hold up and emphasize his or her own philosophy, establish and maintain corporate values (or support those values already in place), and demand much of others in the interest of pursuing those powerful goals. Clearly, the leader must help his organization differentiate itself from other organizations as "the best," and exemplify that differentiation with ceremony and heroes, a point emphasized by Thomas J. Peters and Robert H. Waterman.[3]

Each of the leaders in this book had a strong paternal model and strove to please that model, even when he had only the memory of the model as a guide. We heard about the powerful parental images of most of our leaders from either the leaders themselves or their colleagues. The references to Thomas J. Watson, Sr., Henry M. Wriston, James P. Hanley, Adolph S. Ochs, and Arthur Hays Sulzberger are most vivid in this respect. Thomas J. Watson, Jr., was in business with his father. Walter Wriston turned to his father for advice and guidance. Jack Hanley anticipated being his father's partner. Punch Sulzberger knew he had to carry on a family tradition represented by both his father and his grandfather. (The fathers are less prominent in the other examples, but clearly they were nevertheless important models.) These fathers were also important critics who established and maintained inordinately high standards. Tom Watson, Jr., attributed the practices of IBM to his implementation of his father's standards. Walter Wriston's emphasis on writing and presenting intellectual arguments as the basis for Citicorp's strategy relates directly to his father's intellectual, logical bent. One way or another, the fathers of all the others were occupational models. While rivalry is natural, none was so intensely rivalrous that he had to overthrow his father or to become an entrepreneur.

The achievements of the sons also were consistent with what pleased their mothers, some of whom provided psychological shelter, and, apparently all, psychological support. An observer of Walter Wriston described how he spoke about his mother's influence. Jack Hanley spoke of his mother's probable pride in his contact with world political leaders. Sulzberger believed his mother enjoyed satisfaction in his achievement in diversifying the company.

Certainly, our leaders also developed an attitude about the self in relation to others. As did the Kennedy family, the Sulzbergers moved among the greats; in that intimacy, they must have learned that the greats were just human beings, whom they need not fear or approach by currying favor. The Sulzbergers felt they had every right to be where they were. In a different setting, Watson had something of the same experience. The others worked their ways into their organizational settings, but apparently without that intense overcompetitiveness within the company or drivenness that reflects the discomfort of too much self-doubt.

All also had organizational models and supporters. For Jones there was the series of GE predecessors; for Watson, Red LaMotte and Al Williams; for Hanley, Neil McElroy of Procter and Gamble, together with Earle Harbison and Bob Berra; for Wriston, George Moore; for Sulzberger, Turner Catledge and Ivan Veit. These were sometimes guides, sometimes protectors, sometimes allies, as in the case of Gabriel Hauge and Harold J. Szold on MacGregor's AMAX board.

Our leaders could listen to these people, not always without quarrel.

Jones and Hanley came from lower socioeconomic levels; Wriston and MacGregor from middle-class levels; and Watson and Sulzberger from upper-class, established wealth. Two were in family businesses. At IBM, the father-son rivalry continued in the business unabated. Tom, Jr., was not going to be defeated; he would prove himself to be a worthy son. At the *Times,* there was no immediate organizational rivalry between Punch and his father, although he had to persuade his father of his initiatives, but there was indeed an idealized organizational tradition to be sustained. Watson had to more fully establish a tradition rooted in his father's values; for Sulzberger, the tradition came from his grandfather. Both Sulzberger and Jones carried on the momentum of already established values in organizations in which those values were cherished guides to operations. Hanley, MacGregor, and Wriston made their own personal values dominating forces in their organizations. Wriston was acutely aware of the history of Citicorp, which dated from 1812.

In Harvard's Peabody Museum, there is a world-famous collection of glass flowers created by Leopold Blaschka and his son, Rudolf. Said Leopold:

> "Many people think that we have some secret apparatus by which we can squeeze glass suddenly into forms, but it is not so. We have tact. My son Rudolf has more than I have, because he is my son, and tact increases in every generation. The only way to become a glass modeler of skill, I have often said to people, is to get a good great-grandfather who loved glass; then he is to have a son with like tastes; he is to be your grandfather. He in turn will have a son who must, as your father, be passionately fond of glass. You, as his son, can then try your hand. But if you do not have such ancestors, it is not your fault. My grandfather was the most widely known glass worker in Bohemia, and he lived to be eighty-three years of age. My father was about as old. . . . I am between sixty and seventy and very young."[4]

By tact, Leopold meant skill. His point, however, was the importance of identification with and lifetime apprenticeship to a master who is one of a line of masters. Giving leadership to an organization is as much a skill as any other. The identification and apprenticeship starts very early, as we have seen from these examples. Some, Sulzberger and Watson, carried on a personal line. Jones continued an organizational line. MacGregor, Wriston, and Hanley established new lines of continuity. And, as we shall see later, both the identification and apprenticing tasks became paramount issues for each of our leaders.

The models, both personal and organizational, and the organizational traditions in the case of GE and the *Times*, combined with high personal standards to create almost tyrannical self-demand and, in turn, demand on others. Our leaders pursued these demands with a relentless intensity that reflected underlying, highly controlled fury. All but Wriston and Sulzberger were described as workaholics, and they, too, worked hard. All assumed that they were responsible for making their organizations the best. Though none started his organization, and so none had the problems of entrepreneurs, each had to rebuild or refocus his organization. In most cases, that rebuilding had to take place quickly in the face of a major competitive threat. All were regenerators. Each did, indeed, succeed in turning his organization around and putting his stamp on the enduring character of the organization, as well as maintaining industry leadership and competitive position. Each was concerned with building an enduring organization—the figurative sons of sons—that subsequently could regenerate itself from within.

In each case the leader could verbalize his aspiration: for Jones, to turn over a stronger GE to his successors; for Wriston, to demonstrate the effectiveness of an ideology and to achieve profitability; for MacGregor, to build and transform bigger organizations, maximizing the inherent potential; for Watson, to please his father by being competitively most powerful with highest levels of conduct and product; for Hanley, in his father's tradition, to rescue and rejuvenate; for Sulzberger, to perpetuate the tradition that was the *New York Times*.

They tied people together by repeatedly urging their tradition and their own values and by policing their enforcement. Whether it was GE's "stamp on their behinds" or Jones's budget allocations and repetitive exhortations, there was an imperative to being in GE. Wriston compelled internal and external competition with the conviction that the best would survive and only the best and most logical deserved to survive. MacGregor exemplified personal standards and the imperative of maximizing all resources. There was no question that Watson insisted on the urgency of quality and service and personal behavior. Hanley exemplified the aggressive leadership he hoped would serve as a model for his followers. Sulzberger and his staff were all imbued with the reputation of the *New York Times*. A "we're the best" syndrome pervaded the thrust of each. In the words of Paul Lawrence and David Dyer, they were committed to being "world class" competitors.[5]

However, not only did all our leaders repeatedly emphasize the ideal, they also often punitively reinforced it. True, there was much celebration of achievement and victory, and of the corporate family that attained them, but there were also firings, demotions, transfers, or other forms of punishment for those who could not or did not live up to the standards and ideals. Each leader spoke of the pain and disappointment that accompanied those actions. Each had to be able to face up to them. The attainment of what Levinson has called transcendent purpose or what Richard T. Pascale and Anthony G. Athos call superordinate goals is not possible without the application of negative sanction, as well as positive reinforcement.[6] The theorists of leadership take an essentially naive Skinnerian view of utopian possibilities. We are not making a case for the application of rewards and punishments—"the Great Jackass Fallacy" theme of an earlier book by Levinson. But we do insist, as the experience of our leaders demonstrates, that the followers must know when they are not living up to the ideal and that there is a cost in the organization for not doing so.

Implicitly, but also often explicitly, these leaders saw themselves as having an obligation to society. That, too, was part of their ego ideals. All recognized that they could not survive without social permission. Jones worked at it in Washington. Wriston pushed for what he thought to be the most effective functioning of the system. MacGregor specifically anticipated environmental concerns and the possibility of reaction unless the federal government were treated with a fairness it could not anticipate. In addition to quality of product and service, Watson was concerned about the impact of his company on its environs and Hanley very much with the toxicological issue. Sulzberger voiced the concern of editorial fairness.

Each had international commitments and reputation, and each simultaneously recognized his obligation to his country. Each was patriotic and handled his own and his company's relationships with the government sensitively, while representing his corporate obligations vigorously. Sometimes those relationships were less than friendly. Hanley stayed close to the EPA and the FDA to avoid potential difficulties, yet he fought for removal of inhibiting controls. He fought EPA access to proprietary information on Roundup. Watson served the government as ambassador to Russia and had put his early precomputers at the disposal of the government in the Korean War, yet he had to endure a long, fruitless antitrust suit. Jones stood up to President Carter and MacGregor to the governor of Colorado. Wriston, after decades of battling, won the freedom to compete as a financial institution rather than narrowly as a bank. There is still some public questioning of Citibank's practices vis-à-vis regulatory bodies. And Sulzberger on two occasions had to support a stand against the wishes of federal agencies in the case of the Pentagon Papers and the *Times* story on the CIA.

Each, except Sulzberger, spoke of the need to maintain a congenial, supportive public climate, and Sulzberger was concerned about what the business community thought of the *Times*. And each used his political skills and political wisdom to gain acceptance without formal public encounter, except Wriston who fought at every opportunity to advance the cause of free competition. Though at first none was comfortable in those roles that made them vulnerable to open public hostility, each learned to rise to the uncomfortable challenges and to handle them with aplomb.

Except for Wriston's stand for open competition, none was caught up in doctrinaire positions. All had a broad sociopolitical perspective that incorporated knowledge about what was going on in many parts of the world. And they could articulate their values and beliefs with clarity and firm conviction.

In short, despite their practical concern for profitability, these leaders were powerfully value-driven. Leaders, as the literature indicates, are managers of the values of the organization, but much more. They bring knowledge, intuition, insight, aggressive strength—and their own ego ideals—to that leadership. These together sustain the strong culture of each of these organizations. GE's stemmed from long tradition, as did Citibank's and the Times Company's. MacGregor constructed AMAX's out of people's identification with his implemented vision. Watson expanded on his father's propriety. Hanley shook up Monsanto by making new stringent standards and teaching new methods.

Must Interact

The leader must interact with customers, employees, and other constituencies supportively. That means that he or she must not only touch others in a personal way, but do so warmly and consistently so that all recognize his integrity—managing "the soft S's" as described by Pascale and Athos.[7] Ideally, such a powerful person interacting with others gives them permission to act on behalf of the organization. This, in turn, leads to strong bonding and identification, especially if the leader is intuitive and empathic. As we noted earlier, the leader historically has developed support from others and, having learned to use it, is able to support others. The leader anticipates disappointment and defeat and helps his people cope with them by sharing skills, competences, expertise, and sophistication. He is also a powerful voice upon which people can depend for disapproval. This last quality, a form of aggression, is not touched on in most of the contemporary discussions of leadership. Yet we found it an important part of the leader's role. If one is to hold up an ideal, then one must also reject that behavior which compromises the ideal. It is not enough merely to hold it up.

There were no ivory tower isolates among our leaders, nor were they preoccupied with the customer alone, though they gave careful attention to him and her. Our vignettes are replete with illustrations of interactions with multiple constituencies. The literature of leadership does not touch much on the relationships of leaders with their boards or with their closest confidants. Our leaders tell us they were acutely sensitive to both. In the case of MacGregor, managing those board members who were reluctant to follow his leadership was a major part of his task. Sulzberger specifically built a strong businessman board to guide him. Hanley reconstructed a board to support him. Despite their powerful executive positions, Watson and MacGregor went out of their way to accommodate board members. Jones spoke of earning the respect of his board.

The literature of leadership tends also to ignore the political aspects of leaders' roles. These leaders did not. All of them took an active role with respect to various levels of government, and with overseas governments. They were politically sophisticated and often acted beyond their own self-interests. They became statesmen.

They maintained their organizations as systems open to outside information and capable of acting on it; indeed, they encouraged that response. They seemed to give congruent signals, to say what they meant (except in some intimate, painful personal situations) and mean what they said. They are likeable men even when they do things that hurt. Watson, for example, balanced his attacks with reconciliation that restored the loving image. At the same time his behavior invited attachment because of the relief he afforded after creating so much pain. By "getting in the boat" with their subordinates and accepting joint accountability, they reduced paranoid fears of being up against a hostile environment, alone and vulnerable. They struck others as being "lovers" not haters.

Sometimes even the most brilliant scientific and technical people in the organization did not see the proverbial forest for the trees. Reg Jones maneuvered his GE technologists into electronics against their passive resistance. He recommended, pushed, cajoled, set up task forces, jawboned, almost demanded that they turn to electronics. Tom Watson used cheap transistor radios to compel his people to recognize the electronic age. Walter Wriston insisted that his managers manage the bank as a business, regardless of the tradition of banking, and be judged by the returns of a business. Ian MacGregor steered AMAX into what he knew it could and should become, despite the opposition of less perceptive board members. Punch Sulzberger guided his company into a diversification that contradicted its historical precedents. Jack Hanley didn't even know the business and had to cope with the burden of poor decisions until he could become knowledgeable and change direction.

These leaders were able to be flexible, able to recognize and respond to reality. One of the factors that enabled them to stay clearly focused on reality was that they were eminently practical men, despite their capacity for high-level abstraction. (We think it is that practicality, particularly, that differentiates leaders from those valedictorians who never achieve power.) They "smelled" the marketplace. Wriston's innovations ranged from certificates of deposit and novel ship financing to the international financial conglomerate. Watson not only pushed transistors, but also was said to sense how customers would take to and use a product. Hanley and MacGregor saw the need to depart from overreliance on commodities and to shift to vertical integration downstream to products. Sulzberger supported the novel special sections of the *Times.* Jones also "smelled" the political marketplace and became a business statesman.

Another factor that kept them in touch with reality was their humility. Reg Jones spoke unabashedly about his shaking knees and reported that he had told Fred Borch he was not the man for the job because of his technical inadequacy. Tom Watson told us about the tears he shed as a boy and of underachieving in school because he was afraid he might not be capable of following in his father's footsteps. Punch Sulzberger described his academic achievement as so modest that apparently there was some concern in his parents' minds about his being able to become chief executive in fact as well as in name. An observer of Hanley's behavior suggested that he was not as self-confident as he appeared. MacGregor felt inadequate about not being able to push costs down to maintain margins in a low market.

Between the lines, these reports tell us of feelings of inadequacy in the face of powerful consciences. But the obvious achievements of those leaders tell us also that those feelings, ennervating stimulants though they were, were not so overwhelming that they inhibited the building process. Instead, they served as goals to high level attainment and resulted in conspicuous personal modesty. The personal modesty and the intertwining of person and organization was reflected in the frequent use of "we" rather than "I." That was most conspicuous in Jones's and Hanley's coaching, in MacGregor's comments, and in Watson's dictum not to use the first person singular in correspondence.

Each leader disdained and fought against the self-aggrandizing accoutrements of power. Those who had corporate airplanes had small ones, and complained of the luxurious life styles of some of their peers. For all of their success, IBM's executives have modest offices and entertain conservatively, and Watson wanted no limousines or entourages or special arrangements when he traveled. MacGregor tried to exemplify frugality in travel. Hanley cut back on golf games, club memberships, and other luxury items.

Clearly, these men could be characterized by a sense of restless dissatisfaction. They were not satisfied with themselves or their organizations. They demanded much of both. Reg Jones cut, shaped, pruned, drove, inspired, expanded, and demanded much of GE. No significant detail escaped him. It was in his inches-thick plan book. He was punctuality personified. Walter Wriston stimulated intense competition so that the best people, and thereby the organization, might rise to the top. Tom Watson carried his penchant for perfection from concern for the cleanliness of the washrooms to the design of the working environment. Jack Hanley emphasized the importance of dress and manners, as well as solid analytic method. All three demanded and supported high-level research to be at the frontiers of knowledge.

Ian MacGregor prepared his deals meticulously, and Punch Sulzberger, no lover of detail, nevertheless invested himself carefully in important detail, like the redesign of the *New York Times.* But preoccupation with detail in the absence of purpose and important standards becomes only nit-picking, as Hanley learned. The concern of our leaders with detail, part of the striving to be the best, also yielded the narcissistic gratification that comes from that striving.

Each did his homework and his subordinates knew it, as reflected in Jones's, Watson's, Hanley's, and MacGregor's questioning. The leaders did not stop studying or learning. Monsanto executives knew that Hanley set out formally to learn the chemical business. MacGregor insisted that he know enough about a matter to make a decision based on his own understanding rather than the recommendation of a subordinate.

Watson insisted on exacting staff work and that people be prepared to defend their recommendations. Citicorp managers, too, had to defend their positions. And Punch Sulzberger complained about projects that acquired their own momentum if they weren't stopped soon enough.

The leaders energetically gathered information and pressed toward action with a focus on the main issue. They had a knack for getting to the heart of a matter, amassing information, holding onto it until they could integrate it and act on it. They fostered critical examination of information, positions, and points of view. Each could take an opposi-tional position, deliberately testing views, sentiments, and logic. The Watson-IBM contention concept deflected aggressive hostility into crit-ical cross-examination of problems, followed by responsibility for re-solving them.

Each could change his mind based on that information, particularly from selected, trusted confidants. Each sought information from the outside, from consultants or established sources of basic information, like universities. Wriston used Arthur D. Little and Tempo. He, Jones, and Sulzberger consulted McKinsey. Hanley made extensive use of Robert Stobaugh and Ed Schleh. Watson made an attempt—albeit an abortive one—to use Booz, Allen and Hamilton.

All were aware of the need to touch their own people and made a practice of it. All but Hanley, having grown up in their organizations, could touch easily as they traveled. Sulzberger wandered about the *New York Times* building to do the same thing. This touching was also a device to pick up information. They were especially affectionate with people close to them, while still maintaining an appropriate distance.

Although the leaders set a direction, changed significant personnel, and made heavy demands on their subordinates for exacting behavior and performance, they were also supportive. They were compassionate and empathic. They were sensitive to people's self-esteem and face-saving needs; the lower in the organization, the greater the concern for the person. They did not confront people easily, though they usually did so when required. They did not fire people readily, except for cause. Each spoke of certain subordinates whom he tried to save or of the pain of taking actions that could no longer be avoided. MacGregor was so subtle, one subordinate didn't know he was fired. Jones did personal favors for those in distress. They tried to rescue or defend some people at times when perhaps they should not have made that effort. Jones reports how he took hours with one abrasive executive, only to have to fire him. They went out of their way to extend personal kindnesses. They were loyal friends. Sulzberger insisted that a subordinate talk about the trauma of his divorce. Watson obviously had listened to many family battles as part of his open-door experience.

These men were constantly engaged in touching bases and consulting subordinates, although perhaps Hanley somewhat less so than the others. Jones was attentive to his peers, got letters from the shop floor, shook hands at Belleair meetings, and spoke to management classes, as did Watson. MacGregor called on his network of personal contacts in the company and made himself available at all times for consultations. Although perhaps Hanley did less touching and consulting than the others, even he got feedback from Berra and enough information to stop nit-picking. They were all listeners, but they governed their time and what they would listen to. None could sit still for long or involved presentations. Watson and Hanley made extensive use of their notebooks, which enabled them to recall earlier meetings and gratify subordinates whose words had been taken seriously. Jones used his plan book and his near-verbatim notes.

They were able to maintain an appropriate distance from their subordinates. Despite the easy use of first names in the case of Tom, Reg, and Punch, they did not encourage close intimacy. They did not need to be loved by their subordinates. In fact, they had to take painful stands with some. Jones severed close relationships with subordinates when he became CEO and was evenhanded in his contact with contenders for succession. Each CEO went to great lengths to show no favoritism, although clearly Sulzberger moved Mattson very fast, and Gousseland was MacGregor's obvious successor.

Most were good at sensing nonverbal cues. Usually they could put others at their ease so that their contacts provided them with a wide range of information not available through formal channels. Hanley didn't do that at first, in an effort to establish his formal position and the recognition of his strength, nor had he the long history in the organization to establish such ties. All the others maintained one-to-one relationships, frequently on a first-name basis.

These leaders created a visible management. They were accessible. The open-door policy made Watson ultimately accessible to all employees. For the most part, they tried to treat their subordinates as responsible managers. Though the leaders were not in the habit of issuing edicts, what they wanted was quite clear to their subordinates. Subordinates could evolve ways to protect the leaders from themselves and to persuade them to change their minds. Each leader allowed respectful dissent. Watson demanded it.

They all delegated well and insisted on performance. MacGregor's delegation of operations is one example; others are Sulzberger's insistence that managers generate solutions and Wriston's and Hanley's emphasis on managerial communication and results. Yet none of the leaders functioned as a rubber stamp for managerial decisions, and each held some critical issues to himself. Watson moved quality control into a direct reporting relationship to him. MacGregor's concern with molybdenum and labor relations, and both Jones's and Hanley's control of financial commitments are additional examples. All, except Watson, had to deal with labor relations.

Their interactions, even when sometimes hostile and critical, enabled their people to attach themselves to their leader and to the organization. Indeed, they also facilitated the attachment of the public to the organizations. Many people who respect GE, Citicorp, AMAX, IBM, Monsanto, and the *New York Times* don't even know the names of these leaders. They attribute positive qualities to the organization because of the quality standards the leaders tried to uphold.

In some cases, they failed: GE was accused of not sustaining its leadership in consumer products, of using the units that manufactured those products as cash cows; that is, they provided profits to be invested in other products or efforts instead of being reinvested in themselves. Many people were displaced in the chaotic efforts at Citicorp to master the back office problems. Despite his efforts to ensure regularity of employment, MacGregor could not ensure that stability in the sluggish market. Watson had to fight off monopoly charges. Hanley suffered the Cycle-Safe failure and the loss of personnel that followed. Sulzberger had to fight off the stranglehold of the typographical unions. Yet the public still regarded all of those organizations highly, for the positives of their reputations far outweighted the negatives.

The leaders sought diversity of people and diversification of effort with controlled and guided conflict. In GE, conflict is apparently subdued: it rarely was reported in the interviews. In IBM, it was formally institutionalized in the contention system, and in Citicorp, formally stimulated for competitive position. MacGregor set different task forces to work on the same problem, unbeknownst to each other. Yet each leader insisted that people get along, that they recognize that conflict was necessary for the best people and ideas to rise so that, in turn, the company would flourish. Sulzberger insisted that executives control each other, Watson that they support each other; and, at GE, Jones made much of the concept of the GE family. He emphasized team work in selecting three vice-chairmen. Earlier, he accepted the fact that he would have to learn from those he had inherited from Borch. Hanley insisted that Monsanto executives be polite to each other, particularly in their managerial presentations.

There was a great deal of rapport between the CEO and the top people in the organization. Even when Watson became impulsively angry, most subordinates still wanted to be there, tied to the model and trying to be as good as he expected them to be. When Hanley was no longer in the position of the newcomer who assumed the posture that a good offense is the best defense, people who made it up the ladder found him warm and supportive. Watson, Sulzberger, MacGregor, and Jones all invited "drop in" behavior on the part of their immediate colleagues.

There was a heavy use of involvement of line executives in decision making. IBM's committees for major problems were combinations of salespeople and engineers. Even though no one has yet been able to demonstrate a relationship between the executive bonus and motivation, at four of the six corporations that bonus was tied to performance. Management by objectives could hardly be used with the editorial staff of the *Times,* and MacGregor had little use for that piece of bureaucracy. They all stressed corporate committee work and the use of task forces to solve immediate or pressing problems. The process of bubbling up ideas and developing internal support along the way was most vividly illustrated by Wriston and Sulzberger. In Citicorp, good ideas had to be sold. At the *Times,* Sulzberger was in on their evolution. All developed teams, except Hanley and MacGregor, who tended to prefer one-to-one relationships. Sulzberger, too, made much of one-to-one contacts.

They recognized the need for the consent of the governed inside their organizations as well as outside. Although each could and did take a firm position, override objections, and insist on positions, each nevertheless recognized the need to obtain consensus, a sufficiently large and strong critical mass to support movement. There was most often a soft-sell orientation. Each leaned heavily, therefore, on persuasion rather than edict, except Hanley, who recognized the need to establish himself and change the organizational culture quickly. His meetings frequently had dramatic flair, as, for example, when he had his managers don caps to symbolize the company hat.

Each leader made an effort to create an understanding of his platform, to obtain commitment rather than compliance. Each found it necessary to be able to sell his particular goals and aspirations as well as his immediate decisions. Hanley did this sometimes spectacularly, MacGregor quietly. Each got key people to agree on what the facts were and what the facts meant in a given situation, what should be done about it, and what the next step should be. They were constantly in the process of bringing their people along. Each had to cope with people who couldn't or didn't want to go along. Wriston's subordinates wouldn't give up their intention to manufacture their own card machine despite Walter's opposition. Although each leader did well in this respect, nevertheless each felt that he did not do as well as he should have.

They could and did mobilize their people around them. They took them off for various retreats where they could look at their options, come to conclusions, and get more closely acquainted. Wriston made the most formal use of this device by compelling competitors not only to play golf and tennis with each other, but also to develop the camaraderie of telling jokes and the ability to "take it" from colleagues. GE's meetings at Belleair were frequently inspirational. Hanley's were functional, explanatory, persuasive, and remedial, as were Sulzberger's, except for those that involved confrontational group dynamics. Watson's gatherings were more often offered as rewards. MacGregor did not seem to prefer large discussion meetings or retreats.

Each leader repeatedly changed organizational structures to cope with both power distribution and efficiency of operations. For the most part, these changes were not revolutions but rather evolutions. Except for Hanley in the beginning, they had great depth of knowledge about their businesses. They had imagination about where they could go and stopped with what they knew. Jones fine-tuned the strategic business units and pushed decentralization of responsibility with clear lines of authority, as did MacGregor. Jones created sectors and made the 1970 strategic planning system a way of life at GE. And Hanley inculcated his planning system and results system into Monsanto. Wriston, with his recognition of the future of consumer banking, divided his forces into a consumer group and an institutional group and let them fight out the overlap. As they broke up their organizations into acceptable levels of responsibility, they maintained the integrity of the whole. They did not become conglomerates. Despite the size of their organizations, GE and IBM are still recognizably GE and IBM. The same is true of the others. Out of a consistent internal value system, there is a common unity to what they think, what they believe, what they do, and how they practice management, which enables the pieces to see themselves as part of the larger organization, whether embossed with the GE symbol on their rumps or with the IBM letters in their imaginations or the *New York Times* in their hearts. The ability to forge appropriate structures and to facilitate healthy small group and large group interactions is a major factor in the success of these men and their organizations.

A central issue for all of these leaders, and one inadequately discussed in the literature of leadership, was their involvement in succession. As Fred Borch had said, that was his most difficult task. All of our leaders were intimately involved in the long-range planning for succession. They spent a great deal of time on selection, screening, development, and succession, and they were particularly preoccupied with it at those levels closest to them. GE had long-established formal management development programs, and IBM followed suit. Both companies spent millions of dollars on that training. Hanley brought to Monsanto the development conceptions of P&G and made the development of internal successor management one of his three major objectives. Wriston was involved in selecting and developing people early on in his career. Sulzberger's structure didn't yet allow him to do so.

All were acutely aware of the need for more and more competent managers, and five out of the six saw themselves as teachers of younger managers. Teaching seemed to be an important personal function for them. Watson admittedly defined his role as that of a teacher. Wriston was the son of a professor and carried that tradition into his practice. Hanley was clearly the instructor about both personal behavior and managerial practice, and the instructions MacGregor gave his assistants marked his expectation of what they would learn.

The leaders seemed not to be concerned with developing scientific managers because most of them were not such managers themselves. Only two, Jones and Hanley, were business school graduates. All were, however, concerned with developing professional managers—people who could adapt to rapidly changing competitive conditions while adhering to basic organizational values. Watson put the best salespersons in the most challenging jobs, jobs for which they were otherwise unprepared. Wriston recruited anyone who promised to be broad and aggressive, regardless of his academic background and previous experience. MacGregor, too, looked for all kinds of people.

One way or another, each organization kept track of its promising managers. GE, Citibank, and IBM all had formal tracking processes, and Monsanto was developing one—Hanley spoke of lining up his ducks. He had the names of his top fifty people readily available in his office. They were *his* people, as he told one errant executive.

In their succession preoccupation, the leaders recognized the need for different styles of management at different times. There were no clones. Indeed, when it came to choosing their own successors, Jones,

Wriston, MacGregor, Hanley, and Watson chose men who were quite different from themselves, and who, in turn, would choose different directions.

The leaders knew they were in the business of building enduring corporations. That building was a continuous socialization process: the training and indoctrination of those new to the organization; the continuous articulation and reinforcement of what customs, values, and beliefs the organization held and what models it honored; and the quick rush to turn away from mainstream responsibility those who did not take on the mantle on which all of that was figuratively embroidered.

Each leader was considerate most of the time. He knew whatever he achieved, in the last analysis, had to be the product of the behavior of his people. By and large, the leaders used a mixture of pressure and praise to motivate their people. All, except Sulzberger, were hard-driving, yet their manner was often easy in their tight self-control. Although they presented a relatively unemotional surface, they were capable of being personally cordial.

They might penalize errant performers with something as obvious as Watson's penalty box, or give them the silent treatment, or pass them off, as Wriston did. Yet each shrank from hurting people as individuals or as groups. They had great sensitivity to people's feelings and to the need to save face. They were too easy on some. They made positive efforts for others who became obsolete or redundant and for the communities in which they had operations. They had great loyalty to their people—and got it back. They were straight with their people and trustworthy—although not above manipulation, as reflected in MacGregor's going to subordinates' subordinates and Watson's pattern of criticizing and then apologizing. Each has a tempering sense of humor.

They held out impossible goals and insisted they were going to achieve them. They did: Jones's 10 percent earnings and Wriston's 15 percent growth target; Jones's commitments to run "counter economy"; Sulzberger's acquisition program to undergird the *Times* financial health; Jones's demands on his kitchen cabinet to respond to his needs to deal with the outside political world; and Watson's demands to overcome the Remington Rand lead.

All of this leads to bonding, to strong mutual loyalty. The commitment to GE was so strong that people were reluctant to talk negatively. The bonding was certainly true at least for the winners at Citibank and for certain executives at IBM. It was evident at the *New York Times* and developing for Monsanto.

Permission to Risk

The leader provides permission to risk, thereby encouraging autonomy by offering support for collective decision-making efforts, and the
encouragement and resources to support that permission. If organizations are to satisfy human purposes, then the leader must not only have
a cause but must also create a structure that both supports the development of the bond to the corporation and becomes an instrument for its
continuity. Even promises of lifetime employment have no meaning if
a business organization doesn't remain in business.

The literature of leadership gives scant attention to the utility of
organizational structure and controls, which are important not for their
own sake but for their support of commitment, direction, and
creativity. Leaders must continually modify organizational structure,
but to advocate merely loosening it up, as is so often the case in the
contemporary business literature, is naive and futile. Accountability
must be clear no matter what form the structure takes. Autonomy
without accountability is chaos.

Another form of permission to risk is the example of the risks the
leaders themselves took. The aspirations and standards of our leaders,
coupled with perceptive anticipation of future trends and needs and
supported by their willingness to take great risk by committing millions
to capital investment and more millions to research, showed their followers the seriousness of their intentions. Three of the six massively
funded both inside and outside research, despite downturns in the
economy, to generate intellectual feedstocks for their organizations. By
so doing they were investing in the future of their organizations and
thereby of the people in them. They put their money where their
mouths were. The risks they took were not foolhardy; the men were not
gamblers. The risks were based on careful thought, but ultimately
choices had to be made that were beyond demonstrable logic. The
leaders fell back on intuition—"my viscera" as Watson put it. All of
them could have been wrong.

And, of course, inevitably some of them were wrong some of the
time. Both Jones and MacGregor assumed that the projected shortage
of fossil fuels would boost nuclear generation and lighter vehicles. Hanley committed to capital investments before his analytic methods were
in place, knowing some would fail, and they did. Sulzberger and Jones
mentioned acquisition mistakes. When Sulzberger ignored his intuition

about *Us* magazine, he erred. Jones's Utah International acquisition proved not to have the long-term growth he envisioned. Welch sold it. Wriston's loans to Brazil raise contemporary eyebrows.

The leaders gave support to senior executives and permission to make a mistake, but not many. In IBM and GE, they rotated managers so that no one would get too comfortable in one position. The best sales manager might be precipitously assigned to a new, difficult task about which he knew nothing. The movement from line to staff in IBM and Monsanto fostered the understanding of each for the work of the other. Wriston modified the compensation package of managers in different countries so that it was easier to transfer them and moved successful people rapidly. He would parachute unlikely choices into new positions because of the merit he saw in them.

Exhorting people to risk is of little value unless there is repeated assent from the leader. That comes not only in the form of allocating resources but also from repeated encouragement when people either cannot innovate quickly enough or fail. A leader must give sanction, again and again, to counteract the ever-present harsh self-criticism that inevitably accompanies ambiguity and unconfirmed effort.

Reg Jones, Jack Hanley, and Ian MacGregor did that with the regular use of "we," assuming some of the responsibility for failure. Punch Sulzberger's continual wandering around the *New York Times* building enabled him to be in on ideas early, and to nurture them. Yet he and Hanley accepted others' risky decisions until they had evidence of failure. Walter Wriston insisted on freedom to risk and stood by that thesis, even when it became costly. Tom Watson demanded that his subordinates take risk by standing up to him. Jones and Watson encouraged risk—Jones by initiating a study of technology which led to his urging electronics on GE, and Watson by holding out the transistor radio as a model to be emulated. Both supported the direction they advocated by allocating resources and ultimately by rare edict. Watson said that there would be no more tubes in computers.

Jones, Watson, and Hanley made heavy commitments to research, despite the demand for funds from other parts of the business. By doing so they modeled risk-taking behavior. Watson and Hanley cultivated and supported outside research centers. All three recognized that their competitive positions depended heavily on research. Wriston led Citibank to take big risks in international lending, and MacGregor bet hundreds of millions of dollars on mines where results would not be known for years. Yet none risked without careful analysis, focus on a given area, and a reasonable expectation of outcome. All reorganized their companies repeatedly to support and focus their innovative thrust. All knew that in the last analysis they would be accountable for the risks they had taken—accountable to their boards, to their banks, to their stockholders, to their employees, and to their peers.

Their failures were proof of their risk-taking behavior. Despite their preparation and all of their resources, each leader was caught short at one time or another: Jones and Watson with the threats of obsolescent technology; Hanley with the Cycle-Safe fiasco and the retrenchments required by early misjudgments; MacGregor by the oil glut and the recession; Wriston by the difficulty of getting key government figures to understand the threatened plight of banks; Sulzberger by the crushing burden of seemingly insoluble labor restrictions and the inadequacy of his managerial resources. MacGregor failed in the nickel business and was disappointed in his efforts to make deals for Union Oil and Cities Service. Jones couldn't preserve his price/earnings ratio. These failures necessarily created stress, as did the burden of major decisions in the face of an ambiguous and unpredictable future. Hanley and Watson bemoaned those who promised much but failed to deliver. Each also had to bear the stress of travel, government attack, time pressures, emotional restraint, and controlled anger.

Given their high ego ideals, each wanted to make a difference and make his mark. MacGregor said a retired CEO left little behind and, in effect, was soon forgotten. Yet none acted as if his tenure had only transient meaning. Being analytic, intuitive, and prescient, they were usually three or four steps ahead of their followers and struggled mightily to communicate their vision and to embed it in the organization. That, too, as MacGregor noted specifically and each of the rest mentioned in passing, created its own stress.

Each was imaginative and yet practical, expansive and creative, and tried simultaneously to exert financial controls and free managerial action. They fought bureaucracy. They tried not to make the same mistake twice. Except for Hanley in his early days and Wriston in his effort to stimulate competition, they were not caught up in management by numbers. Theirs was a continuous balancing task of the multiple complex forces that affected their businesses.

All necessarily had to deal with the unrelenting pressures of their roles. Colleagues could observe their tension under such circumstances and sometimes their physical symptoms. Sulzberger had a troublesome back and hives, and, under stress, Wriston's facial tic appeared. Jones had had an ulcer. Hanley recounted how his stomach felt tied in knots in the early days and spoke of his arthritic back. Watson had a coronary that he attributed to his intense effort.

From time to time each lost his temper, but, except for Watson, they had great emotional control. They did not indulge in crude, open displays of sadistic behavior. They were not listed among *Fortune*'s "Ten Toughest Bosses." Nor were they counterdependent, denying their need for other people as they themselves singularly challenged the environment. They were not, for the most part, tough talkers. Sulzberger could handle strong feelings of anger by saying nothing—at all —to the offending executive. MacGregor could be frosty.

To give direction and allocate resources are not by themselves enough to give permission to risk, even supported by frequent approving behavior. People need to be able to take the risk of commitment. In order for them to do that, the leader must also be committed. Commitment is not a matter of being in the organization for a long period of time but rather the result of a sense of dedication to it.

Chief executive officers often are likened to symphony conductors. It is their task to meld diverse components into an integrated whole. Their direction ideally converts cacophony into melody. Interestingly enough, critics say that today's major symphony orchestras have fallen on hard musical times. They aren't what they used to be. The reason, according to the critics, is that contemporary music directors (which is now what permanent conductors are called) are little more than absentee landlords.[8] Unlike the great conductors of the past, who were deeply committed to their orchestras and stayed in their host communities to train and rehearse them, major contemporary conductors conduct less than half of their orchestras' concerts and spend the rest of their time conducting around the world. Guest conductors, associates, and assistants conduct the orchestras the rest of the time. None of the substitutes has responsibility to the orchestra or to the musical life of the community. None is committed. Unlike so many transient chief executive officers, these CEOs were and are attached to and deeply involved with their companies. They were bound to the organizations they served and directed.[9]

The single note of self-criticism struck by all of the leaders was that they hadn't followed their intuition and instincts as assiduously as they should have. Punch Sulzberger recounted his problem with *Us,* Hanley his with plant expansion. MacGregor felt that he hadn't pushed hard enough on several occasions. That brings to mind the advice the late great pianist Artur Rubinstein delivered to conductor Michael Tilson Thomas when Thomas was in his twenties: "Young man, remember always to have the courage of your convictions and if you believe that a certain piece goes a certain way, stick with it because for the first fifty years of my life everybody told me my Chopin playing was absolutely terrible. That I didn't have enough expression and all sorts of other things. The public and the critics were unanimous on this. Then, suddenly, when I got to be fifty-one, they started saying that the only way to play Chopin was the way Rubinstein played it."[10] Like the leaders in this book, Rubinstein thought of himself not as a great pianist but as a "very good one who just happened to play the piano fairly well."

Thinker and Doer

The leader is a thinker as well as a doer. True, he or she should not get lost in obsessiveness or repetitive intellectual exercises, but no great leader "wings it." The leader must have the ability to see ahead and the willingness to try new things in order to meet his anticipated competitive problems; the leader must take risks, but he or she cannot do so without careful thought and clear conceptualization based on specific assumptions. The leader is like the scientist: he or she is always specifying assumptions and testing them in practice.

Nothing is more simplistic than to think of the leader as a doer. Although much is said, particularly by Thomas Peters and Robert Waterman,[11] about companies being action-oriented, as a matter of fact, what we see among these leaders is a great deal of thinking. There is action, of course, but not without considerable prior thought. In addition to its own internal analyses, GE asked for conceptualization by outsiders. Although Walter Wriston was characterized by firm aggressive action, he emphasized the intellectual papers that supported the arguments he was making and directions he was taking. MacGregor was certainly a person of thoughtful and cool consideration. Watson moved fast to cope with competition, but not without a good deal of prior debate and discussion. Hanley installed a new system step by step and rued impulsive action. Sulzberger was slow to act until he had thought his position through and was secure in it.

Many managers tend to premature closure in decision making. They are already too action-oriented. It is likely that that propensity will be fostered by the Peters and Waterman conclusions. Of course, it is hard to make a case for managerial procrastination, nor does any organization profit from protracted discussion and approval procedures before a decision can be made or action taken. That, no doubt, is why Peters and Waterman argue for an action-oriented approach, but that argument does not adequately recognize the level of abstraction, conceptualization, and the tremendous amount of data that leaders must take into account, organize, order, and use as a basis for their leadership action.

Successful companies, as our examples demonstrate, attain their success through purposeful behavior. True, some of it may be unpredictable, but most of it is based on a thrust and a direction. Certainly AMAX and GE did not predict the nuclear fiasco, nor did Citicorp predict the problem of lesser developed countries (LDCs) nor Hanley Cycle-Safe. But at the same time, all made long-range plans and gave their people specific charges. Even in research directions they made specific investments based on well-defined plans. GE and IBM specifically allocated research monies to certain fields and not others, as did Monsanto. Creativity does not necessarily arise out of the tinkerer in the garage, nor out of turning all tinkerers loose to tinker. While some few may be imaginatively creative in the best innovative sense, many others labor in the vineyard. This is true in all disciplines.

The Meaning of Meaning

We set out to delineate the *how* of these leaders' success. We intended to show how they did what they did. We sought to escape the classifications that limited our understanding of leadership behavior and instead to report the behavior itself. Much of the contemporary literature on organizations and leadership speaks of the leader as one who gives meaning to his organization. It is necessary to understand in some greater depth how that meaning comes about and what purposes it serves for both the leader and the led.

What specifically is transmitted? The fundamental communication is that of the meaning of the organization. The meaning of GE as an organization is reflected in the humor about having "GE" branded on the buttocks of its managers ("we are all in it together") and in its tradition of stewardship. In addition to being all in it together, IBM stands for quality of service; the meaning of the *Times* to its people lies in the issues of independence and quality; that of AMAX in being the largest and most respected in its industry; and of Citicorp in being the leading, most innovative, and diversified financial corporation. Each of these companies had a view of its place in the world economy, not merely that of the United States. Each leader strove toward the realization of that image.

There is something grandiose about such striving, but it is that very grandiosity which, according to the late psychoanalyst Heinz Kohut, results in a shared "grandiose self."[12] That shared grandiose self provides the sense of collective purpose which endures beyond the vicissitudes of successes and failures. It is that which, as Rafael Moses puts it, leads to the "pride in 'mine' as opposed to 'yours.' "[13] Similar group narcissistic phenomena occur in a wide variety of groups and organizations. Some organizations are idealized and valued because of the leader who symbolizes the organization—sometimes charismatically, sometimes messianically, Moses notes. He calls our attention to the fact that people take special pride in their jobs, in the small groups on the job to which they belong, their departments, and their organizations— all of which they regard as special. They express these narcissistic feelings by stressing the assets and competences of the organizations and underplaying the problems and liabilities, by comparing the organizations' strong points favorably with those of others. (Citicorp managers saw themselves as the best, all others as lesser beings.) Sometimes the organization achieves a dramatic and impressive victory, such as IBM's emergence into computer leadership, which reinforces such feelings.

However, this idealization is apt to be followed by a period of narcissistic inflation, of feelings of omnipotence, of haughtiness and arrogance, Moses points out. That, in turn, is followed by denial of reality when other threats begin to arise. It was that denial which Reg Jones recognized he had to fight, by taking to the stump and confronting his people with the liquidity crisis. Hanley complained about the hockey stick approach to planning. Watson insisted that IBM not rest on its electromechanical laurels.

Shared grandiose feelings are necessary to safeguard the existence of the organization. Simultaneously, the existence and actions of the organization strengthen the self-esteem of its members and, therefore, the sense of group self. There is a reciprocal, self-supporting, self-esteem mechanism. According to Moses: "Clearly there must be a normal, adequate, not too deviant sense of group self, a group narcissism which provides the group with a positive self-image, positive self-esteem on balance, a sense of worth for belonging to that particular group which is secure and breeds confidence because it is based on reality. . . . The school tie, the alma matter, 'my' firm, 'my' profession . . . all these are treated as extensions of the self, of a more or less grandiose self. . . . At times of crisis there is a greater need for cohesion and a greater need for the group's self to strengthen the sense of belonging, and perhaps a willingness to sacrifice, of members of the group."

If a group is held together by shared ambitions or goals rather than by shared grandiose ideals, its activities are determined by expedient relationships. Group members are bound to each other by the need to vanquish a common enemy. The relationship disappears when the enemy no longer exists. There remains no affiliation or membership. There is only self-interested transient self-aggrandizement. All too many companies are managed that way. Meaning is derived from purpose beyond goals. Goals are specific targets, which often are steps toward organizational purpose. They frequently provide gratification, as does the winning score for a football team. But goal achievement does not endure as inspiration for the present and the future. The goal achieved loses its potency as an attractive force. It results in, "What have you done for me lately? And what will you do tomorrow?"

Nor does a preoccupation with goals generate morality. One of the characteristics of each of these organizations is a shared morality. We heard repeatedly not only of business morality, but also of concern with and fairness to competitors, to the government, to the community, and of actions demonstrating concern for employees. Jones cautioned his managers to anticipate displacements and to prepare for them early. Hanley assumed responsibility for managing the loss and transition of 1,000 employees who lost their jobs overnight because of the Cycle-Safe fiasco. Watson established an open-door policy to protect employees from managerial abuse, and also protected vendors and host communities. MacGregor closed the Blackwell plant and gave the property to the town. True, when AMAX was concerned about the environment, that concern was not purely altruistic, for there were potential consequences of being hostile or unconcerned. When Watson reported errors in the corporate income tax, that, too, may have avoided other possible difficulties. But each of these leaders held out and tried to live up to a code of exemplary behavior, and they enforced it in the organization. There was not only an enemy to be against; there was also something to be for. That is the essence of meaning.

James MacGregor Burns calls giving meaning "transforming leadership":

"Such leadership occurs when one or more persons *engage* with others in such a way that leaders and followers raise one another to higher levels of motivation and morality . . . transforming leadership ultimately becomes *moral* in that it raises the level of human conduct and ethical aspiration of both leader and led, and thus it has a transforming effect on both. . . . Transcending leadership is dynamic leadership in the sense that the leaders throw themselves into a relationship with the followers who will feel 'elevated' by it and often become more active themselves, thereby creating new cadres of leaders [the great grandfathers, the grandfathers, the fathers, the sons]. Transcending leadership is leadership *engagé*. Naked power-wielding can be neither transactional nor transforming; only leadership can be."[14]

What differentiates transforming leaders from others? Certainly, as we have seen, their values, their commitment, their concern with succession. But there is something even more subtle and important. Though these leaders are appropriately aggressive, as good executives must be, and present a visage of control—of their organizations, of information, of time, and of their own emotions—as we noted earlier, they are not driven. They are not significantly compensating for earliest feelings of helplessness.

Outsiders may see leaders as problem-solvers, and only that side of them. Yet, as our data indicate, these men have close, affectionate ties with their key subordinates and colleagues who are integral to the formulation and execution of components of their vision. To have such an affectional bond requires not only that subordinates and colleagues be attracted by the leader's ego ideal, embodied in organizational purpose, values, and beliefs, but also that there be a modulation of aggressive tension that is coupled with personal friendship. There is necessarily love and hate in every relationship. "To our human mind, personal friendship represents one of the most cherished values, and any social organization not built on its basis inspires us with a chilling sense of the inhuman," writes the famed biologist Konrad Lorenz.[15] Our leaders are able to fuse their affectionate and aggressive strivings. They can form intimate relationships with their key people because they don't fear the hostility of those people. Indeed, as in the case of Walter Wriston, they go to extremes to stimulate the expression of that hostility precisely so that people can learn to deal with it and thereby to work together. Because the leaders can fuse both of these strivings, they are attractive people to be around. They are loving. They seek out the company of others, although there are differences in this regard in our sample. Jack Hanley was a bit aloof, though he did work closely with two major support people. MacGregor sought out even low-level subordinates for informal chats. Wriston could be playful at the retreats he set up. That context brings to mind the picture of boys in a schoolyard horsing around in a playful, yet aggressive manner. (The leaders of England who are said to have learned their skills on the playing fields of Eton learned to integrate the loving with the aggressive aspects of themselves in preparation for leadership roles.) Such a fusion is required for lasting leadership, for transforming leadership.

The fusion of the affectionate and the aggressive is given added significance by the fact that these men were in what Erik Erikson calls the stage of generativity.[16] They loved to mentor and to develop others. They were talent scouts and people-growers. Their comfort with the aggressive side of themselves and their sense about what and who they loved allowed them to enjoy the rough and tumble of relating to and with others.

We have referred to their strong, predominantly loving, identifications with their fathers. In *Adaptation to Life,* George Vaillant sees this identification as a critical factor in those who have achieved the best adaptation.[17] It might well be that those early attachments allowed for the hostility of parent/child rivalry to be modulated by the powerful affection that was also part of those relationships.

In addition to their capacity for positive relationships with those around them, the leaders created external targets that simultaneously allowed for the discharge of aggression and for action on behalf of the organization family. Not only were there appropriate avenues for aggression, but also the leader gave the followers permission to pursue those targets on behalf of the organization family. In the process, the bonds to him, and thereby to each other, were strengthened, and their sense of mutuality confirmed. Furthermore, they grew bigger and better for that relationship.

There is something more, something also not touched in the managerial literature. These leaders loved their companies. How else can one understand the narcissistic grandiosity that compelled each to devote his ordinary working life to making his company the best in the world? And, even more significantly, in the service of that grandiosity, when it came time to retire, the ability of each to let go? Entrepreneurs characteristically cannot. Those who use organizations as devices to compensate for their own sense of inadequacy or helplessness cannot. Only the true leader, like the parent who enables his child to leave home when he grows up, can leave his company in the hands of others, having assured himself that his job is done. Not to let go is to manipulate and exploit in one's own self-interest. To be able to endure the pain of letting go takes deep and abiding affection.

Coda

What did we learn from all this? In particular, what did we discover that challenges contemporary social science wisdom?

1. Strong leaders are necessary, particularly for organizations that must undergo significant change. Not good managers, or executives, but strong leaders.

2. Leadership that builds changing organizations into larger and better social instruments will not achieve its ends by consensus. By permission, yes. That permission, as we have seen from our examples, is obtained in many different ways from many different groups and particularly by the creation of identification with the leadership. But consensus, no.

3. The leader must have a highly developed capacity for abstraction, for vision, and the strength to take charge. He must pull his organization into the future.

4. The leader must be not only strong enough to be an identification figure but also attentive enough to detail to be on top of things. He must always fight the tendency to overcontrol but, in formal organizations, he cannot hang loose without creating chaos.

   The required behavior is exemplified by no less a leader than Winston Churchill, as described by Simon Schama: "By sheer force of personality, transmitted to the British Parliament and to the people through radio broadcasts, he turned fear into fortitude. By telling the truth he actually succeeded in making things seem better, not worse . . . in essence, they [the mechanics of inspiration] were the result of the extraordinary effect that Churchill's own unambiguous dedication and his jaunty bravura had on others—on immediate colleagues, on junior ministers, on the people at large."[18] Schama reduced "this peculiar chemistry, the essence of Churchillian charisma" to four elements: (1) his indefatigability in the face of staggeringly hard work; (2) his impressively detailed grasp of military strategy; (3) the passion and dignity of his rhetoric; and (4) his unswerving moral decency. But not these elements alone; there was also the importance of the mundane. Churchill was a stickler for detail.[19] He followed up daily on the performance of his subordinates. He insisted on transmitting instructions in writing, on keeping orderly track of every decision, and on tracing the progress of decision to action. He had an extraordinary mental capacity for combining an infinite grasp of details with a sense of how they fit into a grand strategy. He is said to have had supreme self-confidence, although judging from his early life history, much of his behavior was compensatory and, therefore, like the leaders in this book, he necessarily must have had his share of anxiety and self-doubt. However, he did have a well-defined sense of purpose which gave significance to his attention to detail.

5. When one is in love with one's work, then the extraordinary hours are like play. To take Churchill as an exemplar again, he could work joyfully at full capacity for fifteen or more hours a day. All of the leaders in this book worked long hours as well. Despite its burdens, they enjoyed the work they were doing and made of it a kind of play. We agree with Warren Bennis that the leader's intention is a playground, an arena surrounding an idea.[20] But we go beyond that to affirm that leadership itself is a form of play.

Barbara Tuchman says: "A study of history reminds one that mankind has its ups and downs, and during the ups has accomplished many brave and beautiful things, exerted stupendous endeavors, explored and conquered oceans and wilderness, achieved marvels of beauty in the creative arts and marvels of science and social progress, loved liberty with a passion that throughout history led men to fight and die for it over and over again, pursued knowledge, exercised reason, enjoyed laughter and pleasures, played games with zest, shown courage, heroism, altruism, honor, and decency, experienced love, known comfort, contentment, and occasionally happiness." She points out that one of the ways man has coped with the downs and the problems was to make use of his capacity for pleasure. "*Homo ludens,* man at play, is surely as significant a figure as man at war or at work. In human activity, the invention of the ball may be said to rank with the invention of the wheel."[21]

Leadership, as play, leads to the triumphs of the human spirit. And leadership, as ennobling and transforming, is the enactment of a dramatic human story.

"I want to be a great storyteller and have people come a long way to hear the stories I have to tell. That is what acting is all about. The storyteller has always been at the center of the community, and if we start to ease him out, then we're in trouble politically, as well as socially. If we lose our sense of theatre, then we lose our identity as a nation. In the theatre, you can scrutinize an issue the way you can nowhere else on earth."[22] So says Ben Kingsley of *Gandhi* fame.

He might well have been talking about the leader. The leader has to be a great storyteller. People come a long way to share in his stories, his fantasies. The leader has always been at the center of the community, all communities, any community. We cannot do without him.

Appendix

CEO Questionnaire

OUR INTENTION is to understand more clearly the subtle impact of a uniquely individual CEO on a corporation. For example, given two CEOs with similar training, experience, and background, each is nevertheless likely to affect the same organization in different ways. Some of these ways may be conspicuously self-evident. Others are more likely to be quietly unobtrusive. We are particularly interested in the latter, precisely because they are less widely recognized. We will therefore ask a series of questions to help illuminate these issues.

1. When you took over as CEO, what strong wishes, thoughts, aspirations, ambitions did you have in mind?

2. When you were selected for your CEO tasks, were you given a specific charge by the board? Did that charge differ significantly from what you yourself saw had to be done? What did you hope to be able to do beyond the expectations of the board?

3. What did you see had to be done in and to the organization in order to achieve those goals? That is, what policies, practices, perceptions, methods, attitudes did you perceive had to be changed?

4. How did you go about changing them?

5. Looking back on it now, how well did you succeed in making those changes? Did they produce the effects you were striving for? How do you know?

6. By what mechanisms or modes of operating have your conceptions become embedded in the organization? If you had it to do all over again, how would you do it differently?

7. What modes of operation have proved to be refractory to your effort?

8. Of the various ways in which you had an impact on your organization, some are likely to have been more widely publicized but less important in the long run. Others may have been subtle but highly significant. Are there comparatively little-known initiations that have produced significant effects?

9. If you were to derive one or more major principles of organizational leadership from your own experience, what would they be?

10. If you were to point out one or more major pitfalls for prospective organizational leaders, what would they be?

11. When you left your organization (or when you leave it), what managerial monument did (do) you want to leave behind? That is, what indicated (will indicate) that you had (have) an enduring effect on your organization?

12. What were the dominant problems your organization faced when you took over?

13. What were the dominant problems your successor faced (or will face) when he/she took (takes) over from you?

14. Which were the repeatedly frustrating problems that you experienced while CEO?

15. Which, if any, aroused feelings of guilt or inadequacy? What did you do about such feelings? What did you do about resolving those problems so that they would not recur?

16. If your parents were (are) still alive, and if they were as managerially sophisticated as you would like them to be, of the

many things you did in your CEO role, which would give them the greatest pride?

17. Which would give your former professors the greatest pride? Among your CEO peers, which earns you the greatest respect? Among people in your organization, which earns you the greatest accolade(s)?

18. How do these perspectives differ from your own?

19. Who among your peers has done something in his or her organization that you wish you have been able to do in yours? Why couldn't you do it?

20. Describe yourself as an individual. What kind of person are you?

21. Think of your company as a person. Describe that person to me. What is he or she like?

22. Think of a peer (another CEO that you respect highly). If he or she were in your position as CEO of your organization, what would be different about how the organization would operate? What subtleties of your different behavior might make a significant difference?

23. What stories do people tell about you?

24. What enduring mark do (did) you leave on your organization?

25. What do you want to be remembered for?

(These questions were recast for the non-CEO informants.)

Notes

Chapter 1

1. James M. Burns, *Leadership* (New York: Harper and Row, 1978), p. 2.
2. Kurt Lewin and Ronald Lippitt, "An Experimental Approach to the Study of Autocracy and Democracy: A Preliminary Note," *Sociometry* 1 (1938): 292–300.
3. Michael Maccoby, *The Gamesman* (New York: Simon and Schuster, 1976).
4. Robert R. Blake and Jane S. Mouton, *The Managerial Grid* (Houston: Gulf Publishing, 1964).
5. David C. McClelland, *Power: The Inner Experience* (New York: Irvington, 1975).
6. Douglas MacGregor, *The Human Side of Enterprise* (New York: McGraw-Hill, 1967).
7. Rensis Likert, *The Human Organization* (New York: McGraw-Hill, 1967).
8. Chris Argyris, *Intervention Theory and Method* (Reading, Mass.: Addison-Wesley, 1970).
9. Trudy Heller and Jon Van Til, "Leadership: The Management of Meaning," *Journal of Applied Behavioral Science* 18 (1982): 257–73.
10. Bernard M. Bass, ed., *Stogdill's Handbook of Leadership* (New York: Free Press, 1981), p. 610.
11. Nevitt Sanford, "Social Psychology: Its Place in Personology," *American Psychologist* 37 (1982): 896–903.
12. Richard M. Nixon, *Leaders* (New York: Warner Books, 1982.)
13. Harry Levinson, *Executive* (Cambridge, Mass.: Harvard University Press, 1981).

Chapter 2

1. "Look at It through My Eyes," *Forbes*, May 15, 1971, pp. 59–60.
2. Isidor Barmash, "America's Most Influential Jones," *New York Times Magazine*, September 16, 1979, p. 122.

3. "G.E. Not Recession Proof, But Recession Resistant," *Forbes,* March 15, 1975, pp. 26–35.

4. Louis Kraar, "General Electric's Very Personal Merger," *Fortune,* August 1977, p. 190.

5. Barmash, "America's Most Influential Jones," p. 122.

6. Ibid., p. 187.

7. Ibid., p. 191.

8. Ibid., p. 194.

9. Reginald H. Jones, "Sustaining the Spirit of General Electric" (Presented to the National Meeting of the Elfun Society, Nela Park, Cleveland, Ohio, September 6, 1977).

10. Barmash, "America's Most Influential Jones," p. 34.

11. *U.S. News and World Report.* April 14, 1980, p. 42.

Chapter 3

1. *Wall Street Transcript,* December 4, 1967, p. 1179.

2. Walter B. Wriston, "Let's Stop Making the Wrong Mistakes" (Presented to the 1980 Banking Forum, New York, January 26, 1980).

Chapter 4

1. *Wall Street Journal,* May 2, 1969, p. 15.

2. *Wall Street Transcript,* February 13, 1967, pp. 9–36.

3. *New York Times,* March 23, 1981, p. D5.

4. *E/MJ* (engineering and mining journal) 173 (1972): 157.

5. Ibid., pp. 157–158.

6. "Can Coal Save Pierre Gousseland?" *Business Week,* October 18, 1982, pp. 104–110.

7. Barnaby J. Feder, "Mrs. Thatcher Tests the Miners," *New York Times,* August 28, 1983, p. 3.

Chapter 5

1. *Wall Street Transcript,* April 3, 1972, pp. 27, 821.

2. Aimee L. Morner, "Jack Hanley Got There by Selling Harder," *Fortune,* November 1976, p. 164.

3. Ibid., p. 165.

4. Ibid., p. 175.

5. Ibid., p. 177.

6. Dan J. Forrestal, *Faith, Hope and $5,000* (New York: Simon and Schuster, 1977).

7. Ibid., p. 177.

8. Michael Rothfeld et al., "The Man from Mother Procter: Businessmen in the News," *Fortune,* December 1972, p. 36.

9. Forrestal, *Faith, Hope and $5,000,* p. 233.

Chapter 6

1. Robert Sobel, *IBM: Colossus in Transition* (New York: Times Books, 1981), p. 117.

2. Ibid., p. 119.

3. Ibid., p. 123.

4. Katherine D. Fishman, *The Computer Establishment* (New York: Harper and Row, 1981), p. 43.

5. Sobel, *IBM*, p. 127.

6. Ibid., pp. 161–62.

7. Thomas Belden and Marva Belden, *The Lengthening Shadow* (Boston: Little Brown, 1962).

8. Sobel, *IBM*, p. 165.

9. "The Colossus That Works," *Time*, July 11, 1983, pp. 44–54.

Chapter 7

1. Harrison E. Salisbury, *Without Fear or Favor* (New York: Ballantine Books, 1981), p. 65.

2. Ibid., p. 66.

3. Ibid., p. 66.

4. Ibid., p. 176.

5. Ibid., pp. 174–75.

6. Ibid., p. 175 footnote.

7. Edward Meadows, "The New York Times?" *Fortune*, July 28, 1980, p. 84.

Chapter 8

1. Warren G. Bennis and Philip E. Slater, *The Temporary Society* (New York: Harper and Row, 1968).

2. Abraham Zaleznik and Manfred Kets de Vries, *Power and the Corporate Mind* (Boston: Houghton Mifflin, 1975).

3. Thomas J. Peters and Robert H. Waterman, *In Search of Excellence* (New York: Harper and Row, 1982).

4. Richard Evans Schultes and William A. Davis, *The Glass Flowers at Harvard* (New York: E. P. Dutton, 1982), p. 8.

5. Paul R. Lawrence and David Dyer, *Renewing American Industry* (New York: Free Press, 1983).

6. Richard T. Pascale and Anthony G. Athos, *The Art of Japanese Management* (New York: Simon and Schuster, 1981).

7. Ibid.

8. Samuel Lipman, "U.S. Orchestras Have Problems at the Podium," *Boston Globe*, July 10, 1983.

9. Interestingly enough, the most successful professional football teams are those that have stability and continuity of ownership and management. See Subrata N. Chakravarty, "Character Is Destiny," *Forbes*, October 10, 1983, pp. 114–123.

10. Edgar J. Driscoll, Jr., "Rubinstein—'Always Positive'," *Boston Globe*, December 22, 1982.

11. Thomas J. Peters and Robert H. Waterman, *In Search of Excellence*.

12. Heinz Kohut, *The Analysis of the Self* (New York: International Universities Press, 1971).

13. Rafael Moses, "The Group Self and The Arab-Israeli Conflict," *International Review of Psycho-Analysis* 9 (1982): 55–65.

14. James M. Burns, *Leadership* (New York: Harper and Row, 1978), p. 20.

15. Konrad Lorenz, *On Aggression* (New York: Harcourt, Brace, and World, 1966), p. 142.

16. Erik H. Erikson, *Childhood and Society*, 2nd ed. (New York: Norton, 1963).

17. George E. Vaillant, *Adaptation to Life* (Boston: Little Brown, 1977).

18. Simon Schama, "The Churchillead," *New Republic*, December 5, 1983, pp. 28–32.

19. Martin Gilbert, *Finest Hour: Winston S. Churchill 1939–1941* (Boston: Houghton Mifflin, 1983).

20. Warren Bennis, *Leadership and Empowerment* (New York: William Morrow, 1984).

21. Barbara W. Tuchman, "Mankind's Better Moments," *Wilson Quarterly* (Autumn 1980): 96–105.

22. Sheridan Marley, "Kingsley as 'Kean'," *Playbill*, November 1983, pp. 19–22.

Index